THE KING'S MISTRESS

THE KING'S MISTRESS

The True and Scandalous
Story of the Woman Who Stole
the Heart of George I

Claudia Gold

Quercus

First published in Great Britain in 2012 by
Quercus
55 Baker Street
7th Floor, South Block
London
W1U 8EW

A CIP catalogue record for this book is available
from the British Library

ISBN 978 1 84916 411 5

10 9 8 7 6 5 4 3 2 1

Text and plates designed and typeset by Ellipsis Digital Ltd

Family Trees © Rich Carr Studios

Printed and bound in Great Britain by Clays Ltd, St Ives plc

For my sister Tanya

Contents

Acknowledgements   ix

Dramatis Personae   xi

Family Trees   xv

List of illustrations   xxi

1   A Portrait   1

2   The Mermaid and the Girl   7

3   Venice of the North   15

4   The Mistress   47

5   Beloved   67

6   The Crown at Last   93

7   Germans in England   107

8   A Strange Family   123

9   A City out of Rubble   135

10 Palaces   151

11 Politics and Players   161

12 A Battle   185

13 A Bubble   209

14 Venality   231

15 Diplomacy   243

16 A Marriage?   257

17 Endings   265

Bibliography   277

Notes   287

Index   305

Acknowledgements

I should like to thank my agent, Vivienne Schuster, and my editor, Joshua Ireland, for their encouragement and enthusiasm. I am indebted to Professor Aubrey Newman, Emeritus Professor of History at the University of Leicester, who encouraged me throughout this project and first led me to believe that there was a book here. Huge thanks to my linguist friends who helped me with the translation of German and French sources, particularly Yehuda Shapiro and Jerry Gotel. Dr Amanda Jones at the Borthwick Institute for Archives, University of York, was enormously helpful regarding a morganatic marriage, and I am grateful to Antonio Jimenez-Milian, library assistant at York Minster Library, for his information on Lancelot Blackburn, Archbishop of York. Dr Joanna Marshner, Senior Curator at Kensington Palace, generously gave up a morning of her time to guide me behind the scenes there.

In Germany the curator at Celle Castle, Anke Wiesbrich, helped to make my trip there extremely productive. I am particularly grateful to her for unearthing a portrait of Melusine, previously unknown, in the bowels of Celle Castle, and for her detailed tour of Sophia Dorothea's childhood home. The local historian Rolf Sahlfeld was very generous with his time and gave me an impromptu tour of Barsinghausen. Thanks to the ever-helpful staff at the London Library and the British Library.

The amazing Katy Rose cared for my children while I wrote. My mother Trudy Gold and my sister Tanya Gold were founts of wisdom and childcare.

Above all, my love and thanks go to my boys, Asher and Jake, and to my husband Phil. I am so grateful to them all for their affection, patience, and humour.

Dramatis Personae

An astonishing number of contemporary women were called Sophia, or had Sophia as a prefix to their name. To add to the confusion, George's illegitimate half-sister and his only legitimate sister shared the same name, Sophia Charlotte. George's youngest and favourite brother shared their father's name, Ernst August. Below is a list of some of the main characters who appear in *The King's Mistress*, in the hope that it will help to illuminate and distinguish them.

Caroline of Ansbach, Georg August's wife, later Queen of England.

Ernst August, Elector of Hanover. George's father.

Ernst August, prince-bishop of Osnabrück, later Duke of York. George's youngest and favourite brother.

Figuelotte, see Sophia Charlotte

Georg August, George's eldest son, later King George II.

Maximilian Wilhelm (Max), George's most troublesome brother.

Melusine, see Ehrengard Melusine von der Schulenburg

Sophia, princess of the Palatinate and Electress of Hanover. George's mother. Proud and haughty, she was descended from King James I of England.

Sophia Charlotte (Figuelotte), later Queen of Prussia. George's only sister.

Sophia Dorothea of Celle, George's wife and first cousin, and Melusine's rival.

Trudchen, see Margarethe Gertrud von Oeynhausen

Young Sophia Dorothea, George and Sophia Dorothea's legitimate daughter.

Margarethe Gertrud von Oeynhausen (Trudchen), Melusine and George's youngest daughter. She married Albrecht Wolfgang of Schaumburg-Lippe.

Sophie Juliane von Oeynhausen, Melusine's younger sister. She and her husband accepted Trudchen as their daughter.

Klara Platen, Sophia Charlotte's mother. *Maîtresse en titre* of Ernst August, Elector of Hanover.

Sophia Charlotte von Platen (later Sophia Charlotte von Kielmansegg by her marriage, and Countess of Darlington), George's illegitimate half-sister.

Sophie Karoline von Platen, married to Sophia Charlotte's brother, Ernst August von Platen, and a leader of the anti-Melusine faction at the Hanoverian court.

George Augustus of Schaumburg-Lippe, Trudchen's elder son.

Joanne Sophie, Countess of Schaumburg-Lippe. A courtier in both Hanover and England, she was Melusine's closest friend, and Trudchen's mother-in-law.

William of Schaumburg-Lippe, later Count of Schaumburg-Lippe. Trudchen's younger son.

Anna Louise von der Schulenburg, later Countess Delitz (Louise). Melusine and George's eldest daughter.

Ehrengard Melusine von der Schulenburg, later Duchess of Kendal (Melusine). The mistress of George, Electoral Prince of Hanover, later King George I of Britain.

Frederick William von der Schulenburg, Melusine's half-brother, gentleman of the bedchamber, friend and confidant of George.

Johann Matthias von der Schulenburg. Melusine's eldest brother, an internationally renowned field marshal and diplomat.

Margarete Gertrud von der Schulenburg. Melusine's eldest sister, she and her husband accepted Louise and young Melusine as their daughters.

Petronella Melusine von der Schulenburg, later Countess of Walsingham, and by her marriage, Lady Chesterfield (young Melusine). Melusine and George's middle daughter.

The Melusine family tree

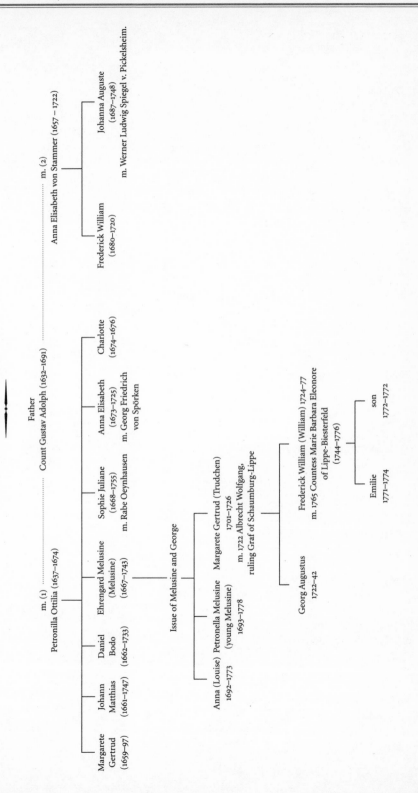

Father
Count Gustav Adolph (1632–1691)

m. (1) Petronilla Ottilia (1637–1674)

m. (2) Anna Elisabeth von Stammer (1657 – 1722)

Margarete Gertrud (1659–97)

Johann Matthias (1661–1747)

Daniel Bodo (1662–1733)

Ehrengard Melusine (Melusine) (1667–1743)

Sophie Juliane (1668–1755) m. Rabe Oeynhausen

Anna Elisabeth (1673–1725) m. Georg Friedrich von Spörken

Charlotte (1674–1676)

Frederick William (1680–1720)

Johanna Auguste (1687–1748) m. Werner Ludwig Spiegel v. Pickelsheim.

Issue of Melusine and George

Anna (Louise) 1692–1773

Petronella Melusine (young Melusine) 1693–1778

Margarete Gertrud (Trudchen) 1701–1726 m. 1722 Albrecht Wolfgang, ruling Graf of Schaumburg-Lippe

Georg Augustus 1722–42

Frederick William (William) 1724–77 m. 1765 Countess Marie Barbara Eleonore of Lippe-Biesterfeld (1744–1776)

Emilie 1771–1774

son 1772–1772

The Protestant / English succession

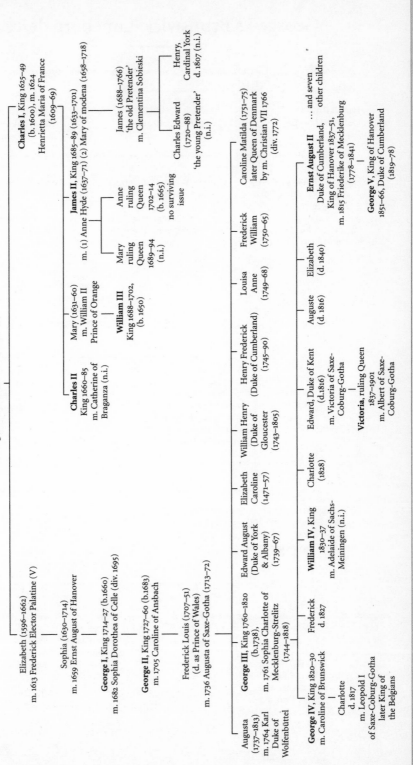

James I, King 1603–25 (b. 1566) = Anne of Denmark
as King of Scotland (James VI) from 1567

Elizabeth (1596–1662)
m. 1613 Frederick Elector Palatine (V)

Charles I, King 1625–49
(b. 1600), m. 1624
Henrietta Maria of France
(1609–69)

Sophia (1630–1714)
m. 1659 Ernst August of Hanover

Charles II
King 1660–85
m. Catherine of
Braganza (n.i.)

Mary (1631–60)
m. William II
Prince of Orange

James II, King 1685–89 (1633–1701)
m. (1) Anne Hyde (1637–71) (2) Mary of modena (1658–1718)

William III
King 1688–1702,
(b. 1650)

Mary
ruling
Queen
1689–94
(n.i.)

Anne
ruling
Queen
1702–14
(b. 1665)
no surviving
issue

James (1688–1766)
'the old Pretender'
m. Clementina Sobieski

Charles Edward
(1720–88)
'the young Pretender'
(n.i.)

Henry,
Cardinal York
d. 1807 (n.i.)

George I, King 1714–27 (b.1660)
m. 1682 Sophia Dorothea of Celle (div. 1695)

George II, King 1727–60 (b.1683)
m. 1705 Caroline of Ansbach

Frederick Louis (1707–51)
(d. as Prince of Wales)
m. 1736 Augusta of Saxe-Gotha (1713–72)

Augusta
(1737–1813)
m. 1764 Karl
Duke of
Wolfenbüttel

George III, King 1760–1820
(b.1738),
m. 1761 Sophia Charlotte of
Mecklenburg-Strelitz
(1744–1818)

Edward August
(Duke of York
& Albany)
(1739–67)

Elizabeth
Caroline
(1471–57)

William Henry
(Duke of
Gloucester)
(1743–1805)

Henry Frederick
(Duke of Cumberland)
(1745–90)

Louisa
Anne
(1749–68)

Frederick
William
(1750–65)

Caroline Matilda (1751–75)
later Queen of Denmark
by m. Christian VII 1766
(div. 1772)

George IV, King 1820–30
m. Caroline of Brunswick

Charlotte
d. 1817
m. Leopold I
of Saxe-Coburg-Gotha
later King of
the Belgians

Frederick
d. 1827

William IV, King
1830–37
m. Adelaide of Sachs-
Meiningen (n.i.)

Charlotte
(1828)

Edward, Duke of Kent
(d.1816)
m. Victoria of Saxe-
Coburg-Gotha

Victoria, ruling Queen
1837–1901
m. Albert of Saxe-
Coburg-Gotha

Auguste
(d. 1816)

Elizabeth
(d. 1840)

Ernst August II
Duke of Cumberland,
King of Hanover 1837–51,
m. 1815 Friederike of Mecklenburg
(1778–1841)

George V, King of Hanover
1851–66, Duke of Cumberland
(1819–78)

… and seven
other children

George I's Brunswick-Lüneburg descent

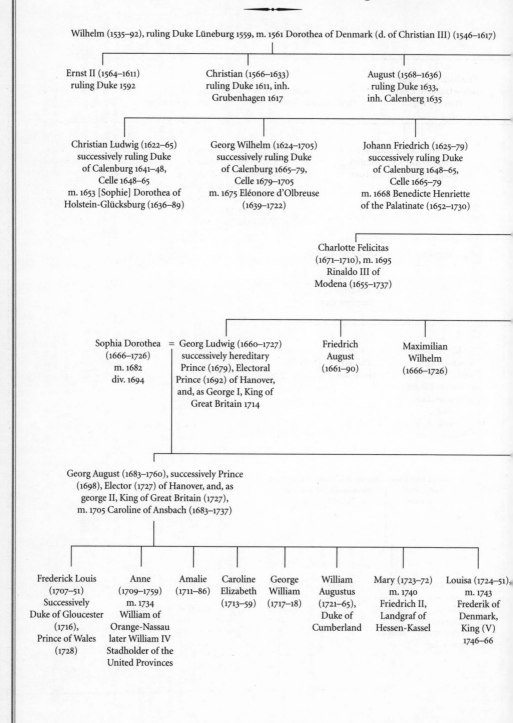

Wilhelm (1535–92), ruling Duke Lüneburg 1559, m. 1561 Dorothea of Denmark (d. of Christian III) (1546–1617)

Ernst II (1564–1611)
ruling Duke 1592

Christian (1566–1633)
ruling Duke 1611, inh.
Grubenhagen 1617

August (1568–1636)
ruling Duke 1633,
inh. Calenberg 1635

Christian Ludwig (1622–65)
successively ruling Duke
of Calenburg 1641–48,
Celle 1648–65
m. 1653 [Sophie] Dorothea of
Holstein-Glücksburg (1636–89)

Georg Wilhelm (1624–1705)
successively ruling Duke
of Calenburg 1665–79,
Celle 1679–1705
m. 1675 Eléonore d'Olbreuse
(1639–1722)

Johann Friedrich (1625–79)
successively ruling Duke
of Calenburg 1648–65,
Celle 1665–79
m. 1668 Benedicte Henriette
of the Palatinate (1652–1730)

Charlotte Felicitas
(1671–1710), m. 1695
Rinaldo III of
Modena (1655–1737)

Sophia Dorothea
(1666–1726)
m. 1682
div. 1694

= Georg Ludwig (1660–1727)
successively hereditary
Prince (1679), Electoral
Prince (1692) of Hanover,
and, as George I, King of
Great Britain 1714

Friedrich
August
(1661–90)

Maximilian
Wilhelm
(1666–1726)

Georg August (1683–1760), successively Prince
(1698), Elector (1727) of Hanover, and, as
george II, King of Great Britain (1727),
m. 1705 Caroline of Ansbach (1683–1737)

Frederick Louis
(1707–51)
Successively
Duke of Gloucester
(1716),
Prince of Wales
(1728)

Anne
(1709–1759)
m. 1734
William of
Orange-Nassau
later William IV
Stadholder of the
United Provinces

Amalie
(1711–86)

Caroline
Elizabeth
(1713–59)

George
William
(1717–18)

William
Augustus
(1721–65),
Duke of
Cumberland

Mary (1723–72)
m. 1740
Friedrich II,
Landgraf of
Hessen-Kassel

Louisa (1724–51),
m. 1743
Frederik of
Denmark,
King (V)
1746–66

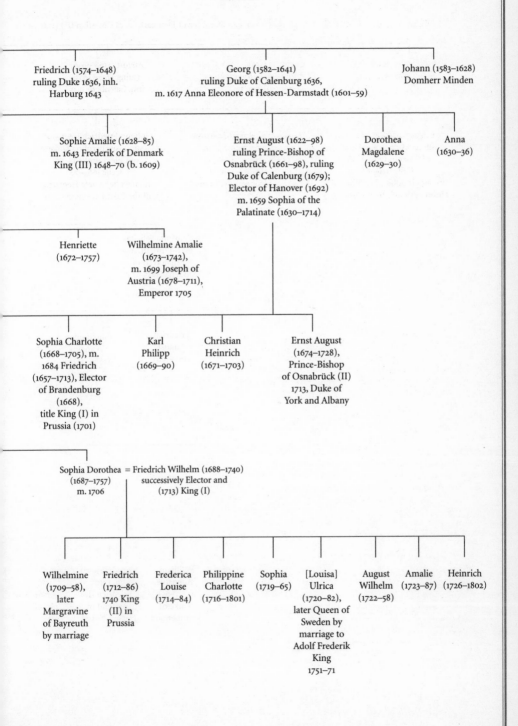

Friedrich (1574–1648)
ruling Duke 1636, inh.
Harburg 1643

Georg (1582–1641)
ruling Duke of Calenburg 1636,
m. 1617 Anna Eleonore of Hessen-Darmstadt (1601–59)

Johann (1583–1628)
Domherr Minden

Sophie Amalie (1628–85)
m. 1643 Frederik of Denmark
King (III) 1648–70 (b. 1609)

Ernst August (1622–98)
ruling Prince-Bishop of
Osnabrück (1661–98), ruling
Duke of Calenburg (1679);
Elector of Hanover (1692)
m. 1659 Sophia of the
Palatinate (1630–1714)

Dorothea
Magdalene
(1629–30)

Anna
(1630–36)

Henriette
(1672–1757)

Wilhelmine Amalie
(1673–1742),
m. 1699 Joseph of
Austria (1678–1711),
Emperor 1705

Sophia Charlotte
(1668–1705), m.
1684 Friedrich
(1657–1713), Elector
of Brandenburg
(1668),
title King (I) in
Prussia (1701)

Karl
Philipp
(1669–90)

Christian
Heinrich
(1671–1703)

Ernst August
(1674–1728),
Prince-Bishop
of Osnabrück (II)
1713, Duke of
York and Albany

Sophia Dorothea = Friedrich Wilhelm (1688–1740)
(1687–1757)   successively Elector and
m. 1706   (1713) King (I)

Wilhelmine
(1709–58),
later
Margravine
of Bayreuth
by marriage

Friedrich
(1712–86)
1740 King
(II) in
Prussia

Frederica
Louise
(1714–84)

Philippine
Charlotte
(1716–1801)

Sophia
(1719–65)

[Louisa]
Ulrica
(1720–82),
later Queen
of Sweden by
marriage to
Adolf Frederik
King
1751–71

August
Wilhelm
(1722–58)

Amalie
(1723–87)

Heinrich
(1726–1802)

List of Illustrations

1. Portrait of Countess Ehrengard Melusine von der Schulenburg, Duchess of Kendal (1667–1743) (oil on canvas). 18th Century. *Private Collection/The Bridgeman Art Library*

2. Portrait of Countess Ehrengard Melusine von der Schulenburg, Duchess of Kendal (1667–1743) (oil on canvas). 18th Century. *Private Collection/The Bridgeman Art Library*

3. General Count Johann Matthias von der Schulenburg by Giovanni Antonio Guardi (1698–1760). 18th Century. *Ca' Rezzonico, Museo del Settecento, Venice/The Bridgeman Art Library*

4. Sophie, electress of Hanover, (1630–1714). Copper engraving, unsigned and undated, *c.*1701. *akg-images*

5. King George I as Prince of Hanover by Kneller, engraved by Richard Tompson after a painting by Sir Geoffrey Kneller. *Fotomas/TopFoto*

6. George I (1646–1723), *c.* 1715, Studio of Sir Geoffrey Kneller. *The Royal Collection © 2011 Her Majesty Queen Elizabeth II / The Bridgeman Art Library/The Bridgeman Art Library*

7. Gertrud von Schuamburg-Lippe, daughter of Melusine von der Schulenburg. *Kloster Barsinghausen*

8. Sophia Charlotte von Platen und Hallermund (1669–1726) by School of Sir Godfrey Kneller. Oil on canvas. *culture-images/Lebrecht Music & Arts*

9. Klara Elisabeth von Platen, Countess of Platen Hallermund, née Meysenbugh (1650–1700). *culture-images/Lebrecht Music & Arts*

10. Sophia Dorothea, (1666–1726), Hereditary Princess of Hanover, with her children Georg and Sophia Dorothea, painting by Jacques Vaillant, *c.*1692.
Mary Evans Picture Library/INTERFOTO/ARTCOLOR

11. Königsmarck, Philip Christoph Count of, (1665–1694), painting by Martin Meytens. *Mary Evans Picture Library/INTERFOTO/Friedrich*

12. King George II Georgius Augustus Electoral Prince of Brunswick (1683–1760). *Fotomas/TopFoto*

13. Princess Caroline Elizabeth by John Faber Jr, after Hans Hysing mezzotint, mid-18th century. © *National Portrait Gallery, London*

14. Portrait of Sir Robert Walpole (1676–1745) (oil on canvas) by Charles Jervas.18th Century. *Private Collection/The Bridgeman Art Library*

15. Melusine von der Schulenburg, unknown artist, *c.* 1720, oil on canvas, © *Bomann-Museum Celle*

16. Frederick William Ernest, Count of Schaumberg-Lippe, *c.*1767 (oil on canvas). *The Royal Collection* © *2011 Her Majesty Queen Elizabeth II*

17. 'The Brabant Skreen', 1721. A satire on the South Sea company. The Duchess of Kendal gives money to Robert Knight (treasurer of the company), to enable him to escape. Illustration from 'Social Caricature in the Eighteenth Century . . . With over two hundred illustrations' by George Paston (pseudonym of Emily Morse Symonds) (London, 1905). *Print Collector/HIP/TopFoto*

18. Herrenhausen Palace (built 1666–1714, rebuilt 1820–66 by Georg Ludwig Friedrich Laves). View of the palace and the Great Garden (established from 1666). Copper engraving, 1714, unsigned; coloured at a later stage. *akg-images*

19. A Royal Hunting Party at Göhrde, 1725 (oil on panel). English School. *The Royal Collection* © *2011 Her Majesty Queen Elizabeth II / The Bridgeman Art Library*

20. Kensington Palace, *c.* 1924 © *Country Life*

21. Kensington Palace, *c.* 1924 © *Country Life*

1.

A Portrait

'As much Queen of England as any ever was; . . . he [George I]
did everything by her.'

– Robert Walpole on Melusine, recorded
in Mary Countess Cowper, *Diary*

On a spring day in 2011, in the storeroom of a provincial museum in Celle, northern Germany, I saw the face of Ehrengard Melusine von der Schulenburg. I had first become aware of her in 2006 while I was researching a book about queens and courtesans. She fascinated me.[1]

She was the mistress and possibly the secret wife of George I, Elector of Hanover and later king of Great Britain. Yet her reputation is appalling. I read that she gleefully purloined Queen Anne's property, particularly her jewels. Several historians have gone so far as to imagine Melusine and her lover George I's half-sister, Sophia Charlotte, nightly plundering Anne's diamonds in the candlelit vaults of St James's Palace. One claims that she was so meticulous in her looting that Caroline of Ansbach, George II's queen, had only one strand of pearls at her disposal for her coronation and was crowned in borrowed jewels.

Few could understand George's infatuation. By contemporary standards Melusine was not a great beauty. Eighteenth-century men preferred their women plump, and 'la Schulenburg' was slim. Her nickname amongst the English, who loathed her, was 'the Maypole'.

Others sources twittered that she was old; she was hideous; she was excessive in her greed; she had no love for George and would have 'sold him to the highest bidder'; she was dim-witted; she was dull; she stood by passively as George pursued younger and more attractive mistresses; she condoned incest, willingly sharing George's affections and his bed with his half-sister, Sophia Charlotte.

Yet this seemingly grasping and unattractive woman managed to wrest George from his beautiful and tempestuous wife, Sophia

Dorothea of Celle, and bind him to her for almost forty years. In doing so she rose from the ranks of minor courtier to become one of the most powerful women in Europe. Her influence led Louis XV of France to write to his ambassador to the Court of St James's, Count Broglio: 'You will neglect nothing to acquire a share of her confidence, from a conviction that nothing can be more conducive to my interest.'[2]

She became the conduit between the king and his ministers and she traded in court places and titles. She was a prime mover in the South Sea Bubble, that unedifying spectacle of greed, deception, stupidity and finally blind panic that resulted in misery and economic ruination. Melusine's part in the scandal would seal her notoriety.

Melusine, a clever woman in a position of power, was one of Thomas Carlyle's notorious 'harlots'. She was not in the tradition of those glorious, vibrant courtesans who for centuries have held sway over kings. But she was extremely powerful. The king's ministers did little without her say-so and she used her position to accumulate fabulous wealth. As I investigated the sources, it became clear that George I was devoted to her.

Although she lived only 300 years ago, the sources are problematic. We have the opinions of those who loathed her and laughed at her foreignness, the coffee-house wags and the court gossips, and the testimonies of those who were indebted to her, whose views were naturally biased. She wrote charming notes to the court glitterati and was forthright in sending instructions and admonitions to the king's ministers. But very little about her personal life comes from Melusine's own lips. The reason is the Königsmarck affair.

In 1694 George divorced his wife Sophia Dorothea of Celle in circumstances that scandalized Europe. The princess was conducting an indiscreet love affair with a Swedish mercenary, Count

Philip von Königsmarck, and it was the letters between the lovers that left no room for doubt.

Count Philip was subsequently murdered, probably on the orders of George's father, and the unfortunate Sophia Dorothea was denied access to her children and locked in Ahlden Castle for the rest of her life. A shocked and humiliated George instructed his mistress that they must never write anything of an intimate nature to one another. Unusually, as her status as *maîtresse en titre* – the king's official mistress – was established both in Hanover and England, no letters survive between the pair. Frustratingly the biographer can only surmise her most intimate thoughts.

Until recently only three portraits of Melusine were known. One is in the British Museum. It is a delightful print of her head and shoulders, etched in her youth; it dates from about 1691. The second, in a tiny room in the sleepy convent of Barsinghausen, shows a haughty and imposing Melusine, in her late forties or early fifties, richly but soberly dressed. The other, in Hanover, is a sumptuous three-quarter-length portrait, which was probably painted in the early 1720s. But as I researched this book, an archivist at Celle Castle told me there was another painting of Melusine in the castle's storage block.

I went out of the spring sunshine to find her. Celle Castle has portraits of queens on its walls, but Melusine in consigned to the vaults. A grave curator accompanied me to a dismal basement and slid her out from amongst hundreds of paintings that may never be displayed again. And there she was, a little faded and in poor condition, but unmistakably Melusine – regal, elegant, her left hand resting on the royal ermine.

2.

The Mermaid and the Girl

'Dear lady ... Please believe me when I say there will be nothing I will not strive to do for your sake, however difficult it might be.'

The Count of Lusignan to the Fairy Melusine

A medieval story tells of a count of Poitou who falls in love with a golden-haired maiden called Melusina. She consents to marry him on one condition: that she can spend one day each week in complete solitude. The count agrees until at last, after many years, his curiosity demands satisfaction. He spies on his wife in her bath, and sees that her lower body is transformed into a serpent's tail. Later, when misery strikes his house with the death of one of their sons, he attacks Melusina with the words: 'Away, odious serpent, contaminator of my honourable race.'

Whatever her parents were thinking as they named her, Ehrengard Melusine von der Schulenburg was always known by her second name.

She was born at Emden, a prosperous town on the estuary of the river Ems, just two miles from the North Sea, on Christmas Day 1667, the second surviving daughter and fourth child of Count Gustav Adolph and his first wife, Petronilla Ottilia.

The Schulenburgs were minor aristocrats, well-entrenched and respectable. Their forebears had been ennobled in the thirteenth century. Family legend claimed celebrated generals, marshals and bishops among their ancestors. But despite past glories, by the time of her parents' marriage the family was poor and their estates in ruin. Melusine's early childhood was spent in relative poverty, in a ramshackle castle.

Her father was named after his father's hero, Gustav Adolph, the legendary king of the Swedes. Gustav studied in Helmstedt, where he was a less than model student. In the autumn of 1653 he was fined a swingeing amount for a now unknown misdemeanour.

After his studies he served in the Swedish army, before turning to the civil service, where his rise was meteoric.

He entered the service of the Elector of Brandenburg, where his talents were rewarded with promotion after promotion. In 1683 he was created Privy Councillor, one of the highest honours in the Electorate. Administrative brilliance brought diplomatic responsibility; he successfully undertook emissaries to Lüneburg in 1682, to Dresden in 1685, and to Leipzig in 1690.

But credit for a turn in the Schulenburg fortunes lies with Melusine's mother, Petronilla. She was a daughter of the Holstein family, another of the myriad of minor aristocrats whose tiny principalities formed the intricate patchwork of separate regimes that occupied the territory we now call Germany, all owing allegiance to the Holy Roman Emperor. (Germany consisted of over 300 tiny city-states, and the number was ever-changing.) Petronilla's financial management was spectacular. Within a few short years she managed to pay off her husband's stupendous debts, to reorganize his estates and to finance the building of the castle at Emden, which became their family home.[1] It was Petronilla who enabled Gustav Adolph to pursue his brilliant career in the service of the Elector of Brandenburg.

Meanwhile the Schulenburg family was growing. Between 1659 and 1674 Petronilla produced nine children, six of whom survived infancy. Melusine's eldest sister, Margarete Gertrud, was born in 1659, followed two years later by her eldest brother, Johann Matthias. Daniel Bodo joined the nursery the following year. Melusine was born in 1667, followed swiftly by her sister Sophie Juliane in 1668, and by Anna Elisabeth in 1673.

When Melusine was only six years old Petronilla Ottilia died, probably due to complications in childbirth. Her youngest daughter, Charlotte, was born on 11 April 1674 and Petronilla died nine days later. Charlotte would live for less than two years.

The children's grief must have been terrible. Their father was frequently absent from home and their primary relationship was with a mother who had created a loving domestic environment where the siblings' deep affection for one another was nurtured. Melusine and her siblings were close all their adult lives. Later, her sisters would accept maternity of her illegitimate children, she would support them financially when necessary, and the family regularly took holidays together, despite being scattered across Europe. Petronilla was considerate, not only to her own children but to the children of the estate's tenants, ensuring that even the poorest children received an education at the local school she established.[2]

At her funeral Petronilla's grief-stricken widower dedicated a Latin song to her.[3] But two years later his grief had abated enough to marry again, to the nineteen-year-old aristocrat Anna Elisabeth von Stammer, who was twenty-five years his junior. Melusine was only eight years old when her father's new young wife took over the running of the household. There was a mere eleven years between them. Anna Elisabeth gave birth to four children, two of whom survived infancy. Frederick William, born in 1680, became one of George I's intimate circle through his sister's intercession.[4] Another sister, Johanna Auguste, was born in January 1687.

Though he may have lapsed into bouts of bad behaviour as a student, Gustav, who had been a pupil of the humanist John Caselius, nevertheless prized education for girls and boys alike. Although only his sons attended the university at Helmstadt, all the children enjoyed the services of a tutor. Melusine received a solid but not particularly inspiring education; she studied arithmetic, literature, music, drawing and dancing. Like most German aristocrats, to whom everything French was the epitome of good taste, Melusine spoke the language fluently.

Many aristocratic families sought positions for themselves and their children outside of their principality; the Schulenburgs were no exception. By the end of the 1680s Gustav decided that, with no imminent marriage prospect, Melusine must be found something to do. Johann Matthias and Daniel Bodo were long gone. They went to school in Magdeburg in 1676, when Melusine was nine. The brothers returned home briefly before continuing their education at Helmstadt, and then in 1680 they spent two years at the University of Saumur in Brittany. When their studies were completed they went to Paris, where Johann Matthias ran up such huge debts that he was forced to remain longer than Daniel Bodo – who returned to the family home in 1684 – to pay them off.[5] Daniel Bodo then pursued his own military career, and by 1687 Johann Matthias, Melusine's favourite sibling, had entered the service of the Emperor and was gone for good. He would eventually become one of the most famous field marshals of the age.

Margarete Gertrud, eight years older than Melusine, had become a mother-figure to her younger siblings after their own mother's death. She married the diplomat Friedrich Achaz, a Schulenburg cousin twelve years her senior, in the summer of 1681 and they moved to Vienna. Of those siblings close to Melusine in age only Sophie Julianne remained at home, but by 1690 her marriage to Rabe Christoph von Oeynhausen, a courtier at Celle who at some point served as Master of the Hunt and a Gentleman of the Bedchamber, had been arranged. The remaining children were very young. Anna Elisabeth was six years her junior and in 1690 her half-brother Frederick William was ten and her half-sister Johanna August only three. It was time for Melusine to fly the nest.

Why did she remain unmarried? It is likely that no one sufficiently distinguished asked for her hand in marriage. To her father's delight, he managed to obtain a position for Melusine as a maid of honour to the universally admired Sophia, Duchess of Hanover, wife of Ernst August of Hanover. Gustav probably hoped that this position would attract a glittering marriage. But the romance that Melusine embarked on when she arrived in Hanover was not what her father had envisaged. The year was 1690, although the exact date, as with so much of her life, is unrecorded. She was twenty-two.

3.

Venice of the North

. . . one of the most agreeable places in the world.
                                    – Lady Mary Wortley Montagu

Hanover was a walled town spanning two sides of the river Leine, with fortified towers, only one of which – the Beginenturm – now survives. It was filled with half-timbered dwellings in the Saxon style, or brick patrician houses with distinctive red-gabled roofs. Broad streets ran parallel to the river and out through the city walls to the countryside beyond. There was a paved market square, a windmill, and four churches – amongst them the strange and glorious Market Church, towering above the square and proudly displaying its pentagon alongside the Star of David.

The Market Church stands next to the gorgeous mass of red-brick gables that was the Town Hall. Hanover's churches, most of which had become Lutheran during the Reformation, reflected the religious tolerance of the principality, which allowed for freedom of worship. Religion played an important part in the lives of most of the population, despite the beginnings of the Enlightenment and the enthusiasm with which the ruling family embraced its principles. The city was less than a kilometre from city gate to city gate. Its population barely topped ten thousand.

Appearances are deceptive. By 1690 the ambitions of Hanover's rulers, Sophia and Ernst August, had turned a city-state that was previously a footnote on the international stage into a dynamic entity with aspirations to greatness. It was Ernst August's and Sophia's determination to create a royal dynasty that would ensure that Melusine would not become the mistress of a minor princeling, but of an elector of the Holy Roman Emperor. Elector was the highest rank in the Holy Roman Empire below the Emperor himself. The chosen few – there were only seven until the Peace of Westphalia in 1648 – were empowered to choose the emperors. To secure the honour, the ruler had to ensure that his dominion was large and wealthy enough to provide the Emperor (at the time Leopold I) with troops and finance for his wars, and ostentatious enough to advertise it.

It was a gamble. The Treaty of Westphalia, which brought an end to the Thirty Years War, allowed for the creation of another elector, and the Hanoverian princes, fuelled by a wild ambition, craved the glory this would bring to their house. Melusine entered a court that was feverish in the pursuit of this single aim. All were expected to act in the service of the rulers' ambitions. The dazzling possibility of the electoral cap overshadowed everything.

The ducal family – Ernst August, Sophia and their children – lived in splendour. Their two main residences were the Leineschloss, a small castle on the river Leine in the centre of the city, and the pretty summer palace of Herrenhausen two kilometres away. The family divided their time equally between the two houses, and moved their enormous household between them. The Hanoverian stable boasted six hundred horses and accompanying coachmen, horse-doctors, grooms and ostlers. Dancing and fencing masters taught the ducal family; twenty cooks fed them; musicians and players entertained them; a legion of pages, gentlemen of the bedchamber and ladies in waiting served them.

During the 1680s the sophisticated Sir William Dutton Colt, English envoy to Hanover, wrote that in 'all Germany there is not a finer court'. He and his secretary, Larrocque, rhapsodized that Hanover had achieved the apex of fine culture and the intellect. Even the indefatigable courtier and acid-tongued English diarist Lady Mary Wortley Montagu agreed and praised it as 'one of the most agreeable places in the world'.

Its chief musician was the renowned composer Agostino Steffani, its philosopher and historian the brilliant polymath Gottfried Wilhelm Leibniz. Hanover was a state of benign autocracy and religious tolerance, whose Protestant rulers encouraged freedom of worship. Catholics, Calvinists, Huguenots and Jews were employed, adding to the richness of the intellectual and artistic tradition that Sophia had worked hard to establish since she arrived in Hanover in 1679. Like many of his contemporary German princes, Ernst August employed his own Hofjude, or Court Jew, the financier Elieser Lefmann Berens-Cohen. His role was essential to the smooth running of the state.

But it was also a court of secret sexual machinations and bitter familial rivalry. To understand the family and court that Melusine encountered in 1690, we have to tell the story of the woman who first employed, protected and finally despised her – the Electress Sophia.

Sophia came of an illustrious lineage. Her parents were the tragic king and queen of Bohemia. She was the granddaughter of James I of England and the great-granddaughter of Mary Queen of Scots. Eventually this genetic inheritance would bring her eldest son George to the Crown of Great Britain as George I – after England's Glorious Revolution of 1688, the country would not accept a Catholic monarch. The historian Alvin Redman tells us:

> In 1658, nine years after the head of Charles I had dropped into the basket at Whitehall, she [Sophia] brought as her dowry, unknowingly and unpredictably, the reversion of the Crown of Great Britain. She was a handsome woman, shrewd and accomplished, and fortunately for the Hanoverian succession she was the only daughter of the luckless Elizabeth Stuart who was a Protestant . . .[1]

Amazingly, considering that Sophia was the twelfth child, she was the closest Protestant to the throne. All her older siblings save Louise were dead by 1682, and of their descendants some were illegitimate, some dead, and the rest married into Catholic families.

Louise, meanwhile, converted to Catholicism in 1657 and became the abbess of Maubuisson.

Nevertheless Sophia was brought up in the uncertainty of exile in a foreign court, away from her father's homeland. She was to have a profound influence on Melusine's life, yet she could barely bring herself to address her and rarely spoke of her to others. The reasons for this are clear; due to her tumultuous upbringing, Sophia craved familial stability and marital fidelity, ideals that she believed were profoundly threatened by the existence of her son's mistress.

When Sophia's mother Elizabeth was sixteen years old she was married to Frederick V, the Elector Palatine and head of the German Protestant Union. It was this marriage that would ultimately destine the heirs of their twelfth child Sophia for the throne of Great Britain. Frederick and Elizabeth were the same age and, unusually for royal dynastic marriages, their relationship was an extremely happy one. They set up court at Heidelberg, Frederick's capital, where they lived an extravagant lifestyle of parties, plays and masquerades. Then, in 1619, politics and wars of religion began to destroy their idyll when the citizens of Protestant Bohemia, having dethroned their Catholic monarch, invited the Calvinist Frederick to take the Crown.

The Jesuits foretold that Frederick would reign for only one season, 'then his rule would melt away like the winter snow'. The new king ruled for only one year and one day before the Catholic Imperial forces defeated him at the battle of Bílá Hora near Prague on 7 November 1620. Everything was lost. Not even Frederick's rule of the Palatinate could be salvaged, despite the (admittedly lukewarm) intervention of his father-in-law King James. His beloved Palatinate was overrun by the Bavarians, his nobility massacred or their lands confiscated, and the population forcibly converted. Henceforth Frederick and Elizabeth, monarchs in exile, were dubbed the 'Winter King and Queen', recalling the priests' prophecy. Frederick's acceptance of the Bohemian throne was arguably the start of the catastrophic 'Thirty Years' War', a conflict between the German princes and the Emperor. It destroyed the fabric of German society, devastated entire communities, and by the war's end in 1648 had reduced the population from 21 million to an estimated 13 million; some historians believe that Germany lost up to half of her pre-war population.[2] Still others have speculated that the widespread destruction of German society led to later aggressive German nationalism, 'the soil of despair which alone can have fed the seeds of virulent German pride that sprouted from the recovery of a later age'.[3]

Sophia was her parents' penultimate child and she spent her childhood watching Frederick and Elizabeth's desperate efforts to recover their kingdom. When Frederick died in 1632 the onus fell on Elizabeth to restore their children to their birthright. Sophia recalls in her extensive memoirs her mother's insistence on etiquette and decorum as she strove to recreate the Palatinate court in exile in The Hague. She was never allowed to forget that she was a princess who, through marriage, could expect to become a queen.

The peace settlement of 1648 that marked the end of the Thirty Years War restored the Rhine Palatinate to Sophia's eldest brother, Karl Ludwig. He set up court at Heidelberg with his wife, the tempestuous Caroline of Hesse-Cassel, and the pair invited Sophia to join them. But although she adored her brother and his children (particularly her niece Elisabeth Charlotte, or Liselotte as she was called by the family) she was drawn into a drama that led her to seek marriage and her own household at any cost.

Karl Ludwig had fallen in love with a lady-in-waiting to Caroline, Louise von Degenfeld. Caroline felt hideously betrayed, particularly as she had befriended and protected the girl. Louise, young and pretty, had also attracted the attentions of Karl Ludwig's brother,

Prince Rupert of the Rhine, the romantic hero of the Cavaliers of the English Civil War, on one of his rare visits to Heidelberg. Caroline, to discourage the amorous prince, encouraged Louise to sleep with her in her own bedchamber for the duration of his visit. She had no idea that Louise and her husband had already fallen in love. When Caroline found out about the affair she became violent and in a fit of rage nearly severed one of Louise's fingers with her teeth. Karl Ludwig was determined to leave Caroline and marry Louise, but Caroline refused to be put aside. Their hysterical rows culminated in a desperate Caroline accusing her husband of incest with his own sister, Sophia. It was not the last time that Sophia would be obliged to refute an allegation of incest.

Karl Ludwig divorced Caroline and married Louise morganatically in 1658. They went on to have fourteen children, nine of whom survived infancy. On their marriage Louise was created a Raugravine – effectively a landless countess – and their children, who became raugraves and raugravines, were regular visitors to the Hanoverian court. But Caroline, slightly unhinged by the betrayal, refused to accept her new status and leave. She stayed with the household.

Sophia's quest for a husband and escape from the emotionally draining and volatile Heidelberg court was not straightforward. She was courted at first by her cousin, the future Charles II of England, but she declined him. In her memoirs she wrote that Charles had told her, with breathtaking tactlessness, that she was more beautiful than Lucy Walter, his current mistress (indeed the two were startlingly similar in looks). She added: 'he had shown a liking for me with which I was most gratified . . . [but I had] sense enough to know that marriages of great kings are not made up of such means'.[4] Furthermore it was not at all clear during Oliver Cromwell's Protectorate that Charles would ever ascend the throne, and this may have influenced Sophia's decision.

Marriage negotiations with Adolf Johann of Zweibrücken also came to nothing, to Sophia's relief. However desperate she was to have her own household, she found the prospective bridegroom extremely unattractive. Then in 1656 salvation seemed to arrive in the shape of Duke George William of Brunswick-Lüneburg, whose large estates were in north Germany. This family was a branch of the ancient Guelph dynasty. When he asked Sophia to marry him, she accepted.

But having secured Sophia's hand the duke got cold feet. He found he was too attached to his bachelor lifestyle and to his frequent trips to Venice, the playground of the German aristocracy. But as he did not want to disappoint Sophia or lose face with Karl Ludwig, he persuaded his youngest brother, Ernst August, to marry her instead.

Ernst August had drawn Sophia's interest from their first meeting. Three years earlier he had visited Heidelberg with his brother, where he had played duets and danced with the princess. They even corresponded after he left the court. But the pragmatic Sophia refused to entertain him as a prospective bridegroom. As the youngest of four sons he could hardly hope to be a ruling prince, and Sophia had been brought up by her mother to expect a glorious marriage.

German rulers rarely practised primogeniture, the inheritance of the entire estate by the eldest son. As every estate was subdivided among the inheriting sons every few years, Germany eventually fragmented into numerous tiny city-states. Duke George, the brothers' father, was no exception, dividing the duchy into two on his death: his son Christian Ludwig was given Lüneburg-Grubenhagen while George William inherited Calenberg-Göttingen – known unofficially as Hanover.[5]

As an inducement to take his place as bridegroom to Sophia, George William offered Ernst August a sweetener. He agreed never to marry, effectively removing any children he might have from the succession. He pointed out that their brother Christian Ludwig had no children, and that their other brother Johann Friedrich (dubbed the fat duke) was also unmarried. So it was likely, he suggested, that Ernst August and his children by Sophia could hope to rule either one or both of the duchies.

Despite the lack of certainty that Ernst August would ever become a ruling prince, the agreement between the brothers was enough for Sophia and she enthusiastically agreed to swap her bridegroom. She was impressed by his lineage: he was descended from the legendary Henry the Lion, Duke of Saxony and Bavaria, who had married the English Princess Matilda in 1168. Sophia had inherited a love of all things English from her mother. Furthermore she was twenty-eight years old – almost past marriageable age by contemporary standards. She also found him extremely attractive. They married on 30 September 1658 at Heidelberg.

Sophia was not vain – she thought herself far too thin – but she evidently delighted in her marriage to the urbane and handsome sybarite Ernst August. She was overjoyed by the passion she found between them and never tired of relating how delighted Ernst August had been with her on their wedding night. Her memoirs are peppered with references to their sex life; after the birth of her second child she returned to the marital bed within two weeks and caught a severe chill. But despite the inconvenience her memoirs record that she had gone there willingly, without coercion and with 'la plus grande joie du monde'.[6]

Sophia and Ernst August initially lived with George William in Hanover. When Ernst August succeeded to the prince-bishopric of Osnabrück, they moved to the castle of Iburg. Elisabeth Charlotte, always known as Liselotte, the only daughter of Karl-Ludwig and Charlotte, was frantic to escape the incendiary atmosphere of the

Heidelberg court, and joined her aunt Sophia on her marriage. In 1671 she left Sophia's care to marry Philippe I of Orléans, the only brother of Louis XIV of France. Liselotte's extensive and gossipy correspondence with princes and princesses throughout Europe, and particularly with Sophia, forms one of the richest historical sources of the late seventeenth and eighteenth centuries. It is from her letters that we know so much about Sophia's family.

Meanwhile Sophia's marriage gamble had already begun to pay off. The death of Ernst August's brother Christian Ludwig in 1665 removed the first obstacle to their ambitions. On Christian Ludwig's death, Ernst August and George William united against their other brother, Johann Friedrich, and took the duchy of Celle for George William. But a complication had arisen in George William's personal life that upset Sophia and Ernst August profoundly and threatened their plans. George William had fallen deeply in love with a beautiful French Huguenot, Eléonore d'Olbreuse. Voltaire wrote that Eléonore 'brought grace to Germany . . .'

Despite the threat that Eléonore posed, even Sophia found her beautiful and wrote of her: 'She was grave and dignified, spoke little and behaved pleasantly . . . Altogether I found her amiable.'[7] Sophia's attitude quickly changed however when she discovered the nature of the relationship. Her brother-in-law's new love would not consent to be his mistress. She was planning marriage. Sophia wrote, in alarm: 'I noticed at once the understanding between the Duke of Celle and Mll [sic] d'Olbreuse by the looks they exchanged, and realised that she was determined to lead him far. She kept him well in hand, impressing on him the warmth of her supposed affection for him on the one hand, and the strict propriety of her conduct on the other.'[8] Sophia went further, referring to Olbreuse as the 'concubine', and, clearly irritated at having to accept her as a sister-in-law, complained that it 'went against honour, for a king's daughter such as I'.

George William had never expected to marry, and had entered into the 1658 convention with Ernst August on that premise. But Eléonore demanded marriage and the respectability it bestowed. She eventually agreed to a lesser 'marriage of conscience', which would render any children of the match illegitimate. In a hasty letter to her brother the Elector Palatine Sophia wrote: 'the marriage of conscience between Duke George William and the Olbreuse was made public, although the consecration was done secretly, without candles or witnesses. This is all I have time to say.'[9] Nevertheless, George William was at pains to stress to his anxious brother and sister-in-law that he would uphold his side of the bargain and deny any future heirs an inheritance.

Later, Sophia recorded the terms of the arrangement in her memoirs:

> As the affection I bear for my brother made me resolve never to marry, for his advantage and his children's; and as I shall never desist from this resolution; and as Mlle d'Olbreuse has decided to come and live with me, I hereby promise never to leave her. I undertake to give her two thousand crowns a year during my lifetime, and six thousand crowns a year after my death; while she, on her part, will promise to be as satisfied with this arrangement as I am. Having taken this decision with my brother's agreement, he has promised to sign it.

She goes on to note: 'That was the contents of the anti-contract of marriage which the four of us signed, the Duke of Celle and the Olbreuse, my husband and myself. After that the two lovers went to bed together without further ado.'[10]

A daughter, Sophia Dorothea, was born to the couple in the autumn of 1666. Eléonore, although overjoyed at her birth, was nevertheless distraught that her daughter was illegitimate and feared for the financial provision of any future sons. However Sophia Dorothea remained an only child; subsequently the unfortunate Eléonore suffered only miscarriages or stillbirths.

Sophia gave birth to George Louis, Sophia Dorothea's first cousin and future husband, and the future George I of Great Britain, on 28 May 1660. Only two years had passed since his parents' marriage. He was much longed for by his mother. Prematurely, she had thought herself barren. Sophia adored him at once, her love fuelled by relief that she could conceive a child. She was in rhapsodies over his big blue eyes, believing him 'as beautiful as an angel'. Seven more children followed, although one boy, the twin of Maximilian Wilhelm, died very young. Friedrich August was born in 1661, Maximilian Wilhelm in 1666, Sophia Charlotte (the only girl, known as Figuelotte) in 1668, Karl Philipp in 1669, Christian Heinrich in 1671 and Ernst August in 1674. Although she loved all of her children, Sophia later commented that perhaps she had had too many.

Sixty years later, Liselotte recalled George Louis's birth:

I remember the day when the King of England was born as if it were today. I certainly was a willful, forward child. They had put a doll in a rosemary bush and wanted to make me believe that it was the child to whom Ma Tante [Sophia] had given birth; just then I heard her screaming dreadfully, for Her Grace was in great pain; and this did not seem to fit in with the baby in the rosemary bush. I pretended to believe it, though, but hid as if I were playing seek . . . squeezed into Ma Tante's reception room where Her Grace was in labour, and hid behind a large screen that had been placed before the door by the fireplace. When the child was born, it was carried to the fireplace to be bathed, and then I crawled out. They should have spanked me, but because it was a happy day I was only scolded.[11]

Sophia called herself a 'nearly stupidly fond' mother; perhaps no woman, neither wife nor mistress, would ever be good enough for her beloved 'Görgen', as he was known to the family. As a child George was eager to please his parents. He was studious and reliable, a solemn boy who took his responsibilities seriously. Sophia vigorously defended him to critics, amongst them Liselotte, who thought him cold. Sophia argued that he was an intensely private individual, not given to displays of emotion but capable of deep feeling. He was loyal: once gain his friendship and he gave it for life. Although his stubbornness irritated her, particularly when he replaced his father as ruler of Hanover in 1698 and they found themselves frequently in one another's company, she thought him the most admirable of her children.

In 1679 another obstacle to Ernst August's ambition was removed with the death of Johann Friedrich. As he had produced only daughters, the dukedom of Hanover passed, at last, to Ernst August, and the family moved to the Leineschloss.

Sophia's father had inadvertently unleashed the horrors of the Thirty Years War. Yet paradoxically it presented his son-in-law Ernst August with the opportunity to reinvent his principality. The 1648 Treaty of Westphalia, marking the end of the war, allowed for the creation of an eighth elector. For the first time since the Golden Bull of 1356 another German prince would be admitted to the Electoral College, the small elite body that elected the Holy Roman Emperor. Ernst August began to entertain a dream: if the electoral cap could be won for his house, the glory days of his medieval ancestor Henry the Lion would surely return.

The Hanoverian electoral cap has been called 'the most expensive bonnet in history', and to secure it, Ernst August was prepared to compromise his religious beliefs, send his people to war, use his children to further his dynastic ambitions and – most damaging to his immediate family circle – establish primogeniture in

Hanover. It could only be achieved if Ernst August could prove that Hanover was large enough and wealthy enough to be of use to the Emperor – and more so than any of the competing German principalities.

In pursuit of electoral status, Ernst August and Sophia spent a fortune on building and patronage. They rebuilt and modernized the Leineschloss, and the small summer villa of Herrenhausen was entirely remodelled by Ernst August's Italian architect, Quirini, who used as his archetype the sublime Palladian palaces of the Veneto. If the Hanoverians could have lived anywhere on Earth they probably would have chosen Venice. Ernst August and George William adored it and kept a permanent residence there. But they were not doges of Venice; they were dukes of a minor German principality with ambitions, and Sophia was determined to make the best of it. Since the assumption of rule in Hanover, with the time-consuming duties it entailed, meant fewer opportunities for Venetian holidays, she would create a little Venice right there in Hanover, at Herrenhausen, for the family and court to delight in. When the work was completed the family spent every summer there, from May until October.

The relatively simple building began life in 1665 when Johann Friedrich dismantled his hunting lodge, Lauenstein, near Coldingen, and took it to Hanover. Its half-timbered frame was remodelled by the Venetian architect Lorenzo Bedoghi, and the foundations of the baroque gardens were laid the following year. Johann Friedrich, a humanist and an enlightened prince, clearly gave much thought to the gardens and their layout. The philosophy behind baroque gardens was man's taming of nature, and he charged his new thirty-year-old court adviser, Gottfried Wilhelm Leibniz – who would achieve renown as a philosopher, mathematician, polymath and the implacable rival of Isaac Newton – to bring his skills to bear on the gardens from the outset.

At Herrenhausen Leibniz's fingerprints are everywhere. Throughout the 50 hectares of the Great Garden, for example, there is not one perfect right angle: they are all precisely 2.8 degrees out of true.[12] Baroque thinking gave rise to the paradoxical theory that perfection appears imperfect to the eye, hence flawlessness can only be achieved by a small discrepancy. Leibniz's mathematical genius had detected that anything up to 3 degrees awry created something even more faultless to the eye than a perfect right angle. The ideal baroque garden aspired to be far more than a pleasing space. It was meant to represent the immeasurable nature of the universe. And at Herrenhausen the long pathways of the Great Garden almost tricked the eye into supposing that they carried on into infinity.

Johann Friedrich continued to extend the house and the gardens until his death in 1679. Although the foundation of something marvellous was already there, Sophia was disappointed with what she saw as rural, dreary Herrenhausen. But she set about her improvements with such passion and determination that the project consumed her. She spent the next thirty-five years turning it into one of the glories of Hanover, and its incomparable gardens made the duke and duchess the envy of many a European ruler. Sophia said: 'The garden is my life.' And by the time she died in the middle of her wonderful creation in 1714 it was the most gorgeous and perfectly baroque garden in Europe.

She summoned the French gardener Martin Charbonnier, who had designed the gardens at their palace of Osnabrück, to help her; in turn he employed other gardeners and sent them on scouting missions throughout Europe. Charbonnier oversaw the design of the Great Garden, the Garden Theatre, the Nouveau Jardin, the Great Parterre, the Gallery, the pavilions and the Great Fountain. Water was everywhere. Sophia would take walk after walk during the summer days, listening to the trickle of the fountain and the gentle lapping of the river against its bank. Heady scents more typical of southern Europe filled the air; the gardens were stocked with exotic plants from far warmer climates, particularly date palms, apricots, peaches, figs, pomegranates and orange trees. The orange trees were housed in the Gallery during the winter, but in the summer when the family and court were in residence they nestled in the courtyard, pervading the gardens with the scent of their blossom.

The roses in the Rose Garden, or Love Garden, imbued the air with their aromatic perfume, and at the centre of the Labyrinth stood a wooden temple filled with doves. During the carnival or summer festivals musicians accompanied the revellers. For those in a philosophical mood, the Lawn Garden was a perfect place to walk, with no distractions. The grotto, built by Johann Friedrich in 1676, offered relief from the burning midsummer sun. And in the Berggarten, opposite the Great Garden, a beautiful garden theatre was created between 1689 and 1692. Here Sophia encouraged the family to perform; one year George acted in Leibniz's play *Trimalcion*, apparently very well. In contrast to the rest of the gardens, the Berggarten was carefully cultivated to present the appearance of being untamed by man, rather than showcasing a mathematical ideal. Here one could lose oneself entirely, and one can imagine the games of chase the ducal children would have played here, and the forbidden liaisons that the frenzied atmosphere of carnival would have encouraged.

Carnival was an established fixture in the calendar in Johann Friedrich's time, but under Sophia and Ernst August it became ever wilder and more elaborate, leading contemporaries to call Hanover 'the Venice of the North'. The canal built at Herrenhausen between 1686 and 1701 provided carnival revellers with gondolas in which to float and contemplate, or to indulge in the debauchery associated with the festival.[13] A Venetian gondolier, Pierre Madonetto, was employed to look after the boats and to ferry those who would not or could not row themselves.

Carnival, Ernst August believed, served two purposes. The first was to throw a huge party that gave the regime a veneer of accessibility; the second was to burnish the glory of the ruling house. Masques and tableaux where family members would dress as gods and goddesses enhanced the notion of rule by divine right; yet equally the populace was distracted by the music, dancing, free food and access to glorious Herrenhausen. They adored the sight of the nobility in their most outrageous fancy dress parading through the town in open carriages or on horseback, accompanied by musicians. By the time of Ernst August's death, the Hanoverian carnival rivalled the Venetian for pomp, debauchery and fun; anyone who could afford a mask could join in. Ernst August was a lotus eater and the pleasure seekers of Europe benefited.

In antithesis to the devastation of the Thirty Years' War, Hanover became a party town. The war created a huge shift in approaches towards life and happiness. Just as the survivors of the Black Death in the fourteenth century became less risk-averse, so the Thirty Years' War created a culture of excess, most visibly amongst the rich. Whole generations had been raised under the yoke of death; many responded with a taste for earthly delights.

If Germany's princes adored Italian licentiousness, they also coveted French style. Writing nearly one hundred years later, George's grandson, Frederick the Great of Prussia, wrote of the enduring attraction of France: 'there is no prince [of Germany] down to the younger member with an apanage who does not imagine himself to be a Louis XIV. He builds his Versailles, has his mistresses and maintains an army.'[14]

The French King Louis XIV's unsurpassable court and palace of Versailles, a former hunting lodge some 25 kilometres from Paris, became the model for aspirational princes throughout Europe.

Louis moved the court there in 1682 in an attempt to curb the intrigues of his courtiers in the vast and labyrinthine Louvre – he wanted the key men in France to remain under his watchful eye. When Sophia visited in 1664 on a grand tour of France and northern Italy, she was struck by the unique formal beauty of the palace and grounds. She admired the pomp and the sophisticated revels. The rigidity of the court structure appealed to her sense of royal entitlement. After she and Ernst August inherited the principality in 1679, Sophia succeeded in creating a court at Hanover that became an eastern reflection of that of the Sun King in France. Whilst Hanover's pleasures reflected the frenzied delights of the Venetian carnival, the style, the fashion, and the language of the court was French – the lingua franca of international diplomacy.

Sophia and Ernst August had inherited the services of the dazzling Gottfried Wilhelm Leibniz from Johann Friedrich, and he became so indispensable to the dynasty that he stayed for forty years. Leibniz became the family's historian, diplomat, adviser and great friend. In him, Sophia found an intellectual sparring partner, just as her contemporary Queen Christina of Sweden, the 'Minerva of the North', had done in the philosopher René Descartes and in her secretary Monsieur Urban de Chevreau, who briefly filled the post in Hanover until Leibniz's arrival. With Leibniz, the new duke and duchess devised a plan to promote the glory of their house, to make them all 'immortal'.

Leibniz was charged with producing a genealogy of the House, the *Historia Domus*, in order to support its claim to the Electorate by claiming descent from heroes of German and Classical history. His excavations in the archives of Germany and Italy produced the hoped-for link with the twelfth-century German hero Henry the Lion. But Leibniz was not the first to delve into the family's past. In 1685 a Venetian scholar, Abbot Theodoro Damaideno, had discovered not only a link to the d'Este family of northern Italy, but also to Rome's second Caesar, Augustus, to the fifth-century BC Accius Navius, a contemporary of the legendary Tarquin, supposed fifth king of Rome, and to Charlemagne, the first Holy Roman Emperor.

Such revered and newly resurrected ancestors prompted a flurry of portraiture and architecture as the dead were brought into play to enhance the glory of the House. In 1664, when Sophia and Ernst August had embarked on their grand tour of northern Italy and France, they had noted how at Versailles and in the Veneto Louis XIV and the Italian princes had exploited architecture and decoration for their own propaganda. Now, twenty years later, the duke and duchess made use of the lesson. Fresh ancestral portraits were commissioned. At the Leineschloss, most prominently in the newly decorated presence chamber, the ducal family were observed by the multitude of German, Roman and Byzantine heroes they claimed as their own. Hanover's link to ancient Rome and the glory of medieval Germany was celebrated not only in portraiture, but in the classical simplicity of Palladian architecture.

The Hanoverian ruling house allowed Leibniz incredible freedom to follow his own intellectual pursuits, and he seems to have formed a warm and genuine friendship with Sophia. Yet he had travelled in London and Paris and felt himself far too urbane for the 'provincial' Hanoverians, despite Sophia's and Ernst August's efforts to make their court a magnet for European intellectuals. He complained: 'Everything that so confines me both mentally and physically derives from my not living in a large city like Paris or London' and he lamented the absence of men from whom he could 'learn'. Perhaps he was frustrated and bored with his research into the family's history. He further complained against the injustice of the divine right of kings: 'It is just as seemly for those whom God has granted intellect but no power to give advice, as it is befitting to those who have been granted power to listen to that advice . . . Where the intellect is greater than the power, the one holding the former may consider himself to be oppressed.' But although frustrated with his position, he did find happiness in Sophia's garden.

Today the Gallery is one of only two buildings from the palace to survive Allied bombing during the Second World War. It was originally designed to house the delicate plants during the harsh north German winters. But Sophia, adamant that the main palace was not grand enough for all the balls and parties she hosted, turned it into a Festival Hall, a glorious confection she hoped would rival Versailles. It is a beautiful building, decorated with elaborate stucco work and filled with glorious classically themed frescos by the Venetian artist Tommaso Giusti. Light floods through the windows and bounces off the ornamental chandeliers to bathe the room in gold. It was in this room that Sophia danced a Polonaise with Peter the Great in 1697 as the Tsar journeyed throughout Europe visiting his royal brothers and sisters. Here the Tsar ogled Ernst August's gaudily attired mistress Klara Platen: Sophia maliciously wrote to Liselotte that Peter singled Klara out 'because of her colourful appearance: thick paint was all the range in Muscovy'. And it was in a suite off this room that Sophia lived.

Even opera was drafted to serve the Hanoverian claim to the electoral cap. Johann Friedrich's theatre was transformed into the most magnificent opera house in northern Europe. The chosen production for its inauguration in 1689, Steffani's *Enrico Leone* was an orgy of operatic theatricality. This elaborate five-hour marathon of a production served to show the family's tenuous link to the twelfth-century hero Henry the Lion and his English wife Matilda. The production of 1689 kicked off the Carnival with an array of mythical characters – Amazons, fauns, nymphs and devils in abundance. Live horses appeared on stage. The thrilling libretto by Ernst August's Italian secretary, Hortensio Mauro, induced Sophia to call him 'notre Apollon' – our Apollo. *Enrico Leone* delighted first the court, and then the general public who were admitted free of charge.

But no matter how much dazzle, glamour and elegance Ernst August and Sophia may have been able to import into their principality, electoral status could only be achieved if Ernst August could prove to the Emperor that his dominions were vigorous enough to provide effective aid to the Habsburgs. To this end he was determined to establish primogeniture in Hanover (thus ensuring that his dominions would remain united after his death rather than being divided piecemeal amongst his sons) and sought the Emperor Leopold's approval. It was granted in 1683 and Ernst August finally announced it to his children at Christmas the following year. George would get everything; his brothers received no lands, only financial compensation. It split the family irrevocably.

George's brother Friedrich August, as the next eldest, was furious and canvassed support against his father throughout the courts of Europe. He had particular success with Duke Anton Ulrich of Brunswick-Wolfenbüttel, a distant cousin who saw the sons' disaffection with the father as a wonderful opportunity to sow discord in a rival state.

One son who, despite Friedrich August's promptings, initially stood by his father was Maximilian Wilhelm – known by the family as Max. He was born in 1666 and was six years younger than George. A portrait in the Historisches Museum in Hanover shows him sporting a red silk bow and a white lace jabot. He was a dandy who believed his parents owed him a living – his mother Sophia said he lacked 'Geist' (spirit).[15] And when Ernst August first raised the issue of primogeniture with his sons at Christmas 1684, Max initially agreed. He was only the third son and he was placated by his father's offer of financial compensation. He left it to his older brother Friedrich August to rail with tantrums against their parents at the injustice of his position. Max even signed the primogeniture clause in 1687. But when Friedrich August died in battle in 1690 (George's brother Karl Philipp also died in battle that year), Max, now the second son and the one with most to lose, broke his promise in spectacular fashion.

A contemporary story claims he tried to poison his father with snuff. He certainly contacted Duke Anton Ulrich to aid him in a plot against his father. But his sister Figuelotte discovered the scheme and told their father, after which Max and two of his accomplices, the cousins Joachim and Otto Friedrich von Moltke, were arrested for treason. Sophia, distraught at the loss of two of her sons in battle and anxious not to lose another in familial strife, possibly aided Max in his machinations. Ernst August certainly suspected her of treason, and she was questioned by privy councillor Albrecht Philipp von dem Bussche.[16] She wrote frenziedly to Bussche, begging him to tell her husband that she had never wished to 'plunge the country into a bath of blood and fire', as Ernst August claimed.[17] Max, cowed into submission by his arrest and by the beheading of Otto Friedrich, finally consented officially to the primogeniture.

Max was to remain an embarrassment to George for the rest of his life. He stayed quiet until Ernst August's death in 1698. Then, easily overcoming his grief for a father he felt betrayed by, he once again reneged on his signing of the primogeniture clause, seeking support for his position from Hanover's foreign enemies. To Sophia and George's dismay, his brother Christian Heinrich also turned on George. George was convinced that it was the younger Christian Heinrich who had led Max astray, but it is unclear who influenced whom. Both went into self-imposed exile, leading a desperate Sophia to seek a reconciliation between George and his brothers. Max, a gambler with an expensive lifestyle, played on George's fears for Hanover's position on the international stage to gain the maximum financial compensation (Sophia subsidized his already considerable income for the rest of her life). He also exploited a new development that drove the European gossips into a frenzy of speculation: the English succession.

England's 'Glorious Revolution' of 1688 had removed the Catholic Stuart monarch James II from the throne and replaced him with the joint rule of his Protestant daughter Mary and her Dutch husband and first cousin, William, Prince of Orange. When Mary died childless in 1694 her sister Anne became William's heir presumptive. By the end of her childbearing years in 1698 Anne had endured eighteen pregnancies, most of which had resulted in miscarriages, stillbirths or infants who only lived for a few months. Only one child survived infancy – William Duke of Gloucester. In 1694 he was five years old and sickly.

Anne's tragic childbearing history prompted a succession crisis. The English would not tolerate another Catholic monarch. The next Protestant in line to the throne – though there were over fifty more eligible Catholic candidates – was Sophia. In July 1700 the young Duke of Gloucester died of hydrocephalus, or water on the brain. His death prompted the Act of Settlement of 1701, which acknowledged Sophia and the Protestant heirs of her body as the heirs to England. This historical fluke, resulting from Anne's misery, was to have drastic implications for George.

But the problem of Max and Christian Heinrich continued, causing further embarrassment to the family. In an act of breathtaking disloyalty, Max converted to Catholicism. The English were naturally appalled. Sophia's succession to the English throne rested not only on her own Protestantism, but on that of the 'heirs of her body'. Max's conversion, as George's sibling, put in jeopardy the prospect of the Hanoverian assumption of the English throne.

Speculation piled upon speculation. Reports spread that not only had Max converted, but Christian Heinrich too. William III was furious and demanded confirmation from Philipp Adam Eltz, a Hanoverian diplomat, as to the truth of the rumours. Eltz, embarrassed, confirmed that Max had indeed converted, but said that to the best of his knowledge Christian Heinrich remained a Protestant.

More promisingly for chances of harmony in the Hanoverian court, after the debacle of Max's treachery of 1692 and Sophia's possible role in its execution, husband and wife were reunited in the spring of 1693. The reason was joy. Emperor Leopold, desperate for Hanoverian troops to fight against the hegemony of Louis XIV of France, had finally agreed to confer the electoral cap on the House of Hanover. It was a long-awaited prize, and an expensive one. For the wars he undertook on the Emperor's behalf and the palaces he built to reflect the glory of his house, Liselotte records that Ernst August paid a million thaler, an astronomical sum.

The arrival of this tiny bonnet, wrought with crimson velvet and ermine, was celebrated with a magnificent gala at the Leineschloss. Everyone at court wore new clothes and everyone attended; immediate and extended family, courtiers and mistresses. Most colourful of all was Ernst August's mistress, Klara Platen, weighed down by the magnificence of her jewels. Although great affection still existed between Ernst August and Sophia, the love affair of the early years of their marriage was long gone.

Whilst his brothers caused havoc, the couple's eldest son, George, was being carefully groomed as the fulfilment of his parents' ambitions. With the establishment of primogeniture everything would rest on George's ability to be an excellent soldier and statesman. In 1675, when he was only fifteen, he fought bravely by his father's side in his first battle at Conzbrücke, helping to drive back the French. Ernst August wrote fondly to Sophia: 'Your Benjamin was worthy of you, he stuck to my side through thick and thin.'[18]

Of all of their children George was the one most suited to military life, and he found that he excelled at it because he loved it. He was also an able scholar, fluent in French and Latin, with some Italian and Dutch. He diligently studied history and geography, the subjects that would improve him as a soldier. His diplomatic skills were honed by visits to France and to England in 1680, he sat in council meetings and enjoyed his father's full confidence from 1688, accompanying Ernst August on several diplomatic visits to Berlin. George became intimately acquainted with his father's ministers: with the trusted Otto Grote, President of the Chamber (and a contemporary of Melusine's father at the university of Helmstadt); with the lawyer Ludolf Hugo, who oversaw the smooth conclusion to the issues of primogeniture and gaining of the electoral cap;[19] and with Friedrich Wilhelm von Görtz, who would form part of George's intimate circle when he became ruler of Hanover and king of Great Britain. George was already well acquainted with another of his father's privy councillors, his former tutor, Abrecht Philipp von dem Bussche.

During George's 1680 visit to his Stuart cousins in England the gossips chattered that, as the heir to Hanover, he was there to view the young Princess Anne as a possible bride. Sophia certainly considered it. Later speculation suggested that Anne and George's subsequent frosty relationship was due to his rejection of her. But there was probably little foundation to the rumours. Anne and her uncle King Charles II greeted George as a cousin rather than as a potential bridegroom. Three years later the princess made a love match with her marriage to the extremely dull Prince George of Denmark. Charles II drolly declared of her fiancé: 'I have tried him drunk and I have tried him sober and there is nothing in him.' But the reason a union between Princess Anne and George was not seriously pursued was that Ernst August and Sophia, and probably George too, had already decided that the only marriage he could possibly contemplate was to his first cousin, Sophia Dorothea of Celle.

In 1675 George William eventually married his mistress, with the blessing of the Holy Roman Emperor, and their daughter Sophia Dorothea's illegitimacy was revoked. Although George William stressed again and again his promise to uphold the convention, Ernst August was alarmed at Sophia Dorothea's engagement to August Frederick, the heir of the Duke of Brunswick-Wolfenbüttel. When George William eventually died, he feared, the might of Brunswick-Wolfenbüttel's army would be employed to uphold Sophia Dorothea's birthright. Conveniently the heir was killed in battle and Ernst August and Sophia determined that Sophia Dorothea would have to marry George.

A union between the first cousins George and Sophia Dorothea had become imperative to the promotion of the state. Hanover and Celle were already acting as one, sharing a single diplomat to represent their interests.[20] Sophia was obliged to overcome her distaste for Sophia Dorothea's initial illegitimacy. She wrote avariciously of her agreement to the marriage: 'if it is gilded with 100,000 crowns [thaler] a year in our full control we may shut our eyes to take it . . .' By 1681 the details of the marriage contract had been decided. Sophia Dorothea, destined to become one of the most pitiful of Europe's princesses, brought the promise of a unified Celle and Hanover, a dowry of 100,000 thaler, as well as an income of 4,000 thaler per annum to her future in-laws. She would have no financial independence; her income was to be under George's control.[21] Although George was undoubtedly attracted to his bride, Sophia noted that his desire to improve the fortunes of their house was so great that he would 'marry a cripple'.[22]

The pair were married at Celle on 22 November 1682. The bride was sixteen years old, her husband twenty-two.

Unlike his bride, George had some sexual experience by the time of his marriage. An affair with his sister Figuelotte's under-governess in 1676 produced a son, to his mother's horror. His father was equally apoplectic, but only because he feared scandal – the girl came from a good Heidelberg family. George never acknowledged the child, as he would never formally acknowledge any of his illegitimate children. After the initial shock of George's first sexual foray, Ernst August took it upon himself to arrange a mistress for him, urged by his own *maîtresse en titre*, Klara Platen. The woman was Maria Katharine von Meysenbug, Klara's younger sister.

Ernst August had allowed Klara, who was eighteen years younger than Sophia, to become a considerable force at court. Their affair had begun in the 1670s, and although he continued to have numerous other romantic adventures, it would endure until his death. Her compliant husband, Franz Ernst von Platen, was rewarded for accommodating the affair with political office – he eventually became Hanover's first minister in 1693.

Klara was exquisitely opulent, with a wide, generous mouth and beautiful hands. She dressed superbly, maddeningly copying Sophia's taste to vex her. Clothes always looked better on Klara, whereas Sophia's frame appeared too small to support the rich furs she favoured. Ambitious, scheming and hungry for wealth, which she used her position to gain, Klara was eventually accepted by Sophia as an annoying fixture.

It was typical of Klara to push her sister into George's arms, largely to extend her own power base. Maria Katherine was five years older than George, mature enough to be exotic but young enough to have the freshness and beauty of youth. Ernst August and Klara believed she was the perfect means of controlling George. But the affair quickly fizzled out and Maria Katherine sub-sequently married Johann von dem Bussche, a Hanoverian army officer. George's split from Maria Katherine frustrated Klara immensely, and from the outset she was Sophia Dorothea's enemy.

Some historians have speculated that George's next serious romantic attachment was to his half-sister, Sophia Charlotte von Platen. She was Klara's daughter by Ernst August and was acknowledged and accepted by the family, even by Sophia, who liked her enormously.[23] Illegitimacy was not a stigma in Hanover and illegitimate children had the right to bear their father's arms, although crossed by the bar sinister. Whether or not they would go on to become lovers later in life, they certainly were not at the beginning of the 1680s: Sophia Charlotte was only born in 1675. But, whatever the truth, George showed her a lifelong devotion. He gave her every honour; after the death of his father this illegitimate half-sister was treated as a sister. As king of Great Britain he gave her lands, titles and income.

Despite its eventual breakdown, the early years of the marriage between George and Sophia Dorothea were relatively companionable. Sophia Dorothea's looks were perfectly in accord with contemporary taste. She was pleasingly plump, with a pretty face, creamy skin, beautiful hands and cascades of dark curls. And although the European gossips later reported that George had found her distasteful from the start, he was initially attracted to her. Sophia, perhaps guilty of a little embellishment, wrote of the 'grand passion' that George had formed for his bride. But their personalities were terribly mismatched. The brothers Ernst August and George William were only concerned that the marriage of their children should elevate their house. They did not consider the consequences of uniting the serious, responsible, hardworking and occasionally dour George to a frivolous young girl. Sophia Dorothea, the doted-on, spoilt only child of parents still completely in love, was shockingly ill-prepared for life as a future duchess.

Sophia Dorothea's in-laws went out of their way to welcome her. Sophia, although 'maddened' by her dizziness and often inappropriate behaviour, did her best to make herself agreeable. Liselotte wrote to Sophia on 7 August 1692, complaining of her own daughter-in-law, 'the most disagreeable person in the world'.[24] But, she continues, 'Your Grace's daughter-in-law is only half as bad as ours, and moreover pleasant and kind as a person, which ours certainly is not. No wonder, then, that I find it more difficult to make the effort for ours than Your Grace for hers.'[25] By contrast, the notoriously lecherous Ernst August, who found her extremely attractive, sought out his niece's company as much as possible. George's brothers were equally entranced, with Karl Philipp playing the courtly lover and Friedrich August calling her the bellissime. Figuelotte, perhaps tired of being the only girl amongst so many men, adored her sense of fun and style. (Sophia found her new daughter-in-law so pernicious an influence on young Figuelotte that she comforted herself, when her only daughter left Hanover in October 1684 to marry Friedrich Wilhelm of Brandenburg-Prussia, that at least Sophia Dorothea could no longer turn her head with frivolities.) There were rumours that Max seriously tried to have an affair with her – Sophia Dorothea felt his advances went too far, beyond the bounds of flirtatious behaviour allowed, even encouraged in court circles – but this may have been part of the allegations of treason later brought against him.

Sophia Dorothea was pregnant by the spring of 1683; in December she gave birth to a boy, Georg August, who would eventually become George II of Great Britain. Hans Kaspar von Bothmer, first gentleman of her household, records in his memoirs how eager the princess was that George should return from campaign in time for the baby's birth. Three years later a daughter followed, named Sophia Dorothea after her mother. She had been conceived during an Italian holiday, when Sophia Dorothea travelled with her father-in-law to see George, who had once again been on campaign with his troops in the service of the Emperor against the Turks (part of the cunning Ernst August's jostling for the electoral cap).

If George had spent more time in Hanover then perhaps the marriage might not have broken down so quickly, if at all. But from 1688 he put himself at his father's disposal to fight in the Palatinate war on the side of the Emperor against the French. (This war broke Liselotte's heart, as she saw the troops of the French royal family she had been forced to marry into break up the beloved home of her childhood.) The spoilt, fragile and bored Sophia Dorothea craved attention, and George, either at war or immersed in affairs of state, refused to satisfy what he saw as her unreasonable emotional demands.

She was still young and very immature. Her chief pleasure seems to have been trumping Countess von Platen in the fashion stakes. George had his mother as a perfect wifely role-model. Sophia was completely at one with his father regarding the promotion of their house; her behaviour, although occasionally idiosyncratic, was always exemplary; and she turned a blind eye to Ernst August's many affairs. George's tempestuous wife was Sophia's antithesis. Sophia Dorothea's lady-in-waiting, Eleonore von dem Knesebeck, tells us that the princess was unhappy a mere four years into her marriage, even before the couple's daughter was born. Whilst George, ever conscientious, threw himself into war abroad and administration at home, domestically they plodded on without either finding a serious antidote to their miserable situation. George had no preferred mistress at the end of the 1680s and beginning of the 1690s. If he did have a mistress at all, she was too insignificant for her name to have been recorded. At this point Melusine enters the story.

4.

The Mistress

Women signify nothing unless they are the mistress of a prince or a first minister, which I would not be if I were young . . .
— Sarah, Duchess of Marlborough

Melusine arrived in Hanover in 1690 at exactly the right time. George's marriage to Sophia Dorothea was crumbling and the primogeniture decision had created fury and suspicion within the ducal family while they were still grieving the deaths of Karl Philipp and Friedrich August on the battlefield. Within this febrile atmosphere Melusine and George met, shortly after she entered Sophia's service. From then on, when George was in Hanover, they were constantly in one another's company.

Melusine was well connected and well educated. Her family was noble and newly rich. Her brother Johann Matthias was already making a name for himself as one of the brilliant military minds of the era, and her father enjoyed the confidence of the Elector of Brandenburg. The wily Ernst August and his wife could not have failed to note the potential diplomatic benefit Melusine would bring to their house, which is probably why she gained the position in Sophia's household.

She entered a court peopled by a very small number of the nobility and their servants, dominated by the lecherous and ambitious Ernst August, the snobbish Sophia and the volatile and tricky Sophia Dorothea. Court was about spectacle, wealth and adventure. There were orgies with beautiful courtesans for those that sought them, meandering conversations with Leibniz for those with an intellectual disposition.

There were two distinct types of women at court – the respectable noblewomen and the courtesans. The latter were usually drawn from the families of the burgeoning middle classes, or less frequently, like Melusine, from the minor nobility. They were typically witty, excellent conversationalists, and most were very pretty. But no matter how accomplished, beautiful and talented they were, they were exchanging sexual favours for gifts and protection; as such they languished on the periphery of respectable society. There was misunderstanding and antipathy between the two groups.[1] Characteristically the nobility, men and women, were extremely proud of their lineage. Ernst August, who always made zealous use of the courtesan, obviously saw them as amusing playthings and never referred to them with any respect in his letters. Respect belonged to the 'proper' court lady, and relations between the two groups, who rarely mixed, could be chilly. George's youngest brother Ernst August tells in his correspondence of the outrage expressed by an established court grande dame, Frau von Reden, at the courtesan Katherine von Meysenbug's temerity in calling on her in her rooms. So furious was she that a mere courtesan should dare to visit her as a social equal that she called her a 'cat', a huge insult.[2]

Perhaps the duke's regard for Sophia had encouraged the court to divide along these lines. Although he kept mistresses and allowed at least one to grow powerful, he never treated Sophia with anything less than absolute respect.

Why did Melusine accept George as a lover? Had he not divorced Sophia Dorothea then Melusine would have been condemned to the margins of polite society. Her father and stepmother were hopeful that the Hanover appointment would lead to a good marriage – her old, respectable family demanded it. Melusine must have known that her liaison with George would be detrimental to any future marriage, and his track record suggested he would discard her quickly, even if she became pregnant. In 1690 Melusine had little to gain from such a relationship. Even so, this provincial virgin embraced George enthusiastically when there was absolutely no material reason for her to do so. It seems that Melusine – quiet, shy, not conventionally beautiful and possibly lacking in confidence – fell in love.

George has suffered at the hands of historians, who for the most part cast him as narrow-minded and a cultural philistine who was sometimes monstrous to his own family. The scandal of Sophia Dorothea and Königsmarck so horrified Europe that the Frenchman Charles Perrault may well have had George in mind when he penned his bloody folktale 'Bluebeard' in 1697, and Charlotte Brontë may at least in part have modelled her anti-hero of *Jane Eyre*, Edward Rochester, on George: both effectively imprisoned their wives in the attic. But the historian Ragnhild Hatton has done much to rehabilitate his character. She produces strong evidence to suggest that George was actually sensitive, wise and capable of great love, sharing Melusine's huge interest in art, architecture and music. He was also a brilliant soldier and an able administrator. George did not govern lightly either in Hanover or England. He was extremely active, and effective, both as elector and king, whereas many of his contemporary monarchs relied on ministers and courtiers to govern.

Sophia noted with derision the attention George lavished on Melusine, while in his letters George's brother Ernst August is kinder, quickly accepting George's new mistress as part of the family's odd extended circle. From the beginning, Melusine worked hard to create a warm domestic bubble for George, away from the machinations of the court and his appalling marriage.

When she became aware of the relationship, Sophia was simply amazed – and angry. Melusine, newly arrived at court, was technically under Sophia's protection. The duchess never reconciled herself to the fact that her charge chose to place herself outside 'proper' society and had thus betrayed her class.

Sophia found Melusine's slim, tall figure ugly and thought her unfashionably thin, perhaps evoking memories of her own tiny figure, which she detested. She was forthright in her opinion of Melusine's looks in casual conversation; for example, her rude remark to Henrietta Howard, an English noblewoman and future mistress of George's heir Georg August, was, according to one source, uttered in Melusine's hearing. 'Do you see that maukin [scarecrow]?' she asked, as Melusine, she knew, stood directly behind her. 'You would scarcely believe that she had captivated my son.'[3]

In fact, Melusine was an extremely attractive young woman, but her looks were far more suited to modern tastes. In an age where small, plump women were in vogue, a figure like hers commanded little admiration. It was Sophia Dorothea who embodied everything that was fashionable in beauty: petite, buxom, plump and full-featured. Yet Melusine had a sweet face, wonderful dark hair, pale, flawless skin and large, almond-shaped eyes. For George, the fact that she was the antithesis to Sophia Dorothea's magnetic 'beauté tyrannique' was the most attractive thing about her.[4]

Sophia would never accept her eldest son's liaison with 'La Schulenburg'. Mistresses, she knew, were a fact of life. She had tolerated her own sexually incontinent husband's plethora for years. Ernst August expected Sophia to entertain his current and former mistresses, and for the sake of harmony she complied. She even shared an Italian holiday with Ernst August and several of his sexual partners. But it seems her tolerance had limits; she had baulked at his suggestion that she appoint the Marchesa Paleotti, a former mistress from Bologna by whom he had a son, to her staff. (Later Liselotte wrote of a romance between the young man and Sophia Charlotte, Ernst August's daughter by Klara Platen. 'Disgusting,' thrilled the bored Liselotte, '. . . they are probably brother and sister.')

In the many volumes of Sophia's surviving letters, which detail almost every aspect of her life, Melusine is mostly an absence. Sophia rarely committed herself to paper about her, and when she did she dismissed her as 'la Schulenburgin', with various spellings. Ever the drama queen, Sophia wrote in exasperation to her niece the raugravine Louise in 1702 that Melusine could 'hardly be reck-oned to her court-ladies any more'.[5] If Sophia did refer to her by name it was with disrespect. For example, in September 1701 she wrote to Louise: 'My son is not here yet; the three ladies who accompanied him did however arrive back yesterday: the Schul-lenburgin, Madame Wey, Enhausen, Schullenburgin's sister.'

What Sophia resented most – and perhaps felt threatened by – was her son's complete attachment to Melusine, to the detriment of his marriage to the beautiful, opulent, volatile and immensely silly Sophia Dorothea. George's marriage would ultimately unravel amidst the scandal of a lover, a murder and a divorce. Sophia probably thought his relationship with Melusine was the catalyst.

Melusine was pregnant with her first child by the late spring of 1691 – but as she absorbed the news, her father Gustav died, in October. Melusine was grief-stricken and possibly terrified for her future. However, if she had had any reservations about upsetting her family with the affair, her father's death removed them. Her mother was dead, her stepmother was respected but did not inspire the intimacies of a mother, and she enjoyed excellent and appar-ently non-judgemental relationships with her siblings. Melusine was still grieving for Gustav when her daughter, Anna Louise Sophia (always known as Louise by the family), was born in the depths of the German winter, in January 1692.

George, cautious through experience and under pressure from his father, would not accept paternity of Louise. His refusal left his mistress in a fix. Melusine was vulnerable from the birth, mourning for her father, forced to endure the silent rebukes of a formidable and disapproving Sophia, who blamed Melusine for George's increasingly dreadful marriage, and she found herself the mother of an illegitimate child with an unnamed father in an environment that snubbed courtesans. All the court knew the child was George's, but he had let her down in the most public fashion.

It is unlikely that Melusine complained – George would not abandon one volatile woman, whom he found distasteful, to take up with another. Melusine was much more inclined to seek a practical solution to her difficulty than to cause a fuss. She called on her extremely close relationships with her siblings, formed in their motherless years in Emden. Rescue came in the form of Melusine's eldest sister, Margarete Gertrud, and her husband Friedrich Achaz. The pair gallantly agreed to accept the child as their own. Baby Louise, however, would reside with her 'aunt' – Melusine.

Why was George so set on failing to acknowledge Louise? From the day she was born we learn, chiefly through his brother Ernst August's letters, that George was a devoted father. But he remembered the excruciating embarrassment of having fathered a child with Figuelotte's under-governess when he was only sixteen, and his parents' furious reactions. This was also the year that Hanover would finally be raised to the electorate; both George and his father were determined that nothing, least of all the birth of an illegitimate child, should jeopardize such long-held hopes. And despite his detractors' claims that George detested Sophia Dorothea, he was heartbroken at the failure of his marriage.[6] By 1692 the couple were so unhappy that neither could see a way back to harmonious relations, and George was concerned not to heap misery upon misery by acknowledging Louise as his daughter.

Melusine evidently decided to accept the situation for what it was and, if she felt any rancour towards George, to forgive him. If she felt betrayed, it seems she bore it in silence. It is probable that they discussed the issue of paternity before the baby was born, and that George shared his familial pressures – a disapproving mother, a father's single-minded pursuit of glory for their house, unruly siblings and a volatile wife – with a sympathetic Melusine.

Melusine, marginalized, stoically resigned herself to a life in the shadows as George's mistress. Her future depended on her ability to continue to please George, who was married to Sophia Dorothea and had two children by her. Any permanent rupture in George's relationship with his wife could endanger the all-important succession. But in 1692 limitless possibilities opened up for Melusine when a desperately unhappy Sophia Dorothea took a lover.

Sophia Dorothea, in a rare moment of accord with her mother-in-law, was furious with George for his relationship with Melusine. Melusine was admittedly slightly younger than her, but she thought her an inferior in everything that mattered – looks, rank, dress. Sophia Dorothea prided herself on her beauty and allure; it seemed to her that everyone at court was in love with her except her husband. She utterly failed to understand George's attraction for this gentle young woman and she feared Melusine's influence over him. George had virtually moved in with Melusine and shared her apartments in the Leineschloss when in Hanover, although he still expected Sophia Dorothea to remain a faithful wife. Ernst August had paraded a multitude of mistresses before Sophia, and Countess Platen enjoyed huge influence at court, but the Elector had never set up home with another woman under her nose. After her husband so publicly relinquished his affection for her by his entanglement with Melusine and the birth of their daughter, the forlorn princess saw no reason not to be persuaded into bed by a man who had courted her relentlessly for two years – the dashing and charming Swedish Count Philipp Christoph von Königsmarck.

Sophia Dorothea, bored, unhappy and ripe for a flirtation, had first met Königsmarck in 1689, when George's brother, Karl-Philipp, brought him to her rooms in the hope of amusing her. Königsmarck was a mercenary, presently employed by the Hanoverian army. His grandfather, Hans Christoff von Königsmarck, had risen from a common soldier to the rank of general in Gustav Adolph of Sweden's army and had amassed a fortune of nearly two million thaler during the Thirty Years War.[7] Now his grandson made his living as a soldier of fortune. He was handsome, charming, sophisticated and seemingly enraptured by the neglected princess. Sophia Dorothea was enchanted. Writing of an affair that still gripped European gossips a century later, Thackeray noted acidly: 'one cannot imagine a more handsome, wicked, worthless reprobate.'[8] Königsmarck was certainly profligate. It is recorded that he had twenty-nine servants. Even very grand ministers only had twenty.[9]

Sophia Dorothea allowed Count Philipp to write to her. But what began as an innocent flirtation, accepted by the court and ignored by George, soon became far more dangerous. Sophia Dorothea began to write back, prompting a flurry of letters between the pair – she seemed addicted to their correspondence.

Philipp's first letter to her dates from July 1690, the year that Melusine came to court.[10] However the princess, jealous of George's new mistress and beguiled by her admirer, began to take risks, and the tone changed fast, from generic courtly charm to jealousy and longing. By March 1692, just two months after Melusine had given birth, they were probably lovers. There was no harm in having a courtly lover who could yearn for, but not consummate, a passion with his adored. But whilst an admirer would have been tolerated, a lover could never be, as it would put a question mark over the succession. Ernst August had worked hard to establish primogeniture and the birth of his grandson Georg August assured it into the second generation.

Today we have access to roughly half of their correspondence. The count imagines her in bed, and coquettishly switches from German to French when he does so. He begs her to elope with him. He writes of the intimacy of seeing her amongst 'thousands' at court where they can use the language of their eyes. He reveals his delight when she comes to his room and finds him in his 'natural state'. He expresses thanks for receiving him the night before, in the hope that he may come again that night. She writes of how life would not be worth living should he die, she swears she is true to him alone, and flatters him that he has changed her. She is no longer a social butterfly, but a more thoughtful creature who craves solitude to think of him.

Königsmarck also loved to regale Sophia Dorothea with his gossipy stories. He tells how a letter to George's brother Ernst August in which he made fun of Melusine ended up in George's hands. He writes of an orgy he attended at the home of a Georg Friedrich von Offener with five girls from Ghent, two extremely beautiful. George, he gleefully relates, was in attendance, but he (Philipp) 'was very good' and just ate and drank.[11]

They were careful to send their letters away from prying eyes at court, to the safe keeping of Königsmarck's sister Aurora.[12] Sophia Dorothea had known Aurora for some time and trusted her. She was married to a Swedish count who served in her father's army. Some were found sewn into Sophia Dorothea's curtains, others at the bottom of playing-card boxes. For a while at least the pains they took to conceal their affair paid off. Liselotte's letters to Sophia show that even in the summer of 1692, Sophia Dorothea's behaviour was still not seen as at all alarming or threatening to the regime.

As time went on, though, the exact nature of the relationship became an open secret. Sophia Dorothea's lady-in-waiting Eleonore von dem Knesebeck was in their confidence and acted as messenger. When apart (as they were for much of their relationship while Königsmarck was on campaign), they wrote more letters, making them more vulnerable to disclosure. Königsmarck's sisters and brother-in-law all knew of the affair. Königsmarck at times wrote to Sophia Dorothea in the presence of tens of courtiers, amongst them Melusine. On at least one occasion he listed his witnesses at the bottom of his letter.[13] His letters are peppered with references to conversations with various female courtiers about his unhappy love.

We know that they were warned to terminate the relationship – Sophia Dorothea by her mother-in-law, her sister-in-law Figuelotte when visiting from Berlin, and even by her mother; Philipp by his superior and head of the Hanoverian army, Field Marshal von Podewils, and by George's brothers.[14] Ernst August was aware of the relationship and talked of dismissing Königsmarck. And George certainly knew.

The lovers used guile to continue the affair. Both swore that nothing was going on. Sophia Dorothea used Max's passion for her as a smokescreen, claiming his pestering of her, and a make-believe illness, as pretexts to escape Hanover to visit her parents in Celle. George did not believe her excuses. He was a diligent letter writer to his wife while away on campaign. Although much of this correspondence has been lost, we do know that he sarcastically likened Sophia Dorothea to Lucretia, a martyr of classical Rome who, when she was raped by the king's son, chose to commit suicide rather than face her husband with her 'shame'. George seemingly commended Sophia Dorothea for her hasty flight from the flirtatious Max, thrilling that his honour was 'very safe' with such a 'veritable Lucretia' for a wife; we know about this today because she was alarmed enough to quote it in a letter to Königsmarck.[15]

Concurrent with the threatened discovery, a darker element entered the relationship. Sophia Dorothea grew hysterical if Königsmarck attended parties with girls present. But at the same time she tormented him with news of her flirtatious behaviour with other men, and her sexual relations, or *monter à cheval* (literally 'horseback riding'), with George. For George's relationship with Melusine had not stopped his conjugal visits to the princess. She was his wife and their duty was to produce heirs. Königsmarck resented George, but he also accused Sophie Dorothea of taking other lovers.

Königsmarck found he had spent his fortune on fripperies. Sophia Dorothea's sizeable dowry was at the disposal of her husband. She begged her parents to give her an income; they refused, knowing by now that she hoped to end her marriage.

That the lovers were allowed to continue their affair for so long probably owes something to more pressing contemporary events. Max was plotting against his father, the Danes threatened Celle in 1693, and Hanover's army was on campaign in the service of the Emperor. All this time, during 1693 and the first half of 1694 Melusine wisely kept a low profile at court.

But when Königsmarck left Hanover to lead a Saxon regiment in 1694, Ernst August, probably with George's knowledge and consent, determined to put a stop to the affair. The Elector feared Sophia Dorothea would flee to her lover in Saxony, or even worse, to Ernst August's enemy Anton Ulrich of Brunswick-Wolfenbüttel, putting the succession into question. He had worked too long and too hard to establish primogeniture in Hanover for his plans to come to dust in the second generation. If Sophia Dorothea eloped, her children's paternity would be questioned and the succession would be in crisis. In London court gossips would soon refer to her son by George as 'young Königsmarck'.

In July 1694, exactly four years after Königsmarck had sent his first charming missive to Sophia Dorothea, Ernst August moved against the lovers. George was conveniently absent in Berlin, visiting Figuelotte. Königsmarck had returned to Hanover, ostensibly to formally resign his commission, and Sophia Dorothea rushed from Celle to her apartments in Hanover to wait for him. But the couple had no immediate plan to elope. Lack of funds limited their options. The lifestyle Sophia Dorothea expected to enjoy, even if they eloped to some 'little corner of the earth', as she bucolically wrote to Königsmarck, was expensive.

Although it was summer and traditionally Ernst August should have been at Herrenhausen, away from the heat of the city, he moved back to the Leineschloss to observe Sophia Dorothea. He ordered his spies to watch Königsmarck and his daughter-in-law.

On 1 July Count Philipp Christoph von Königsmarck was seen entering the Leineschloss. He did not leave the palace alive. Königsmarck was murdered on the orders of Ernst August, probably by four Hanoverian courtiers. A Danish diplomat, Otto Mencken, recorded that it was the architect Nicolò Montalbano who had actually administered the lethal thrust of his sword. Ernst August gave him 150,000 thaler shortly after the murder (a considerable bonus, considering that his salary was only 200 thaler a year), which probably confirms him as the killer.[16] Mencken concluded his report with Königsmarck's sorry fate. His body was tied in a sack, weighted with stones and dumped in the Leine river.

The events of the next few days were crucial to Melusine's future. Sophia Dorothea was immediately placed under house arrest. She begged her accomplice Eleonore von dem Knesebeck to stay with her, pleading that she would be presumed guilty if Eleonore fled. Incriminating correspondence was found in the princess's apartments and her lady-in-waiting was arrested and threatened with torture. The brothers Ernst August and George William decided Sophia Dorothea's fate. She and George would be divorced. The fabricated pretext would be the princess's refusal to cohabit with her husband. Königsmarck's name would not be mentioned in the hope of avoiding further scandal and any question as to the paternity of Sophia Dorothea's children.

Sophia Dorothea, as yet unaware of her lover's fate, eagerly agreed to the divorce. It is arguable that she had wanted it as early as 1690, when she first fell in love with the count. Now, she presumed it would mean freedom and a new life with Königsmarck. She was sent back to her parents' territory of Celle, but not to her beloved childhood home. Instead she was exiled to the tiny and provincial backwater of Ahlden Castle, an ugly, cheerless, fortified house. Under the Acte de Disgrâce drawn up by Ernst August and George William, she became her parents' responsibility, and was given an income of 8,000 thaler per annum. She was desperate to be rid of George and the marriage was dissolved on 28 December 1694.

It slowly dawned on Sophia Dorothea that something was wrong. Her father would not see her, she was allowed no contact with her children, her divorce stipulated that she could not remarry (although it specifically stated that George could), and she was virtually a prisoner in the castle. Yet she still had no idea of what had happened to Königsmarck.

Sophia Dorothea's actions had made her a liability, and Hanover and Celle maintained a stony silence over the affair. The Electorate would not be assured until 1708 – although Hanover had received the electoral cap in 1692, they were not admitted to the Electoral College until 1708 – and nothing, the ruling family believed, should detract from that goal. So the officials who knew of the affair remained tight-lipped despite the pleas of foreign diplomats for the gossip their rulers craved, poor Eleonore von dem Knesebeck was kept prisoner in the fortress of Scharzfels to ensure her silence, and Sophia, unusually, neglected to write anything to anyone. Sophia Dorothea remained a focus for opposition to Hanover for the rest of her life, from Brunswick-Wolfenbüttel's attempts to prevent their ancient enemies obtaining the electoral cap, to the Jacobite rebellions in Britain after George's accession in 1714.

The international community was outraged at Königsmarck's disappearance. But despite fevered enquiries by his family, and the efforts of his employer Augustus of Saxony to discover his fate, his body was never found. Although the facts of the murder were detailed in correspondence between Duke Anton Ulrich and the Danish diplomat Otto Mencken, the truth of the affair was not accepted until the 1960s, when the German historian George Schnath published his corroborative findings.[17] To this day we do not know the full extent of George's involvement.

When Sophia finally began corresponding with her legion of relatives again, Liselotte wrote back in sympathy from Versailles in February 1695: 'Does the young duchess [Sophia Dorothea] not know that a woman's honour consists of having commerce with no one but her husband, and that for a man it is not shameful to have mistresses but shameful indeed to be a cuckold?'[18] Liselotte had summed up the situation in Hanover perfectly. It was fine for a woman to flirt with a man, but forbidden for her to sleep with him. By setting up house with Melusine, George had proven that the opposite was true for men.

As to whether his former wife should ever see their children again, George was immovable, despite Sophia Dorothea's pleading letters. She swallowed her pride and begged him to 'permit me to see and embrace our beloved children; my gratitude for this boon, so ardently longed for, will be infinite since I desire nothing else to enable me to die content.' To Sophia, she added: 'I beseech once more your Electoral Highness to forgive all I have done which may have offended you and to speak a little on my behalf to your son the Elector. I implore him to grant me the forgiveness which I desire so intensely and to allow me to embrace my children. It would also be my passionate desire, Madame, to kiss the hands of your Electoral Highness before I die.' Both letters went unanswered.

When in 1705 George William died and the two duchies were finally united, George immediately stripped the picturesque palace of Celle with its creamy white walls and scarlet roof, and took the contents back to Hanover. Today we can only get an inkling of what beauty was once housed there; all that remains is the sublime stucco work and parquet floors.

There is a suite of apartments in the castle that is heartbreaking to see. With her husband's death, Sophia Dorothea's mother, Eléonore, moved to a dower house. But George allowed her to come back to the castle frequently so that she could visit her daughter more easily at her prison at Ahlden, some 20 kilometres away. The flooring in Eléonore's rooms is noticeably far more worn than in the rest of the castle, suggesting that she spent much of her time pacing and ruminating on her only child's fate. As she grew older and her eyesight failed, she never neglected to write prodigious notes to her daughter, compensating for her lack of sight with increasingly large letters, until just two or three words filled a page. The grief-stricken duchess died in her eighties in 1722, just four years before Sophia Dorothea's own death.

We do not know if Melusine attempted to intervene with George on Sophia Dorothea's behalf. After her escape from her fortress prison, Sophia Dorothea's accomplice Eleonore von dem Knesebeck spoke of throwing herself on the mercy of George and 'my good friend Mlle von der Schulenburg'; she, at least, thought Melusine 'kind'. This however came to nothing, and Melusine was too pragmatic to help her without George's approval. Furthermore there was no political role for Melusine in Hanover through which she could exert influence, not least because of her cool relations with Sophia. She dedicated herself to creating a secure family life for George and their daughters, and for the most part stayed in the domestic sphere. There was no advantage to interceding on her rival's behalf. Sophia Dorothea's divorce and imprisonment meant Melusine's promotion to first lady of Hanover – save for the Duchess Sophia – in all but name.

George's treatment of Sophia Dorothea was universally condemned. The limited sources suggest that his primary motivation was not vengeance for his cuckolded state, but rather the grave political ramifications of Sophia Dorothea's indiscretion. George had reason to feel aggrieved: in her letters to Königsmarck, which he had seen, she complains that George is a bad lover and she longs for his death in battle. All the same, George had found domestic harmony with Melusine and it is likely that, had she been more prudent, he would have turned a blind eye to Sophia Dorothea's affair. But her actions had put Hanover's ambitions at risk. To lose the electoral cap would have rendered Ernst August's entire career a failure, and his total alienation from his sons, and George's rows with his brothers over primogeniture, would have been for nothing. Rival states, jealous of Hanover's success, were still jostling to exclude Ernst August from the Electoral College. Sophia Dorothea and Königsmarck had considered flight to Hanover's enemy, Brunswick-Wolfenbüttel, and had Sophia Dorothea not been imprisoned after her divorce she might still have fled, creating a diplomatic crisis. Similarly she was an easy target for those British enemies of the Protestant succession, the Jacobites. Even her father, George William, saw the political necessity of her detention. She was too dangerous to be free. Sophia Dorothea's numerous portraits were quietly removed and destroyed, and her name eliminated from the State Prayers. It was as if she had never existed.

Sophia Dorothea's incarceration was probably the source of the rabid antipathy that would grow between George and his son, Georg August. The boy was only nine years old when his mother left Hanover. He never enjoyed a good relationship with his father, blaming him for his mother's fate. Their lack of empathy for one another developed into open hostility and the eventual removal of Georg August's children from his care. The young Sophia Dorothea, possibly because of the scarring events of 1694, became in turn a dreadful mother to her own children.[19] In her extensive diaries her eldest daughter Wilhelmine records vicious beatings, both at her mother's hands and from an abusive governess, encouraged by her mother.[20]

The affair of the princess who had paid for her indiscretion with humiliation and imprisonment captivated Europe and spawned a rash of dubious romantic literature. Sophia Dorothea's former maid, Eleonore von dem Knesebeck, swore for the rest of her days that the Countess Platen had orchestrated Königsmarck's murder and Sophia Dorothea's imprisonment and divorce. She claimed the havoc wreaked sprang from Platen's jealousy of the young and pretty Sophia Dorothea. Contemporaries besides Eleonore von dem Knesebeck believed that Königsmarck was sleeping not only with Sophia Dorothea but also with the countess, in a bid for power and influence. Moreover Eleonore claimed the countess gave Ernst August syphilis and that both eventually died of the disease. This story, true or not, continued to entrance audiences well into the twentieth century, when a film, *Saraband for Dead Lovers*, starring Stewart Granger as Königsmarck and Joan Greenwood as Sophia Dorothea, was made in 1948.

The events of 1694, so devastating for Sophia Dorothea, finally allowed George to begin, very slowly, to allow Melusine a public role. But although now divorced he continued to be cautious, not least because of the developments that were taking place in England, where the succession, despite the legislation that had been enacted in favour of the Hanoverians, was far from assured. Whilst the birth of Melusine's second daughter Petronella Melusine – known to everyone by her second name – in April 1693 only added to George's adoration of his mistress (throughout his letters his youngest brother Ernst August refers to the pleasure George found with his growing illegitimate family) once again Melusine's sister and brother-in-law stepped forward to accept the baby as their own, although she would continue to reside with her 'aunt'. Melusine and her namesake would not be parted for the rest of her life.

Meanwhile after the upset caused by the Sophia Dorothea affair, Ernst August's health quickly and dramatically declined – she was after all his niece. Perhaps his ambition was his undoing: he had sanctioned murder and his conscience was stricken. Cures at the spas of Bad Pyrmont and Wiesbaden had little effect on his 'nervous condition' – he was growing more and more shaky and his speech was slurred, prompting some historians to speculate that he suffered from a succession of strokes. With his father's illness, George effectively became ruler of Hanover. Despite their rocky marital history Sophia was distraught, but comforted herself that at least Klara Platen was marginalized; now that the Elector was ill he only wanted his wife. She would read to him for hours, or offer him her arm as he briefly shuffled around the gardens. He died in January 1698, possibly of a stroke, in Sophia's garden in Herrenhausen. With his death his detractors, chiefly Sophia Dorothea's sympathizers, repeated the allegations that he died of syphilis caught from Countess Platen, who in turn had contracted the disease from lovers such as Königsmarck, and the orgies held at Linden, the Platen home near Herrenhausen.

5.

Beloved

. . . Mademoiselle Schulenburg . . . is a lady of extraordinary merit.

– John Toland, *Hanover*

Ernst August's death precipitated Melusine's rise. For four years she had been in a strange kind of limbo. George, out of respect to his parents, and particularly to his father, whose illness he had not wished to exacerbate with any hint of a scandal, still refused to acknowledge her status as mother of his two illegitimate daughters and *maîtresse-en-titre*. Furthermore Sophia still resented her for her part – albeit passive – in the breakdown of George's marriage. But with the death of his father and his becoming Elector in turn, George conferred almost every honour possible on Melusine. Once he took power in Hanover, she gained in confidence. When Sophia was absent she presided at all official functions; when the dowager Electress was present, Melusine was the second most important woman in the room.

Melusine was fundamentally conservative. She was born into an ancient and noble family that expected a glorious marriage, and she evidently did not possess the temperament to relish the life of a courtesan, for all the freedoms it brought. Despite her love for George, she craved respectability. She was no Countess Platen or Madame du Barry, women who probably had little love for their patrons. The relationships they had were financial and social transactions. Melusine's character and situation was more in the mould of the highly regarded Madame de Maintenon, the likely second wife of Louis XIV. Melusine had been George's mistress for seven years, and so an acknowledgment of her status must have brought enormous relief.

To Sophia's chagrin, Melusine was raised to a position above all the ladies of court save Sophia herself. The dowager Electress was irritated not least because she had formed a plan to invite her raugrave and raugravine nephews and nieces, the illegitimate children of her brother Karl and his morganatic wife Louise von Degenfeld, to live with her in Hanover. Sophia took her responsibilities to the children of Karl and Louise seriously. Their mother had died in 1677, and the death of their father in 1680 made them orphans.

But Melusine's elevation created problems of precedence. Although Melusine was a noblewoman, Sophia's nephews and nieces were royal. The dowager duchess refused to put her beloved relatives in the uncomfortable position of deferring to her son's mistress as court protocol required once George had decreed it – he thwarted, for example, Sophia's attempts to lodge them in state rooms at Herrenhausen. They continued to visit but the plan for a permanent move was abandoned. Melusine now dined publicly with George, and as her daughters grew, Sophia acknowledged them with positions in her own household. Although the dowager Electress continued to spare only the briefest of nods to Melusine's existence, she formed good relationships with her illegitimate granddaughters. The girls were charming, opinionated and clever, and Sophia always liked clever people. Louise was beautiful, and young Melusine gained a reputation for telling George exactly what she thought. Sophia, enchanted with the girl's precociousness, appointed her a lady-in-waiting, just as her mother had been before her. Sophia famously paid her ladies-in-waiting very little, and Melusine was obliged to supplement the meagre income given to young Melusine by her grandmother.[1]

Despite Herrenhausen's beauty and tranquillity, Melusine could never bring herself to think of it as her home. It was completely Sophia's domain, not least because Ernst August bequeathed the house, gardens and surrounding farms to her for the duration of her lifetime. The palace that Melusine could truly call home, particularly while Sophia was alive, was the old hunting lodge, or Jagdschloss, at Göhrde, some 120 kilometres from the city.

Göhrde began as a simple hunting lodge in the middle of an ancient forest. It was in Celle territory, but George knew it well. He had often joined his uncle's hunting parties there and George William had developed the shoot until it offered the best hunting with hounds in northern Europe. But when George William died in 1705 and George inherited Göhrde, he and Melusine renovated it to suit their own taste. It was already the place where they were happiest and they determined to put their mark on it.

George employed the French architect Rémy de la Fosse to build a new palace. It took four years to complete. There is an anonymous painting on display at the Royal Collection at Windsor which, although dated 1725, shows a hunting party at Göhrde in 1723.[2] From the painting we can see it has mellow golden walls and a bright red roof. But it is not a rustic retreat. Elaborate gates lead to a grand Palladian building, perfect not only for the private life Melusine and George craved, but also for entertaining on a large scale. George bought 500 paintings for the refurbished palace. Melusine, in keeping with her almost pathological desire for privacy, is not shown in the painting, but many of the family and courtiers are. George is there with his Prussian son-in-law Friedrich Wilhelm – the young Sophia Dorothea's husband – and George's grandson prince Frederick. Also present are two servants of whom George was extremely fond – the Turks Mehemet von Königstreu (literally 'true to the king') and Mustapha de Mistra. Mehemet, who had been captured by the Hanoverian army in Turkey and later converted to Christianity, was far more than just a servant to the couple. He became a friend and confidant. They both followed him to England. With so many members of his court and family present, the painting testifies to the centrality of this palace in George's life.

Herrenhausen and the Leineschloss were Sophia's homes, and the dowager Electress endeavoured to avoid Melusine as much as possible when both were in residence. At Göhrde Melusine was truly mistress; Sophia loathed visiting because she found herself too much in Melusine's company. For both Melusine and Sophia, the situation was rendered even more awkward after the old Elector's death. Sophia relied on George completely. Figuelotte was in Berlin, Max was sulking abroad, and Christian constantly badgered her for money. Her youngest child, Ernst August, was so inexperienced compared with George that she found herself gravitating towards her first-born as a confidant, adviser and sparring partner. Although Melusine was quiet and patient, she must have felt the strain of a difficult 'mother-in-law', particularly as there were few opportunities to completely escape her company. Sophia was a fact of life who had to be borne for the sake of harmony.

In 1701, at the age of thirty-three, Melusine gave birth to her last child, also a daughter. The large gap between her second and third daughters – young Melusine was eight years old when the baby was born – suggests that there may have been failed pregnancies during the intervening years. But typically discreet, Melusine makes no reference to her childless years in any surviving correspondence. The addition to their family only added to Melusine and George's domestic joy.[3]

Once again George did not acknowledge the child, even though he was now the Elector, divorced, and no longer had a father to please. Perhaps it would have been too awkward to admit that he and Melusine had effectively lied about the parentage of the two older girls and they thought it best to keep it an open secret. The newly gained electoral cap was still, George believed, precarious, and he wished to avoid any scandal.

Melusine's family stepped in yet again to save her honour. Her adored eldest sister, Margarete Gertrud, who had so willingly accepted the maternity of Melusine's first two daughters, had died in 1697. This treasured sister, wife and mother was honoured with the epitaph on her headstone: 'Here lies this fine woman, and a true heart is buried.'[4] Melusine, as a mark of her great feeling for her sister, named her baby daughter Margarethe Gertrud, but the child was always known by the affectionate diminutive Trudchen. Now it was Melusine's sister Sophia Juliane and her husband, Rabe Christoph von Oeynhausen, who claimed Trudchen as their own daughter.

As Trudchen grew older she was known as 'die schöne Gertrud' (the beautiful Gertrud). A portrait survives which today hangs at the convent of Barsinghausen, near Hanover. It was probably painted when she was in her early twenties and it shows an extremely beautiful young woman with long dark curly hair and a rosy mouth and cheeks. She resembles her mother.

During these years, Melusine was seemingly liked and admired by everyone – save for the chilly Sophia. John Toland, an Irishman who served as a diplomat to the court of Hanover, wrote to his patron William III in 1701 on the occasion of the deliverance of the Act of Settlement to Sophia by Lord Macclesfield: 'The Electress's [Sophia's] maids of honour are worthy of the rank they enjoy, especially Mademoiselle Schulenburg, who in the opinion of others as well as mine is a lady of extraordinary merit.'[5]

Toland was obviously enamoured of Hanover. Many Englishmen imagined the state a mere provincial backwater, but Toland disagreed. He was impressed by the 'fine, and richly furnished' palace apartments and 'a pretty theatre'. He observed that: 'the opera house in the castle is visited as a rarity by all travellers, as being the best painted and the best contrived in all Europe . . .'

As to court life, he observed that it was 'extremely polite, and even in Germany it is accounted the best, both for civility and decorum . . . Strangers of figure or quality are commonly invited to the Elector's table, where they are amazed to find such easy conversation . . .' He thrills at 'well-bred . . . obliging' and 'hand-some' court ladies and singles out Sophia Charlotte, daughter of Klara Platen and George's half-sister, who was growing into an intelligent and vivacious woman. Her sister-in-law, Countess Platen, he comments, 'may pass for a beauty in any court whatsoever.' He was equally enamoured of the intellectual life of the court, which despite Leibniz's complaints that it was not up to London or Paris, Sophia had made into one of the most interesting in Europe.

Toland was particularly impressed with George, and his writing glowed when describing England's putative future monarch:

> He understands our constitution the best of any foreigner I ever knew; and though he be well versed in the art of war, and of invincible courage, having often exposed his person to great dangers in Hungary, in the Orea, on the Rhine, and in Flanders . . . yet he is naturally of peaceable inclinations . . . He is a perfect man of business, exactly regular in the economy of his revenues, reads all dispatches himself at first hand, writes most of his letters, and spends a very considerable part of his time about such occupations in his closet, and with his ministers. I hope therefore that none of our countrymen will be so injudicious as to think his reservedness the effect of sullenness or pride, nor mistake that for state which really proceeds from modesty, caution and deliberation: for he is very affable to such as accost him, and expects that others should speak to him first . . .[6]

Significantly, Toland was writing around the time when George's position was strengthened both in England and in Germany. The Act of Settlement automatically naturalized him as an Englishman in anticipation of his inheriting the throne. Sophia was thirty-five years older than Queen Anne, leading many to assume that it would be George, and not Sophia, who would succeed her.

For Melusine, irrespective of the developments regarding George's likely succession to the English throne, life continued to revolve around her immediate family circle – George, her daughters, and her brothers and sisters who were frequent visitors to Hanover. From 1695, the year of his father's illness, George remained in Hanover rather than going on campaign, enhancing his intimacy with Melusine. Family life was enriched by the arrival of Melusine's clever and ambitious half-brother Frederick William around 1700, who relied on his highly-placed sister to advance his career. George, who obviously had an immediate liking for the young man as well as an obligation to Melusine, undertook the completion of his education. The Elector was impressed, and used him on at least one diplomatic mission during the War of the Spanish Succession.[7] Friendship followed; when George went to England he appointed Frederick William a gentleman of his bedchamber. Melusine's young brother was now officially a member of her lover's most intimate circle.

Another of her brothers who moved in the couple's orbit was Johann Matthias, who served the Doge of Venice for much of his career but had come to use his sister as a sounding board. He took up residence at the Palazzo Loredan in Venice when he retired from fighting the battles of European princes, and became an art collector. George regularly sought his opinion and advice, and Melusine's relationship with her eldest brother enhanced her stock at Hanover. He was a gifted soldier and astute statesman who made it his business to know all the European gossip and was enormous fun to be with. Johann Matthias visited Hanover to see his sister as often as possible, on average once a year between 1705 and 1713. Melusine probably never visited Venice. Once George became Elector he took his responsibilities far too seriously to journey far from home for a holiday, preferring to visit Göhrde and the spa town of Bad Pyrmont, and it is unlikely that Melusine would have gone without him.

That Melusine's advice was valued by her brother Johann Matthias is evident from a letter he wrote to her in February 1706.[8] He writes to her in distress and disbelief following his rout at Sorau (now in Poland) during the Great Northern War, in the service of Augustus of Saxony against the Swedes. This debacle was unusual in Johann Matthias's otherwise highly successful career. He had obviously discussed the war in depth with Melusine, as he begins the letter: 'Your predictions, my dear sister, have been but too just.' He speaks frankly: 'There is no army in Europe worse disciplined than this: the thefts, cruelties, and murders which the dragoons and troopers committed after their flight are unheard of, and that even from the field of battle itself to Saxony ... and I am inconsolable for having been at the head of the army in this infamous action, which cannot fail to cause the greatest disorder in his [Augustus of Saxony's] affairs.' He promises to tell her more at a later date. But meanwhile, he asks her to communicate the news to Leibniz, now an important diplomat in Hanover: 'Have the goodness at once to show and communicate the plan and the relation, which has been drawn up in haste, to M. de Leibnitz [sic], to whom I cannot write at full.' Significantly, it was Melusine, and not Leibniz – who was the official channel of communication – who was informed of the disastrous news first.

George's youngest brother Ernst August was also in the inner circle. He was fourteen years George's junior and he saw his eldest brother as something of a father figure. According to Sophia he followed George 'like a dog' and regularly stayed with them at Göhrde. Ernst August never questioned primogeniture, not simply because of his loyalty to George, but because he was probably homosexual and as such, unlikely to have children. Primogeniture and the resultant loss of inheritance was therefore not an issue for him. He remained fiercely devoted to George and Melusine and was one of only two of George's siblings who remained on speaking terms with the Elector.

Melusine was pivotal to the maintenance of friendly relations between George and the rest of his family. This would continue until George's death. Melusine and Figuelotte kept up a regular correspondence, George's only sister pragmatically making the leap of forming a friendship with the mistress once the wife was removed. More important was her relationship with his legitimate children. George was a formal and distant parent with the son and daughter he had with Sophia Dorothea. Though Liselotte's judgement of him is perhaps unfair, in March 1707 she wrote to the raugravine Louise: 'It is not surprising that the old gay good humour is no longer to be found at Hanover. The Elector is so cold that he freezes everything into ice. Neither his father nor his uncle were of that nature.'[9]

Young Sophia Dorothea and Georg August were not allowed to mention their mother's name in their father's presence, which must have had a terrible impact on such young children. Hatton repeats a story, possibly apocryphal, of how, on his father's death, Georg August put up a portrait of his mother. She notes that: 'His presumed change of attitude to her memory (he became noticeably less enthusiastic about his mother) in his own reign has been attributed to his reading of a document after 1727 in the Hanover archives which convinced him of her adultery.' The children were obviously sheltered from the 'Königsmarck' affair. It is unclear if any explanation was ever given as to their mother's complete removal from their lives.

But while George could be reserved towards his legitimate children, Melusine was warm and loving. Her friend Joanne Sophie, Countess of Schaumburg-Lippe, described her desire 'to do all the good she can'.[10] She might have added that this was particularly true when her 'goodness' facilitated George's well-being. Melusine's kindness was possibly tinged with pragmatism: it served her interests to be on good terms with George's legitimate children and it pleased him.

Although for years Melusine had patiently stayed in the shadows to avoid embarrassing her illustrious lover, his children by Sophia Dorothea liked her and accepted her as one of the family. Georg August, like his sister, was very fond of Melusine. This is extraordinary considering George's treatment of his mother and is testament to Melusine's empathetic nature.

In 1705 Georg August married the attractive and clever Princess Caroline of Ansbach in Hanover. Although the court was grieving for George's uncle, George William, who had died in late August, mourning was temporarily suspended to enable the prince and his new bride to celebrate their marriage.[11] The courtship and marriage had fairytale beginnings when the young prince journeyed incognito to Ansbach to propose.

The following year young Sophia Dorothea, now nineteen, left court to marry Figuelotte's son, the volatile and not entirely sane Frederick William of Brandenburg-Prussia. And in 1707 Melusine shared George's delight when Caroline gave birth to George's first grandchild – a boy, Frederick Louis. This child would receive all of the love and attention that George had never given his own son.

Relations between the Electorates of Hanover and Prussia had become, with young Sophia Dorothea's marriage, even more personal. The marriage tested Melusine's skills as an unofficial diplomat and conduit to George as she maintained a friendly correspondence with Sophia Dorothea, the new Prussian queen, who had been encouraged to think of Melusine as a stepmother. (Her own daughter Wilhelmine in turn thought of Melusine as a grandmother.) This relationship exemplified the way in which Melusine's role was changing as she began to prove her usefulness to both foreign diplomats and family members. She gradually moved away from an exclusively domestic role to become an unofficial gatekeeper and counsellor, best able to deal with the less approachable George.

The young Sophia Dorothea actually enjoyed a welcome renaissance in her relationship with her father when she left Hanover after her marriage. George, often shy, felt freer to express his affection via correspondence rather than in person, and the forty-five letters to her found in the Prussian archives are full of warmth.[12] He addresses her as 'ma chère Fille' (my dear daughter), he worries over her health, he sends his physician, La Rose, to attend her at the births of her children, and he assures her of his 'véritable tendresse' (true tenderness) for her.[13] Sophia wrote in delight: 'With even greater pleasure I could now witness, how much her father loves her – which has been concealed from us so far due to his frosty nature; but now everything finally emerges.'[14] Even his mother thought him at times cold towards his legitimate children.

By contrast he lavished his huge reserves of affection on the children – his daughters by Melusine, and eventually his grandchildren – who were present in Hanover. His brother Ernst August's letters are filled with comments about the girls – Louise, young Melusine and Trudchen – managing to twist their father around their little fingers, and George's obvious delight in their precocity. It was George, and not the comparatively strict Melusine, who allowed his daughters to hunt from an early age, who listened with rapt attention to their remarks on the day's political events, and who eventually sheltered Louise from a string of failed love affairs.

Louise was beautiful, wild and independent, and Melusine – increasingly strait-laced as she aged – disapproved. Louise married Philipp von dem Bussche-Ippenburg, a Hanoverian courtier, in 1707. She was only fifteen years old. Ernst August's letters suggest that Louise forced the marriage against her parents' wishes because the couple believed themselves to be deeply in love. There is a vague implication that they may already have slept together. Melusine was furious, not least because Louise had been promised to her dear friend and George's, Alexander von Hammerstein.[15] Hammerstein was the same age as George, and it is unlikely that the young Louise found him an appealing prospect. Even so, Melusine could not even bring herself to speak to Louise, but George came to his daughter's defence and obviously talked his mistress round. The marriage took place.[16] But to Melusine's annoyance the haughty von dem Bussche family approved of neither the alliance nor her daughter. They took years to properly acknowledge Louise.[17] George, at Louise's cajoling, had shoehorned Melusine and the von dem Bussche family into accepting the match at least superficially. When it failed at some point before 1714 her father, perhaps feeling guilty at acting against Melusine's wishes, ensured that Louise obtained a divorce. She would never marry again, preferring the freedom of an independent life and lovers rather than a husband. Of Melusine's three daughters, her relationship with Louise remained the most uneasy.

Melusine offered her own lover her complete loyalty and consistently provided a tranquil haven from the upheavals of the outside world. She was calm when William III died in 1702, making Sophia Queen Anne's heir. She provided solace to George's racking grief when Figuelotte died while visiting Hanover in 1705. George's servant Mehemet later recalled how his master had barricaded himself in his room, kicking at the walls while he grieved for his only sister. George loved Figuelotte, and considering the fractured nature of his relationship with his other siblings (with the exception of Ernst August) their relationship was extremely important to him. The death of his uncle, George William, in the same year was perhaps sweetened by the change in status and influence it effected. The unification of Hanover and Celle brought vast

increases in population, territory and income. Hanover's population doubled to roughly 400,000, and her territory increased from
7,000 square kilometres to nearly 20,000.[18]

Melusine put herself entirely at the disposal of her princely lover.
She was very much a 'helpmeet', ready to perform the duties of a
consort alongside the more informal diplomatic role she had
become so proficient at performing. For example, in 1713 she had
supper in Hanover, probably at the Leineschloss, with the sisters
of Princess Ursula Katherina Lubomirska, mistress of Augustus the
Strong, Elector of Saxony and king of Poland. The Holy Roman
Emperors were adept at recognizing their Electors' affairs of the
heart. Ursula was created a Reichsfürstin, or Princess of the Empire,
by Emperor Leopold I soon after the birth of her son in 1704 and
Melusine became a Princess in 1722, in acknowledgement of her
high standing with George.

She lived an extremely privileged lifestyle, a round of parties, balls,
salons and the hunt at the Leineschloss, Herrenhausen and Göhrde.
For holidays, there were the spa towns of Bad Pyrmont and Wiesbaden, and occasional visits to Vienna. Such a lifestyle demanded
exquisite clothes. Sumptuary laws which strictly controlled the
clothing that could be worn by each class or profession had caused
costume to become synonymous with status. Even though the rules
had relaxed by the end of the seventeenth century, high fashion and
superb fabrics were still the province of the aristocracy and the
wealthy. All fashionable life centred upon the court, and attendance
required high standards of costume. For members of the royal family
and their courtiers, such as Melusine, it was expected that they wear
only the best. And the best, typically, was French.

The court enthusiastically embraced the emulation of French
dress. The pomp of Louis XIV's Versailles had created a certain
stiffness in clothing, with increasingly elaborate and impractical
wigs. When Liselotte's son, Philippe duc d'Orléans, became regent

in 1715 for his five-year-old nephew Louis XV, fashion in France underwent a radical change, favouring a less formal style, which reverberated throughout Europe. But, as the costume historian Aileen Ribeiro has shown, as with all seismic shifts, the old continued to coexist alongside the new for a considerable time. Those who clung to the older fashions were not without their critics. In 1711, three years before Melusine and George came to England, Jonathan Swift, the Tory propagandist who was to become such a critic of the new king and his mistress, bitchily said of the Duchess of Grafton that she wore at dinner 'a great high headdress such as was in fashion 15 years ago and looks like a mad woman in it'.[19]

Elaborate curls and, if a woman could achieve them, cascades of ringlets were de rigueur in Hanover, as we can see from Melusine's and Sophia Dorothea's portraits from the 1680s and 1690s. Because a woman's coiffure and dress was so elaborate, even when the so-called 'freer' style of the French Regency took hold, women such as Melusine needed assistance dressing. Stays needed to be laced tightly, hair needed to be curled, and help was needed to put on the heavy dresses themselves. Court costume was predominantly the so-called open-robe. The shape was made up of a bodice joined to an overskirt, with the skirt open to show a petticoat beneath. Petticoats were worn over wide hoops, which grew so wide as the century progressed that in France in the 1720s, gentlemen complained they had no room to sit at the theatre because the ladies' skirts took up all the room.[20]

The 'mantua', a formal court gown of the beginning of the century, began as a loose-fitting negligee, almost like a male nightgown. It developed to have wide pleats at the back with a small train. In 1712 the author of *The Present State of France* remarked that 'The Quality trail behind 'em a long tail of gold or silk, with which they sweep the churches and gardens.'[21] This fashion certainly found its way to Hanover.

The styles were elegant, but the fabrics and the finish were what made these dresses gorgeous. Elaborate patterned damasks, woven silks, fur petticoats, embroidery in gold and silver thread, delicate floral patterns, striped or plain silks, painted silks, lace, muslins – the list of materials is mouth-watering. In 1724 Mrs Delany wrote adoringly of Lady Sunderland's – an English courtier's – dress that it was 'the finest pale blue and pink, very richly flowered in a running pattern of silver frosted, and tissue with a little white . . .'[22]

Wide hoops made the skirts swing as women walked. With the swing, a tantalizing view of ankle and shoe was revealed. The stockings beneath were brightly coloured. The delicate shoes, made of silk, leather or damask, had an attractive heel of up to three inches. It was the first time fashion had allowed the foot to be on show, and many found it remarkably alluring.

Underwear was always fine linen edged with lace or linen at the neck and sleeves, which remained visible beneath the gown. Stays were laced over the linen shift, and the gown was placed on top. For riding there were attractive riding habits with long sleeves and waistcoats, and for walking out of doors there was the ubiquitous cloak, usually hooded. The cloak served three purposes; for warmth, to cover increasingly low-cut dresses, and for its comfortable fit over the large hoop.

Dress was about theatre and show, and most women wore masks when walking out of doors. Some used them to enhance their allure with mystery, but others were more practical, sporting a mask to hide a disfigurement (many had suffered from smallpox). In 1717 the author of the poem *The Art of Dress* wrote: 'When for the morning Air abroad you steal, the Cloak of Camlet may your Charms conceal; . . . That, with a Mask, is such a sure Disguise, T'would cheat an Argus, or a Spaniard's Eyes.'[23]

In each of the four portraits of Melusine that survive, she wears the very best that fashion had to offer. The portrait of her head and shoulders dating from about 1691 shows her curly dark hair parted in the middle, with short curls framing her face and longer ringlets resting on her bare shoulders. White flowers, possibly jasmine, are braided through the right side of her hair, and the flowers are repeated in the centre of her neckline. Her dark dress is edged with pale lace, and lace is visible at the bottom of her sleeves, suggesting a three-quarter-length sleeve finished in lace.

Then there are the three three-quarter-length portraits, painted in Hanover or Celle when she was in her late forties or early fifties. One shows her with an elaborate fanning of lace at the top of her extremely low-cut dress her chest is practically exposed. Her gown is made of heavy silk in contrasting colours and her hair is dressed closer to her head with a solitary thick ringlet resting on the left side of her neck, following the French fashion. The second, at the convent of Barsinghausen, shows her wearing an elaborate blue and gold damask gown, with a more modest but still low neckline edged with lace. A scarlet and orange velvet stole rests on her shoulders, and she wears a thick rope of pearls. Interestingly Trudchen wore a dress in the same fabric when sitting for her portrait, which was probably painted at the same time as her mother's.

Today they hang together in the same tiny picture cabinet of the convent. The third portrait reflects her near-royal status. It was commissioned by George sometime between 1716 and 1725. Here, Melusine wears sumptuous blue velvet and lace cuffs adorn her wrists. Grecian columns flank her and scarlet drapes denote the theatricality of the portrait. This portrait is all about rank, and the high esteem in which George holds his mistress. Most tellingly, she is portrayed sitting amidst a swathe of ermine. In the painting Melusine is no longer the 'scarecrow' that Sophia complained about. Three pregnancies left her fuller in the face and her figure was now more in keeping with the contemporary preference for plump women.

A typical day at Göhrde or Herrenhausen, with either a large party including extended family and foreign envoys, or even on occasion George's grand Prussian relatives, or a more intimate family affair, would have begun in George's anteroom at eight o'clock for hot chocolate, prior to a hunt in the lush forest. The greater the number of foreign dignitaries, the grander the affair.

After a strenuous morning's exercise the family and their guests would dine in the big hall. Following a large meal all those who felt sociable would go to Melusine's apartments to drink coffee – still a luxurious and exotic drink, having reached Europe only very recently from the Ottoman Empire – and to chat. In the evening there would be a play – Göhrde, like Herrenhausen, had its own theatre – or a ball. For the immediate family circle of Melusine, George, the three girls, Ernst August, on occasion Melusine's sisters and their families, and Johann Matthias, the day followed a similar pattern but was far less grand.[24]

For the girls there were lessons with private tutors, with an emphasis on the study of music. Both Melusine and George were passionate about opera and the theatre – a love that George had inherited from his parents. When Agostino Steffani, who had so added to the glory of the house with his opera *Henry the Lion*, retired in 1710 he was replaced as Kappelmeister by George Frideric Handel. Handel became music master to Louise, young Melusine and Trudchen, and eventually to Georg August's and Caroline's growing family.

Melusine was an enthusiastic churchgoer – far more so than Sophia – and prayer was an integral part of her daily routine. It is interesting to speculate how she reconciled her religion with her domestic arrangements, for she took her faith seriously and the absence of a marriage with George, at least while Sophia Dorothea lived, must have troubled her.

A letter from her brother Johann Matthias to his dear friend Friedrich Ernst von Fabrice, a Hanoverian courtier and diplomat who was also close to Melusine, shows us that the nature of her relationship with George often left her feeling anxious and insecure. Although the letter was written in March 1728, after George's death when she was still in deep grief, it is relevant to Melusine's state of mind at the turn of the century. The letter is worth quoting in full as it throws light on Melusine's passivity and Johann Matthias's frustration with his sister at allowing George to treat her, in his view, so poorly:

> ... I finally received a letter from my dear sister, whom I honour and respect as much as I pity her. Neither advantage nor luck were of permanence or long duration for her. If one is not able to draw immediate benefit from a stroke of fortune, afterwards it becomes almost impossible to undo any wrong step one has taken. Without question one must know the difference between destiny and luck. However, I am firmly of the opinion that luck, whether good or bad, relies principally on our disposition. One should investigate without prejudice whatever generally comes the way of mortals, and one will duly recognise that they themselves almost always represent its direct or indirect cause. I am sure that, wherever passions or tempers rule, neither reason nor healthy human understanding can find a place. If my sister is not one of the happiest human beings of her time, and if she is currently not in an agreeable situation and not completely independent, then she really only has herself to blame. She was wary of opening her heart to anyone, even those closest to her, and proved even less ready to listen to her friends or her relatives; rather she put her trust in those who hardly considered what would be conducive to her interests – may that last comment remain between you and me! I know very well what she would say to me on this, to which I could only answer: If one

knows the people with whom one is dealing, then one knows how one must behave; if, moreover one realises the nature of the matter, then it is only right and proper that one should in many cases reconcile oneself with a situation and that, as and when, one should attempt to influence circumstances oneself, with the aim of achieving one's aims at a decisive point and in the proper place. For this one needs much perspicacity and an unshakeable patience, and that does not grow on trees . . .[25]

While Johann Matthias thought George had been selfish to put his sister in such a precarious position, Melusine rarely gave her lover a hint of any misgivings at her insecurity over her financial situation, over the future of the girls, who were never legitimized, or concerning what would become of her should George discard her. All was perfect harmony in their household. Except, that is, for the tempestuous and 'difficult' Sophia Charlotte.

Sophia Charlotte, George's illegitimate half-sister, was a vibrant and vivacious woman who courted intrigue. Later, Sophia Charlotte was teased for her enormous bulk – English wags bitchily described her as the 'Elephant' to Melusine's 'Maypole'. But in her youth she was a plump and fashionable beauty – lively, clever, and at the centre of court gossip. Contemporaries were convinced that George and Sophia Charlotte were lovers, and even Liselotte mentioned it. George's mother, aware of the rumours, felt compelled to deny these charges of an incestuous relationship, stating in 1701 that 'to her certain knowledge, it was not so'.[26]

Considering George's personality, this alleged incestuous affair does seem unlikely – he enjoyed domestic bliss with Melusine, and this was coupled with a strong sense of duty. But although he found Sophia Charlotte at times irritating she was very much at the centre of his intimate circle, a fixture entrusted by George with politically sensitive tasks such as choosing presents for his Prussian daughter.

Sophia Charlotte was his sister, and his siblings were precious to him, particularly after the treachery of Max and Christian Heinrich, and Figuelotte's untimely death. Furthermore she remained loyal to George until her death, a quality he had learned through experience to value highly. She may have been difficult, but she was also witty, pretty and entertaining. And George liked flirtatious, attractive women.

In 1701 Sophia Charlotte married Johann Adolf von Kielmansegg. He and George got on immensely well, sharing a love of music and the hunt, and George appointed him Master of the Horse, a lucrative position. But Sophia Charlotte created discord. She was often careless of the feelings of others, and in 1701 she upset a volatile Georg August to the extent that the diplomat of the family, Ernst August, had to intervene to calm everyone down.[27] Caroline naturally took her husband's side, and although we do not know the nature of the 'offence' given by Sophia Charlotte, the episode marked the beginning of ill-feeling between the two.

Here, Melusine chimed with Caroline. Neither could abide Sophia Charlotte, and they failed to understand George's favour towards her. Sophia Charlotte's relationship with Caroline swiftly deteriorated; perhaps both were too opinionated to enjoy one another's company. And Sophia Charlotte was extremely jealous of Melusine. This jealousy would eventually lead to her forming a faction with her sister-in-law, Sophie Karoline von Platen (whom we will meet later), against Melusine, which frightened Melusine enough to make her turn to George's ministers for help in maintaining her position.

Later, in England, Caroline went so far as to refer to Sophia Charlotte as a 'wicked woman'.[28] Wilhelmine, George's Prussian granddaughter, wrote of her great-aunt that she 'held the second rank, [and] was the natural daughter of the late Elector of Hanover and a Countess of Platen. It might be truly said of her that she possessed the disposition of a devil; for she was altogether inclined to work evil. She was vicious, intriguing, and ... ambitious ...'[29]

But Sophia Charlotte was not 'wicked'. She was a charismatic and divisive character whose illegitimacy compelled her to fight harder for respect and recognition at the frequently febrile atmosphere of the court.

Two momentous events occurred in 1714. The first was Sophia's collapse and death in her garden at Herrenhausen on 8 June, at the age of eighty-four. She was walking with Melusine's great friend Joanne Sophie, Countess of Schaumburg-Lippe, and Caroline.

It was suitable that Sophia died in her beloved garden. It was here she had sought solace from the horror of the family's fracture over primogeniture, here that she grieved for her sons lost in battle, here she licked her wounds when her husband suspected her of treason. Just months before her death Sophia had written: 'I am sitting in my cabinet, right in the sun, like the melons in the hothouse, I have twelve canaries that make a noise as if I were in a thicket. I must thank God for my good constitution, that I can still make the grand tour around the Herrenhausen garden without effort because I very much like to go walking in these beautiful pergolas.'[30] She was buried in the Leineschloss church, but after the destruction of Hanover during the Second World War her remains were moved to the beautiful nineteenth-century mausoleum in the grounds of her garden at Herrenhausen.

Sophia had insulted and ignored Melusine for twenty-three years. The Hanoverian residences were not vast and Melusine had borne Sophia's ill will in close proximity with extraordinary good grace.

The second event was the death of Queen Anne on 1 August. Days before Sophia's death she had received an extremely harsh letter from Anne (actually dictated by Robert Harley, Earl of Oxford), admonishing Sophia's arguably reasonable request that Georg August, created Duke of Cambridge in 1706, might come to London to take up his seat in the House of Lords. On Sophia and George's part, it was a measure to safeguard the Hanoverian succession. Anne was furious. Like Queen Elizabeth before her, she could not bear to think about her death or the succession. She wrote to Georg August that 'nothing can be so disagreeable to me'.[31] Thus rebuked, Sophia died three days later. We do not know if the English monarch's words stung her enough to contribute to her death.

Anne's response to Sophia's death was callous – she felt dogged by her Hanoverian successors during the latter part of her reign. When Sir David Hamilton 'ask'd her [Queen Anne] if Princess Sophia's Death added any thing to Her quiet or disquiet . . . she said, that Princess Sophia was Chipping-Porridge [a thing or matter of little importance], it would neither give more Ease, nor more uneasiness.'[32]

Anne died at 7.45 a.m. There are rumours that on her deathbed a guilt-stricken queen repented her part in excluding her Catholic half-brother James Stuart from the succession, thereby denying him the throne. But this may be Jacobite propaganda. George was proclaimed king at four o'clock in the afternoon. The proclamation, signed by 127 signatories, read:

> We therefore, the Lords Spiritual and Temporal of the Realm, being here assisted with those of her late Majesty's Privy Council, with numbers of other principal gentlemen of quality, with the Lord Mayor, Aldermen and Citizens of London, do now hereby with one full voice and consent of tongue and heart, publish and proclaim that the High and Mighty Prince George Elector of Brunswick Lüneburg is now by the death of our late sovereign of Happy

Memory, become our lawful and rightful liege Lord, George by the Grace of God King of Great Britain, France and Ireland.[33]

At the age of forty-six, Melusine's position was about to change dramatically.

Later that month George and his courtiers went to Britain. Melusine followed slightly later. She was evidently anxious about leaving her home of the past twenty-three years, and according to her friend Joanne Sophie of Schaumburg-Lippe she 'wept bitter tears'. Melusine was never to reside in Germany again, although she accompanied George on each of the five visits he made back to his Electorate. Britain would be her home and George would give her the titles Duchess of Munster in 1716 and Duchess of Kendal in 1719. She had already mastered English, something her lover was never able to do with complete fluency.

It was typical of Melusine that as it became ever more likely that George would inherit the British throne, she learnt the language. Even so, once in England, she found herself at the mercy of the Jacobite pamphleteers and the free press. They would give Melusine one of the ugliest reputations a British royal mistress has ever endured. In England, the 'good', gentle and benevolent aristocrat became the avaricious and grasping 'Maypole'.

6.

The Crown at Last

And what men that little rustic England could breed! A nation of five and a half millions that had Wren for its architect, Newton for its scientist, Locke for its philosopher, Bentley for its scholar, Pope for its poet, Addison for its essayist, Bolingbroke for its orator, Swift for its pamphleteer and Marlborough to win its battles, had the recipe for genius.

– The historian G. M. Trevelyan, describing the country
that George became king of on 1 August 1714

Great Britain was a very different prospect to the benign autocracy of Hanover, with its tiny population of 600,000. The seventeenth century had been one of the most turbulent in the country's history, a century that had moved away from autocracy and the notion of the divine right of kings towards constitutional monarchy. It had forged a people suspicious of dictatorial government who closely guarded their rights. James I's declaration in 1609 that 'Kings are justly called Gods . . .'[1] and its implicit autocratic doctrine had arguably set in motion the severing of his son Charles I's head at his glorious Banqueting House at Whitehall on a freezing January day in 1649 – an event that precipitated the Hanoverian claim to the throne. This unprecedented act of legal regicide, when Charles I went 'from a corruptible to an incorruptible crown', heralded the moment that England said farewell for ever to absolutist monarchy. Cromwell's ten-year Protectorate, the Catholic James II's disastrous and short-lived reign, the Protestant William III's successful invasion, albeit by invitation, and continuous wars against Louis XIV's France between 1689 and 1713 fashioned a desire not only for stable government, but more importantly for Protestant government. England's Glorious Revolution of 1688 had forever entwined Catholicism and repression, and Protestantism and freedom, in the national consciousness.

The turmoil had created a nation whose self-confidence was out of all proportion to its relatively small population of eight million.[2] National pride was enhanced by the flamboyant Duke of Marlborough's brilliant military victories against the French. His reward from a grateful people and monarch – Blenheim Palace – was more beautiful than any of the royal palaces.

What set Britain apart from her continental and predominantly absolutist neighbours? As the historian W. A. Speck has argued, it was England's unique constitutional monarchy, precipitated by the absolutist Charles I's beheading – mixed rule by monarchy and parliament, which in turn led to the growth of liberalism. With liberty grew trade, which would otherwise have been 'stifled by absolutism'.

A pamphlet of 1757, *A Tract of the National Interest*, asserted that 'riches, trade and commerce are nowhere to be found but in the regions of freedom, where the lives and properties of the subjects are secured by wholesome laws. Nowhere else, in no other soil can they grow or subsist . . .'[3] That great barometer of liberalism and trade, the Jews, had returned to England with Oliver Cromwell during his Protectorate. They had been expelled by Edward I in 1290; by 1665 the wealthy merchant Menasseh Ben Israel, who had moved to England from the Netherlands, noted: 'And so 'tis observed, that wheresoever they [the Jews] go to dwell, there presently the Traficq begins to florish . . .'[4] With wealth came a desire for education. Towards the end of the seventeenth century many cheap schools were established, reflecting Londoners' desire to give their children the tools to do better.[5]

By the end of the seventeenth century the essayist Addison could proclaim: 'this Metropolis [London] [is] a kind of Emporium of the whole Earth'. And by the time Melusine and George arrived in the capital it was the most important commercial centre in the world. As Peter Ackroyd notes in his *London, the Biography*, the start of the eighteenth century 'was the age of lotteries and flotations and "bubbles". Everything was for sale – political office, religious preferment, landed heiresses – and, said Swift, "Power, which according to the old Maxim, was used to follow *Land*, is now gone over to Money".'[6]

The establishment, of course, loathed the new monied classes

created by the burgeoning of trade. In 1715 the dramatist and poet
John Gay complained:

> Now gaudy Pride corrupts the lavish Age
> And the Streets flame with glaring Equipage;
> The tricking Gamester insolently rides,
> With Loves and Graces on his Chariot's sides;
> In sawcy State the griping Broker sits
> And laughs at Honesty, and trudging Wits.[7]

But trade had grown so entrenched in the national character that
the author Daniel Defoe felt able to write:

> the Blood of Trade is mixed and blended with the Blood of
> Gallantry, so that Trade is the Lifeblood of the Nation, the Soul of
> Felicity, the Spring of its Wealth, the Support of its Greatness, and
> the Staff on which both King and People lean.[8]

Parliament was dominated by two political parties, the Whigs
and the Tories. During George's reign the country was effectively
ruled by an oligarchy – the king and his ministers, all powerful
Whiggish parliamentarians. Although the king still enjoyed an
enormous amount of power, George was required to work with
parliament, not least because he depended on it to approve his civil
list. The country was still far from a democracy: an archaic system
of property qualifications decided who could vote, and it has been
estimated that this privilege was enjoyed by, at best, 5 per cent of
the adult male population.

The terms Whig and Tory had their origins in insults – Whig
meant horse thief in Scottish Gaelic; Tory was an Irish term mean-
ing outlaw, or robber (it eventually came to mean 'Papist outlaw').
The parties had emerged out of the 'exclusion crisis' of 1679 in

which the group of noblemen and parliamentarians who would become known as the Whigs argued heatedly for the exclusion of the Catholic James, Charles II's brother, from the succession.

By the time of George's accession the Whigs were associated in the popular imagination with trade, new money and urban life, while the Tories represented the privileges of the Anglican Church and the landed classes, with their roots in the countryside.

Charles, famously libidinous (he had at least fifteen mistresses), had fathered many illegitimate children. But his wife, Catherine of Braganza, was unable to conceive. This meant that the throne would pass to the next Stuart male in the line of succession on Charles's death – his brother James. But shockingly to a fiercely Protestant England, James converted to Catholicism, in either 1668 or 1669. Charles was furious. James's young daughters by the commoner Anne Hyde, Mary and Anne (both future queens of England), were removed from his care and made children of state, to be brought up as Protestants. James further alarmed and infuriated the king and the nation by marrying the Catholic princess Mary of Modena on Anne Hyde's death.

In 1678 a maverick Anglican priest, Titus Oates, caused mass panic when he fabricated his tale of the 'Popish Plot', a scheme to assassinate Charles and place James on the throne instead. Although Oates was tried and found guilty of sedition, many believed his story, a mark of the strength of feeling against Catholics amongst much of the population. Three successive parliaments attempted to exclude James from the succession, and the opposing factions – those who advocated his removal (the Whigs) and those who did not (the Tories) – hurled vile insults at one another across the floor. Ultimately the Whigs were defeated.

Despite the hysteria, James came to the throne on the death of Charles in 1685. It was his daughter Anne's machinations that aided his deposition three years later. James's eldest daughter Mary had married her cousin the Protestant William of Orange in 1677. Mary was childless and the younger Anne was second in line to the throne on her father's accession. Her young stepmother had had numerous miscarriages and Anne believed she could not carry a child to full term. But to her horror, in June 1688 she gave birth to a son, James Francis Edward. The zealously Protestant and fiercely ambitious Anne convinced her sister and brother-in-law that the baby was a changeling; William took the bait and, at the invitation of a group of the nobility, successfully invaded England to save the country from the Papists.[9]

The joint rule of William and Mary firmly established a Protestant dynasty in England, first with their sovereignty and then with Anne's. It was Anne's reign, a second 'Golden Age', that oversaw such artistic and military glories as the architecture of Hawksmoor and Vanbrugh and Marlborough's victories. And, as we have seen, it was Anne's childless misery that ensured the Hanoverian succession. Catholicism had become such an emotive subject that the majority of Englishmen were determined never to tolerate rule by a 'Papist' again.

Since 1688 and her 'Glorious Revolution', England had truly become one of Europe's great powers. Under the successive reigns of William III and Anne, Britain had entered the Grand Alliance with Austria and the United Provinces to fight against the hegemony of Louis XIV's France in the War of the Spanish Succession, a pan-European struggle. John Churchill, first Duke of Marlborough and Anne's brilliant general, had delivered phenomenal military victories for the country. But towards the end of Anne's reign her leading Tory ministers, St John, Viscount Bolingbroke and Robert Harley, Earl of Oxford, had taken England out of the war in 1713 by signing a separate peace with France, the Treaty of Utrecht. George was horrified. Hanover was an ally of the Grand Alliance and according to the terms of the founding treaty, should have been consulted on any peace. He saw it as a betrayal; he would never, forgive the Tory ministers who had engineered it.

Although Anne's natural inclination was to favour the Tories, with their more royalist sentiments, she endeavoured throughout her reign to appear impartial. The absolutist tendencies of English monarchs did not vanish overnight with the deposition and death of Charles I. Anne reputedly enquired of the young Robert Walpole what the cost would be to enclose Green Park within her garden, to which the Whig minister replied: 'A crown, Madam, a crown.'

George, like Anne, hoped to rule without seeming to favour either party. But by the time he entered a London covered with thick fog on 29 September 1714 to take up residence at St James's Palace, the Tories had little chance of forming a ministry under the new monarch. They had been labelled, somewhat unfairly, the anti-Hanoverian party. The most prominent men in Anne's last ministry, Viscount Bolingbroke and the Earl of Oxford, were suspected by George of favouring the accession of the Stuart claimant over the Hanoverians;[10] he loathed them for their part in the Peace of Utrecht; they were associated in George's mind with Anglicanism and the correlating prejudice towards Protestant dissenters; and the enmity between the Tories' leading lights, Bolingbroke and Oxford, meant that the party was hopelessly fractured.

The Tories did little to help their cause with the publication of scurrilous poems by Tory satirists. George was thrust into the arms of the Whigs in part because of the sentiments of poems such as 'The Blessings Attending George's Accession', which contained the lines:

> Hither he brought the dear Illustrious House;
> That is, himself, his pipe, close stool and louse;
> Two Turks, three Whores, and half a dozen nurses,
> Five hundred Germans, all with empty purses.[11]

George duly filled all of the posts in his Cabinet bar one with Whigs – the Earl of Nottingham was the only Tory – and the privy council was stocked with Whigs and a few loyal Tories. Similarly the only Tories who survived George's purge of the state departments were those known to be loyal Hanoverians. By the time parliament was dissolved on 15 January 1715, George had given power over to the Whigs.

A desperate Bolingbroke fled to France knowing there was no hope of favour, and into the arms of the Pretender James Stuart, the son of James II. He became his secretary of state. His actions could not have been more damning to the Tory party. The earls of Oxford and Stafford were impeached in the wake of his flight and Oxford was sent to the Tower. The Whigs were overjoyed and capitalized on the appalling image the Tories had in the king's eyes. They enthusiastically dubbed the Tories who had served under Anne 'Jacobites' – that is, sympathizers with the cause of 'The Pretender'. But not all Tories were Jacobites; many, such as Oxford, fully supported the Hanoverian succession. Others retreated into an apathetic silence. In February 1714 Baron Schutz, George's envoy to Britain, presciently wrote: 'it is certain that of fifteen Tories there are fourteen who would not oppose the Pretender, in case he came with a French army.'[12]

The turbulent events of George's first year as king ensured that the Tories would be out of office for nearly half a century. A leading Whig, James Stanhope, stated somewhat smugly in 1716: 'His majesty's affairs are, thanks be to God, at present in a more settled and prosperous condition than his most sanguine servants could ever have expected.'[13]

It is hardly surprising that George's accession to the throne of Great Britain and Ireland was so fiercely contested. Had Catholics been allowed to reign, George would have been very far back in the line of succession – there were fifty-three other candidates who were more eligible. Even Liselotte was a little sniffy about George's claim. In January 1715 she wrote to her half-sister the raugravine Louise: 'I can't think where he gets his haughtiness from; if I had been a Protestant, he wouldn't be King. I was nearer to the Crown than he, and it is only through my family, and that of his late mother, that he is King now . . .'[14]

The most emotive Catholic contender for the throne and the next in the Stuart line of succession was James Frances Edward Stuart, the son of James II and Mary of Modena and Queen Anne's half-brother – the Pretender. James had died in 1701 in exile in France, and his son became heir to the Jacobite cause. At Anne's death in 1714 James Stuart was twenty-eight, in exile in Lorraine – and therefore closer to Britain than George in Hanover – and a hugely popular figure amongst many Tories. He also had the backing of his cousin Louis XIV of France.

George's accession and arrival in London had been relatively quiet, with public displays, both organized and spontaneous, of joy at the expectation of what a new reign would bring. Queen Anne had been so dogged by ill health and her court so dull in the last years of her reign that bored courtiers hoped for a more dazzling display with the accession of George. Lady Dupplin wrote to Abigail Harley, Anne's last favourite: 'all the town was gazing at the fine show . . . there were great bonfires and illuminations at night . . . Aboard the yacht the king made the Earls Berkley and Dorset Gentlemen of his Bedchamber . . .'[15]

However, on the day of George's coronation at Westminster Abbey on 20 October 1714, there were altercations in the south and the Midlands, in Birmingham, Bristol, Chippenham, Norwich and Reading. In November of that year, the Pretender proclaimed to his 'loving subjects' (with shades of the great orator Queen Elizabeth I) that 'for some time past he could not well doubt of his sister's good intentions towards him . . . which were unfortunately prevented by her deplorable death'.[16] Many Tories, realizing how desperately marginalized they were by George I, made overtures to James. They persuaded him to invade to claim his birthright.

London continued to see frequent Jacobite disturbances on every significant anniversary – Queen Anne's coronation, George's birthday, Charles II's restoration. On 29 May 1715 a bonfire was lit in Chancery Lane and rioting lasted all summer throughout the Midlands.[17]

And it was London in particular that saw a torrent of anti-Hanoverian ballads, pamphlets and prints. In his extensive diaries Lord Egmont accused the Tories of using:

> very vile acts to alienate the minds of the people from the king and proceeded at last to printing and dispersing a pamphlet called advice to the English freeholders etc. which is full of sedition, personal reflections on the royal family and notorious untruths ... It would dirty my pen to write the load of lesser scandal invented by the king's enemies to serve their purpose among the vulgar ... I shall give only a specimen: they say the prince ... has given the princess the pox. That he has sent £40,000 into the country to bribe elections ... that the King goes into the chocolate houses and coffee houses incognito to hear what is said of him. That he is frantic often times and walks about in his shirt. That he keeps two Turks for abominable uses. That he gives his hand behind his back to the English to be kissed, that they may at the same time kiss his Breech. That the prince says he knows a Tory and a common whore by their looks ...[18]

Even Liselotte was worried for her cousin, and wrote a typically vague letter to Louise in September 1714:

> It is hard to believe that the English could ever be content with any king, let alone ours. I feel just as children do when they say 'J'aime

papa et mama'. I love our Elector, who has now become King, and the King of England here, and his mother, are dear to me too. I wish our Elector could have another kingdom, and our King of England his own, for I confess that I don't trust the English one iota, and fear that our Elector, who is now King, will meet with disaster. If his rule in England were as absolute as our King's here, I have no doubt that right and justice would reign, but there are altogether too many examples of the unfair way in which the English treat their kings. But my meal has arrived. Today I am eating earlier than usual because of the hunt.[19]

Although the Jacobite ranks in Scotland would eventually swell to 10,000 men, George and his ministers perceived rebellion in the south to be the greater threat. George's spies reported that James was planning to invade and the king responded by suspending Habeas Corpus on 21 July 1715, 'to impower his majesty to secure and detain such persons as his majesty shall suspect are conspiring against his person and government'. Arrest followed arrest – Lord Lansdowne and Lord Dupplin amongst others – and warrants were issued for the arrests of the Earl of Jersey, Sir William Wyndham and Thomas Forster. Wyndham and Forster declared for James at Warkworth and Alnwick, then joined the Scottish Jacobites. But the rebellion quickly fizzled out.

The Pretender's resources were pitiful and Louis XIV, although he promised all, delivered nothing – no military or financial aid was forthcoming to his cousin's campaign. When the French king died in September 1715, to be replaced by his five-year-old great-grandson, James's venture seemed lost.

However the Scots, France's ancient allies against the English, took up James's cause, and on 6 September 1715 the Earl of Mar raised James's standard at Braemar. Although union between Scotland and England had been achieved in 1707, many Scots felt ignored and disaffected. When the Earl of Mar declared that the Pretender would restore the 'ancient free and independent constitution' of Scotland, James's cause, despite his Catholicism, became the perfect excuse for a rebellion.

It was a lost cause. The Pretender was still in France, and without a strong leader the disparate army surrendered to Hanoverian troops on 14 November. The English Jacobite army was left in tatters; only the Scots remained. James's half-brother, the Duke of Berwick, remarked: 'I shall always consider it a folly to think that he [James] will be able to succeed in his undertaking with the Scotch alone.'[20]

James, realizing he had no hope of a successful invasion of England, headed for Scotland. But his Scottish supporters were on the run and he left again for France at the beginning of February.

George and his Whig ministers were brutal in their reprisals. Twenty-eight were hanged, and hundreds sent to exile in Britain's colonial territories, chiefly the Americas. The Earl of Nottingham, the sole Tory in George's Cabinet, begged for mercy for the rebel peers. George had wanted to execute them all, but Nottingham's intercession ensured that only two, Lords Derwentwater and Kenmure, were hanged. Nottingham then departed the king's service, leaving the Whigs as George's sole British advisers.

The Whigs were dominated by huge personalities, particularly Charles, second Viscount Townshend, and Robert Walpole. They were brothers-in-law whose families were neighbours in their native Norfolk – Townshend had married Walpole's sister Dorothy in 1713. She was his second wife. The alliance facilitated a close political partnership between the pair, who otherwise had little in common. Townshend, an astute politician, was refined, charming and hard-working. His contemporary John Mackay called him a 'Gentleman of Great Learning, attended with a sweet Disposition;

a Lover of the Constitution of his Country; is beloved by every Body that knows him'.[21]

Walpole was loud, coarse, fat, rude and brilliant. An early member of the Whiggish political and literary Kit-Kat club, he was obsessed with politics. He was the son of a wealthy squire and was originally meant for the Church, but the death of his older brother made him his father's heir and destined him for other things. Melusine's brother Frederick William, not easily impressed, was struck by Walpole's skilful handling of his fellow politicians, which he communicated in his extensive missives to Baron Görtz, one of George's Hanoverian ministers. Walpole was extremely attractive to women and had many mistresses, despite his two marriages. We know the name of at least one – Carey Daye – with whom he had a daughter, named Catherine. Walpole embraced life and always lived beyond his means. He was constantly dogged by debt.

During the last years of George's reign, Walpole would preside over an oligarchy. He would realize Melusine's full political potential and ultimately save her from absolute disgrace.

7.

Germans in England

England is a mad country.

— Liselotte to Louise, 23 April 1715

In spite of an unfamiliar country, new and forthright ministers, political upheaval, riots and an invasion, family life went on. Theirs was no longer a young family. Melusine was forty-six when she arrived in Britain, George fifty-four, Louise twenty-two and young Melusine twenty-one. Only Trudchen remained too young, at thirteen, to fully enter society, a detail that has led some historians to overlook her, and even to speculate that Melusine had only two daughters, or 'nieces'.

Melusine initially lived with George and the girls in St James's Palace, together with Caroline, Georg August and their daughters the princesses Anne, Amalie and Caroline Elizabeth. Their eldest child, Frederick, remained in Hanover as a mark of George's continued commitment towards the principality. He was determined to rule both his dominions and gave his directions to the Hanoverian Chancery in London. Young Frederick became the charge of his great-uncle Ernst August, who took care of his upbringing and education. About ninety Hanoverians – ministers, courtiers and servants – accompanied Melusine and George to London, staffing George's bedchamber, his kitchen and his Hanoverian Chancery. They had come with the king only as an interim measure until the places in his household could be filled by Englishmen. Most of them would return to Hanover in 1716.

St James's Palace had been built by Henry VIII on the site of a leper hospital dedicated to St James the Less. Not the most comfortable royal household, it had been meant to be only a temporary replacement for Whitehall after it burned down in 1697, but it remained the royal residence in central London and it is still the palace to which ambassadors are formally called.

It was universally loathed for its small, labyrinthine rooms. Daniel Defoe called its apartments 'mean'. In 1734 James Ralph, in his publication on the buildings of London and Westminster, declared that: 'so far from having one single beauty to recommend it . . . 'tis at once the contempt of foreign nations, and the disgrace of our own.'[1] St James's did not impress either the family or their visitors. J. Gwynn, the author of *London & Westminster Improved* of 1766 lamented that the royal family should 'reside in a house so ill-becoming the state and grandeur of the most powerful and respectable monarch in the universe'.[2]

It was difficult to house the entire family and their staff under its roof, and many of George's English and Hanoverian servants were lodged instead around Whitehall and in Somerset House. Most of the Hanoverians who had come over with Melusine and George were found rooms in surrounding houses. St James's saw a frenzy of building as kitchens, cellars and sculleries were put in to feed the new royal family.

Despite the inadequacy of the palace, Melusine's apartments were 'lavishly furnished' and her rooms the best St James's could offer.[3] The palace was dark and dank, but its location near the river was wonderful and Melusine and the girls used their early days in London well, exploring the parks, which were the envy of Europe. St James's Park in particular was a magnet for those wanting to be seen:

> [It] contains several avenues of elm and lime trees, two large ponds, and a pretty little island; in a word, this is an enchanting spot in summer time. Society comes to walk here on fine, warm days, from seven to ten in the evening, and in winter from one to three o'clock. English men and women are fond of walking, and the park is so crowded at times that you cannot help touching your neighbour. Some people come to see, some to be seen, and others to seek their

fortunes; for many priestesses of Venus are abroad, some of them magnificently attired, and all on the look-out for adventures, and many young men are not long in repenting that they have become acquainted with such beautiful and amiable nymphs . . .[4]

Court was a round of public and private parties, of jostling for power between the Hanoverian and the English courtiers, of familial rivalry, corruption and bribery.

The English had high hopes of a social renaissance with a new monarch. The latter years of Queen Anne's court had been so dreary that many had stayed away. In 1711 Swift wrote to Stella, after one particularly dull afternoon:

There was a drawing room today at Court; but so few company, that the Queen sent for us into her bed-chamber, where we made our bows, and stood about twenty of us around the room, while she looked at us round with her fan in her mouth, and once a minute said about three words to some that were nearest her, and then she was told dinner was ready, and went out.[5]

The queen was so bloated and ill with dropsy that she could barely move, and every movement achieved was at the expense of great pain. She was steeped in grief for her dead children and her dead husband. There were none of the glamorous parties or intrigues that had marked the beginning of her reign at the height of her relationship with her magnetic favourite, Sarah, Duchess of Marlborough. After the death of Anne's husband, Prince George of Denmark, even Sarah stayed away, sparking a shattering fall from grace and the installation of Sarah's cousin, the Tory Abigail Masham, later wife of Robert Harley (the Earl of Oxford), as Anne's new favourite. The historian G. M. Trevelyan wrote of Anne's tedious life: 'for a dozen weary years the invalid daily faced her office work . . . In order to do what she thought right in church and state, she slaved at many details of government . . .'

The reporting of early eighteenth-century court life is comparable to our own fascination with celebrity. Court notices, with their accompanying descriptions of the royal family, the aristocracy and other 'persons of note', were today's equivalent of gossip columns, recording the appointments, the illnesses, the parties and the holidays of the major characters. For example, on 18 May 1722 the *Daily Journal* reported: 'On Tuesday the Duchess of Kendal gave a magnificent entertainment to most of the Foreign Ministers etc at her apartment in St James's House.' The same column, reflecting what typically economically minded and sensation-hungry Londoners wanted, lists stock prices and convicted criminals to be executed the following Monday:

> Yesterday the dead warrant came to Newgate for the execution of the following malefactors on Monday next at Tyburn, viz; John Bootini, a youth, for a rape on a young girl, and giving her the foul disease, Thomas Smith alias Newcomb for felony and burglary, Leonard Hendry for felony, Jeremiah Rand for a street robbery, Richard Whittingham for felony and burglary. John Hawkins and George Simpson for robbing the Bristol Mail; the two last are afterwards to be hanged in chains near the place where they committed the acts . . .

But if the British aristocracy and gossip-hungry Londoners expected George and Melusine to head a more exciting court, they were to be disappointed. A newsletter dated 4 September 1714 happily speculated: 'His Majesty brings with him 17 sets of fine coach horses. We hear the king will keep here a noble and splendid court.'[6] But Melusine and George, immensely private, did all they could to avoid the trappings of kingship.

George and Melusine always preferred the intimacy of family life and close friends to a large and impersonal court, and this desire strengthened as they grew older. Melusine had begun to correspond with various English women whose husbands were important politically while still in Germany, and she created a good impression with all who knew her personally. But she was far more comfortable in informal surroundings, presiding over small dinner parties, attending the opera with her daughters or one or two ladies, or drinking coffee in her rooms. The newspapers are full of reports of outings to the opera or theatre with one of her 'nieces', and she was in the habit of spending evenings with just one or two ladies. Lady Bristol, one of Caroline's Ladies of the Bedchamber, for example, wrote in her diary of seeing a great deal of Melusine in 1715. 'I go to the opera a Saturday with Madam Shulenberg and her niece . . .' she reported, and later in the year: 'I went to court, where I was received more graciously than ordinary. And stayed till three a clock, and am to be at half an hour after four with Madam Shulenburg to drink coffee before we go together to the opera . . .'[7]

Similarly the conscientious George took his duties to the state extremely seriously. But as far as he was concerned those duties did not include providing entertainment for his courtiers and visiting dignitaries. He would provide no public spectacle with a levee and a coucher – the public putting to bed and getting up of the monarch – open to high-ranking courtiers, and he refused to dine in public.

Some English sovereigns had been happy to receive courtiers and ministers in their bedchamber – George was not. Instead he received them in a private closet beside his bedchamber. Entrance was strictly controlled and by arrangement with his Gentlemen of the Bedchamber only. Even peers must wait their turn.

George, if not exactly a misanthrope, only desired the company of trusted friends, family and servants. He saw the frivolities associated with monarchy as distractions from the business of government and he did his utmost to avoid them. English courtiers and foreign observers obviously thought his habits strange. Even the dying Queen Anne, they muttered, had kept a court more fitting to monarchy than this new Hanoverian king.

The Prussian envoy Bonet, in a private report for George's daughter and son-in-law, described the awkwardness George felt at being on 'show'. George, he reported to his master:

> is not seen at his lever, nor at his dinner, nor at his supper, nor at his coucher. Only during some minutes is he seen as he returns from the chapel, and this by stopping in a passageway to the chamber, which is lined on one side and the other with a double hedge of courtiers who touch all walls, of the type of whom there are not ten people of whose faces he takes note, and to whom he might speak ... As His Majesty never appears in public, one may not speak to him of business except in a formal audience ...

Bonet, shocked that a monarch could be so reticent about showing himself to his people, continued:

> Withdrawn into his palace of St. James, rather into one room and one cabinet, the other apartments being for the Courtiers, His Majesty never ventured out to Kensington, to Hampton Court or to Windsor, which are spacious, more commodious, and which have a more royal air. In this room, he slept and ate, and in the neighbouring cabinet he gave audiences. He has made no plan to designate certain days for business, and others for recreation and for the examination of those who are presented to him in audiences.

He goes on to observe that English courtiers rarely had the opportunity to get near their king: 'He had established some lords as his Gentlemen of the Bedchamber, who would have served at table, and some other lesser gentlemen to dress him, but he never wanted to receive the services of either one or the other, and he wanted to receive only the service of his Turks and of his German valets de chambre.'

George, he continues:

> stayed alone every morning in this chamber until midday when he passed into the cabinet in order to give audiences to the ministers of State of the two nations until two o'clock, when he went to his table for dinner; after dinner, he walked alone in the Garden of St. James, or he went to the rooms of the duchess of Munster, and in the evening to the circle of the Princess [Caroline], until midnight, or else to the opera, where he went incognito in a hired chaise, or to the rooms of Madame de Kielmansegge [Sophia Charlotte] . . . and it happened very rarely that his ministers of State spoke to him in the afternoons.

Both George and Melusine had brought their trusted servants from Hanover, and they very much kept to their inner circle – the girls, the extended family and old friends. If anything Melusine, during the early years of the reign, was more gregarious than George, ensuring that she visited and received the noblewomen who could be useful to the king, and taking outings with her daughters.

Two of George's servants served to excite the most interest: the Turks Mehemet and Mustapha, who had served George in Hanover. As a trusted friend and confidant, Mustapha was party to his most private disappointments and pleasures. We know of George's pitiful despair over his sister Figuelotte's death, for example, only because Mehemet told Mary Countess Cowper, a Lady of the Bedchamber to Caroline and the wife of William Cowper, George's Lord Chancellor, and a prolific keeper of her diary, who recorded it. This scene provides us with an image of George as a man of passion, far removed from the taciturn soldier of the popular imagination.

Coxe, the early biographer of Robert Walpole, comments on the importance of these Turkish servants: 'Their influence over their master was so great, that their names are mentioned in a dispatch of Count Broglio to the King of France, as possessing a large share of the King's confidence.' He continued: 'These low foreigners obtained considerable sums of money for recommendations to places.'

Nor did their influence escape Alexander Pope, who mentioned Mehemet in his *Moral Essays*, 'Epistle II, to a lady':

> From peer or bishop 'tis no easy thing
> To draw the man who loves his God, or king,
> Alas! I copy (or my draught would fail)
> From honest Mah'met, or plain Parson Hale.

Mehemet and Mustapha were also immortalized by William Kent in his glorious mural on the grand staircase at Kensington Palace, with the Turkish touches in Mehemet's dress adding to his exoticism. In the mural, alongside the two Turks and George's jester-dwarf, Kent shows Peter the Wild Boy, a feral child, possibly mentally disabled, who had been abandoned by his parents and was living in the woods in northern Germany. George brought him over to England, where he was treated as a curiosity at court. In the minds of many Englishmen, particularly the Jacobites, this strange group – 'heathen' Turks, a dwarf, a 'Wild Boy', a half-sister who all thought was a mistress, and Melusine, who many laughed at simply because she was ageing yet continued to captivate the king – were established as corrupt and bizarre, in antithesis to poor, beautiful, imprisoned Sophia Dorothea.

Melusine also brought her favourite German servants to London with her, but she was typically discreet about her household, and many of their names are lost to us. We do know that in December 1721, one of the women on her staff won the lottery. The *Daily Post* reported: 'We hear that the prize of 300 l. per annum for life that was drawn in the York Buildings Lottery on Wednesday last, fell to the Duchess of Kendal's gentlewoman.' All we know of her identity is that she was a 'German Lady, servant to the Duchess'.[8] She was possibly Mrs Shrieder, Melusine's chief gentlewoman, whom she employed until at least the end of 1727. Another servant important enough to her household to merit mention in the newspapers was Monsieur de Anthony, Melusine's secretary. Melusine's writing was an illegible scrawl, and Monsieur de Anthony must have taken dictation for those letters that are easier to read.

Despite their distaste for display and the commotion of the early years, certain duties towards the court continued. Melusine was frantic with worry at the effect the rebellions and his fractious English ministers were having on George's health, and Mary Countess Cowper reported: 'Mademoiselle Schulenberg [*sic*] in great concern.'[9] Nevertheless the countess recorded in her diary the celebrations for Georg August's birthday: 'I never saw the court so splendidly fine. The evening concluded with a ball, which the prince and princess began.'

But they retreated as much as possible and happily allowed the more sociable and gregarious Georg August and Caroline to perform the social functions associated with monarchy and to provide the royal family with the requisite glamour.

Thus from the beginning of the new reign two courts existed side-by-side – the monarch's and the far more lively ambience created by Georg August and Caroline. It would eventually have disastrous consequences for the entire family. The separation would harden into a near-irreparable breach, splitting court, aristocracy and parliament.

Georg August and Caroline, now Prince and Princess of Wales, enthusiastically embraced the role of society leaders. Lord Hervey, a writer and a gossip at the centre of court life (he became Georg August's vice-chamberlain in 1730), recorded the different temperaments of father and son, and perceived that 'the pageantry and splendour, the badges and trappings of royalty, were as pleasing to the son as they were irksome to the father'.[10] Caroline held a drawing room in the evening twice a week, and gave balls at Somerset House and St James's. She and her husband delighted the English courtiers by including them fully on their staff.

Melusine and George lived at St James's from October or November until May or early June. George's birthday fell on 28 May, and they often stayed for the elaborate celebrations in London before departing for one of the summer palaces. Late spring was spent at Kensington, and high summer at glorious Hampton Court or Windsor. The movement between seasonal residences reminded them of Hanover, and the progression of its court between the Leineschloss, Herrenhausen and Ghörde. Courtiers followed them; in the winter receptions were held at the inadequate St James's Palace, and in the summer at Kensington, Hampton Court or Windsor.

Melusine's days were spent with her daughters, her friends and her new English acquaintances, and her evenings with George. Melusine's siblings were welcome visitors. Johann Matthias came to London in 1726 and George made sure that he reviewed the troops in Hyde Park. The king wore him out with his long and habitual hikes through the palace gardens, which could last up to three hours.[11] There were some familiar faces already in England:

the raugravine Caroline was married to one of William III's officers, Meinhard von Schomberg, Duke of Leinster, and the two
women were on excellent terms. Melusine and George dined
together most evenings, either alone or with the girls. In 1717 she
was given the generous sum of £3,000 per annum to maintain her
own kitchen to feed George and their guests, and was allocated a
great deal of beer, sherry, claret, bread and candles. Sophia
Charlotte was typically jealous of Melusine's allowance, and
badgered George for an equal amount. She too was awarded £3,000
to maintain her own kitchen.[12]

Melusine happily kept in the background while George's days took
on the familiar rhythm of Hanover. He woke early and worked in
his room until noon, when he received his ministers in an adjacent
room until about three o'clock. The king then ate alone in his bedchamber, served only by Mehemet or Mustapha. He exercised in the
afternoons by taking long walks in the gardens at St James's.[13]
Liselotte knew his character well. In October 1714 she wrote to the
raugravine Louise: 'Just between us, I believe that the King of England would have a better time at his Göhrde than in all his splendour
in England. For my good cousin the Lord King is no more taken with
ceremonies than his old cousin, my Excellency . . .'[14]

Once a week George dined with Sophia Charlotte who, naturally more gregarious, arranged for the most interesting artists and
wits to be at a lively supper. George and Melusine frequently went
to the opera or the theatre together, whether alone or with the girls,
or sometimes in an uncomfortable trio of Melusine, Sophia
Charlotte and George. George was either unaware of the antipathy
between his half-sister and his mistress, or he pragmatically chose
to ignore it.

The court was relatively informal. In 1725 a Swiss visitor to
London, César de Saussure, managed to gain access to court easily,
to his evident surprise. He has left us with a lovely description:

On the Sunday following my arrival a friend asked me to accompany him to Court, and at midday we went together to St. James's Palace. We passed through several rooms in which were noblemen and officers awaiting the opening of the King's apartments. As soon as the signal was given, all these people disappeared inside them, we being unable to follow on account of the crowd. Knowing there was a gallery leading to the chapel through which the Court must pass, we posted ourselves on it, and had not long to wait. Six Yeomen appeared at the head of the procession; they reminded me very much of the Swiss Guard at Versailles, being dressed in the same quaint fashion. They carried halberds on their shoulders and walked two and two. These Yeomen were followed by several gentlemen of the Court, by the Duke of Grafton, the King's Chamberlain, and by the Duke of Dorset, Master of the King's Household, each carrying a long white wand of office. Two sergeants-at-arms, or mace-bearers, followed, carrying their maces on their shoulders, these being of silver-gilt, surmounted by crowns of the same precious metal. A nobleman of the Court followed, carrying the sword of state . . . The King then appeared, followed by the three young Princesses who reside with him in the Palace; they are the Prince of Wales's three eldest daughters . . . I was surprised at seeing everyone making a profound reverence or bow as the King went by, which he in his turn acknowledged by a slight inclination of the head. The English do not consider their King to be so very much above them that they dare not salute him, as in France; they respect him and are faithful to him, and often sincerely attached to him. I speak, of course, of those who favour the reigning family . . .

From this room you go into that of the Gentlemen Pensioners, called the Presence Chamber, which is furnished with antique hangings, and from thence into another room, where the gentlemen of the Court await the opening of the King's apartments. The King's chambers consist firstly of a big room which leads into the bed-chamber, the bed being covered with crimson velvet, braided and embroidered in gold. The bed stands in a sort of alcove, shut off from the rest of the room by a balustrade of gilded wood. To the right of the grand ante-chamber is the drawing-room, where the King gives audiences and receives ambassadors. In these two chambers there are canopies of purple velvet. All these rooms look on to the park gardens, and are hung with beautiful old tapestries ...

... Three Drawing-rooms are held every week, one on Sundays from two till three, and the other two on Mondays and Fridays from eight till ten or eleven in the evening. These evening circles are much pleasanter than those held on Sundays, for the apartments are magnificently lighted, and more ladies attend them, and the latter are always an ornament to society ...

But the court was not all pomp and glitter. Many needed the financial security that a place offered. John Gay wrote of the demoralizing necessity of attending evening after evening in the hope of finding courtly work:

> Pensive each night, from room to room I walk'd,
> To one I bow'd, and with another talk'd;
> Enquir'd what news, or such a lady's name,
> And did the next day, and the next, the same.
> Places, I found, were daily given away,
> And yet no friendly Gazette mention'd Gay.
> I ask'd a friend what method to pursue;
> He cry'd, I want a place, as well as you.

8.

A Strange Family

Nor are the Hanover womankind his Majesty has about him, quasi-wives or not, of a soul-entrancing character; far indeed from that. Two in chief there are, a fat and a lean: the lean, called 'Maypole' by the English populace, is 'Duchess of Kendal', with excellent pension, in the English Peeragy [sic]; Schulenburg the former German name of her; decidedly a quasi-wife . . . who is fallen thin and old . . . Then besides this lean one, there is a fat . . . Kielmannsegge by German name, was called 'Countess of Darlington' in this country with excellent pension, as was natural. They all had pensions . . .

– Thomas Carlyle, nineteenth-century historian and writer

Jacobite propaganda was largely responsible for George's reputation for sexual rapacity. He was said to use his Turkish servants both as his pimps and his lovers. The historian Lucy Worsley repeats the rumours that George was besotted with a courtier, Molly Lepell, who was famously beautiful. She continues: 'It was said that Melusine had paid Molly £4,000 to break off her increasingly flagrant relationship with the king.'[1] The bitchy Lord Chesterfield and William Pulteney wrote a spiky little poem about Molly:

> Or were I the King of Great Britain
> To chuse a Minister well,
> And support the Throne that I sit on,
> I'd have under me Molly Le[pel]l.[2]

In 1720 the Jacobites in London added fuel to George's reputation as a deviant philanderer, excitedly gossiping that 'a cargo of new German ladies of the largest size are coming, and Mohammed . . . is to be chief over them'.[3]

Reliable contemporary accounts tell us that when George was relaxed, he could be flirtatious. The Prussian diplomat Bonet reported home of the 'passion' the Italian Duchess of Shrewsbury had conceived for the king.

> But shocking above all are the great familiarities which the duchess of Shrewsbury, an Italian lady whose reputation is not the best established, affects to take with the king in public and in private . . . everyone observes that she only eats what the king touches, or from the plates on which he is served; that she speaks to him with more

boldness than respect; and it was not a little surprising that she spent an evening at the theatre in her box, with the King, the singer San-clos, in her costume, and placing his hands on the latter's bosom, she said to him, even before witnesses, 'voilà, Sire, a beautiful throat'. The familiarities of this duchess give much to consider, but I shall not speak further.[4]

This duchess was not liked at court. Sarah, Duchess of Marl-borough, was disgusted by her behaviour, complaining to Mary Cowper how she set about 'entertaining everybody aloud, thrusting out her disagreeable breasts with such strange motions'.[5]

And César de Saussure observed how George loved to kiss pretty women:

> At about two o'clock we returned to the chamber called the circle or drawing-room . . . Three ladies were then presented to His Majesty; he kissed them all affectionately on the lips, and I remarked that he seemed to take most pleasure in kissing the pret-tiest of the three . . .[6]

Were these innocuous flirtations? Perhaps. Sir Robert's son Horace Walpole, whose gossipy and often unreliable writings still make such entertaining reading today, was convinced that towards the end of his reign George became so enamoured of an Anne Brett, daughter of a colonel, that he wished to replace Melusine with her. But, as with so much of Walpole's chatter, the evidence is very sketchy. Intriguingly, just after George's death on 24 June 1727, *Mist's Weekly Journal* reported: 'We hear Mrs Brett has a grant of a pension of 800 l. per annum for 30 years.' I have been unable to find any evidence to corroborate a pension. This may be idle gossip, or it may show that George, on occasion, sought the company of other women.

Saussure tells us:

> The King is fond of women; he has a mistress, sister of the Duke of
> Schulenburg, officer in the service of Venice. The King has created
> her Duchess of Kendal and Munster in Ireland; she is a fine, hand-
> some woman, and said to be very benevolent and charitable. The
> King is very fond of her, yet he is not always quite faithful to her,
> amusing himself with passing intrigues every now and then.[7]

True or not, he always came back to Melusine.

The English enthusiastically repeated the rumours suggesting
that George was having affairs with not only Melusine but also
Sophia Charlotte, and Sophia Charlotte's sister-in-law Countess
Platen, who had remained in Hanover. A typical verse decrying
George and two of his supposed mistresses – Melusine and Sophia
Charlotte – ran as follows. It would have appeared in a pamphlet
and been shouted in the streets:

> He preferred Hanover to England
> He preferred two hideous mistresses
> To a beautiful and innocent wife.
> He hated all art and despised literature . . .
> And he had Walpole for a minister,
> Consistent in his preference for every kind of corruption.[8]

Horace Walpole said this of the pair:

> Lady Darlington [Sophia Charlotte] whom I saw at my mother's in
> my infancy, and whom I remember by being terrified at her enor-
> mous figure, was as corpulent and ample as the Duchess [Melusine]
> was long and emaciated. Two fierce black eyes, large and rolling
> beneath two lofty arched eye-brows, two acres of cheeks spread

with crimson, an ocean of neck that overflowed and was not distinguished from the lower part of her body, and no part restrained by stays – no wonder that a child dreaded such an ogress and that the mob of London were highly diverted at the importation of so uncommon a seraglio![9]

Horace's description, like so much of his writing, was hugely exaggerated. Sophia Charlotte had put on weight in her latter years but she was certainly not the 'ogress' he described. And as for Melusine, we can see from the three portraits painted around 1720 that she was no longer the 'maukin' that the Electress Sophia had called her in her youth. But his unfavourable account is one of the sources that fuelled the myth of the insatiable and grotesque 'Maypole and Elephant'. It endured at least until the last quarter of the twentieth century when Ragnhild Hatton's research did so much to disprove it.

Although court gossip was rife with rumours that both Melusine and Sophia Charlotte were George's mistresses, the only instance recorded in which it is clear that George was aware of gossip about a relationship with his half-sister led to a dismissal. In 1716 George had appointed a confectioner, Charles Burroughs – he had a very sweet tooth. The confectioner had apparently used 'such indecent expressions concerning the King and Madam Kielmanseck [Kielmannsegg] as are not fit to be inserted . . .'[10] and George sacked him.

Contemporaries such as Lord Chesterfield believed that George had a preference for large women, from whom he was open to offers. Chesterfield claimed that candidates for a liaison with the king would 'strain and swell' themselves to put on weight. And he believed that George was hugely attracted to any woman who was 'but very willing, very fat, and had great breasts'.[11] Considering that Melusine was famously slim, these rumours probably compounded the tales that George was unable to resist a large woman (Sophia Charlotte) who was living in such close proximity to him, even though they shared a father.

Court rumours abounded that Sophia Charlotte's lovers numbered not only the king but one of George's English ministers, Paul Methuen. Mary Cowper claimed he made 'sweet Eyes at Madame K.' at a dinner. As her husband was still alive at the beginning of George's reign Sophia Charlotte was mortified, particularly when she was told that Georg August, who could not stand her, was in the habit of telling anyone who would listen 'that she had intrigued with all the men at Hanover'.[12] Sophia Charlotte, responding to the charge, did an extraordinary thing. According to Mary Cowper:

> She [Sophia Charlotte] came to complain of this to the princess, who replied, she did not believe the prince had said so, it not being his custom to speak in that manner. Madame Kielmansegge cried, and said it had made her despised, and that many of her acquaintance had left her upon that story; but that her husband had taken all the care he could to vindicate her reputation; and thereupon she drew forth out of her pocket a certificate under her husband's hand, in which he certified, in all the due forms, that she had always been a faithful wife to him, and that he had never had any cause to suspect her honesty. The princess smiled, and said that she did not doubt it at all, and that all that trouble was very unnecessary, and that it was a very bad reputation that wanted such a support. I believe it is the first certificate of the kind that ever was given.[13]

We do not know if these rumours were true. We can be fairly sure that Sophia Charlotte did have an affair with the minister James Craggs the younger, as the contemporary sources are so unanimous, but probably not until after her husband's death in 1717. The ease with which Sophia Charlotte attracted men suggests that she was a beauty with sex appeal, although Liselotte cattily mused to Louise: 'Perhaps she has got so fat from drinking English beer . . .'[14]

The rumours of incest did not end with George's generation. John Hervey, an intimate of Georg August and a diarist, made incredible claims regarding Melusine's eldest daughter Louise. He wrote that she had an incestuous relationship with her father George, her half-brother Georg August and her nephew Frederick. Louise, he said, had 'a thousand lovers' and had been discarded by her husband because he had caught her with one of them. Much later in the century George's great-great granddaughter Sophia claimed that her brother, the Duke of Cumberland, had raped her. It was easy in the light of these allegations for Victorian historians to look back at the previous century through the prism of later events, and to give credence to erroneous contemporary reports of a sexual relationship between siblings.

If we assume that Sophia Charlotte and George were not lovers and we take sexual jealousy out of the equation, then it is probably best to attribute the ongoing antipathy between Melusine and Sophia Charlotte to the latter's difficult nature. She was volatile – a little like her nephew the Prince of Wales – tempestuous and argumentative. A newsletter of 1717 reported that Sophia Charlotte flounced from Hampton Court in a sulk after a disagreement, real or imagined, with Melusine: 'Madame Kilmanseck [sic] came to town some weeks since on pretence to be with her husband, who has been indisposed, but as others say upon a difference with the Duchess of Munster [Melusine], and they add that when she complained to the king, he owned to her that the other was in the wrong, but he would not interpose . . .'[15] So George was aware of the antipathy between the two but he closed his eyes to it. Although he believed Melusine to be in the wrong in this instance, he refused to reprimand her.

We know that Sophia Charlotte was jealous of Melusine's elevated status. In 1716 John Clavering, Mary Cowper's brother, wrote to his sister from Hanover:

> I cannot express the surprise we are in here at Mademoiselle Shulenberg [*sic*] being naturalized and made an English Duchess. The Countess de Platen [Sophia Charlotte's sister in law] is mightily mortified, for you must know that we have two parties here more violent than Whig and Tory in England (which are the Schulenberg and Platen factions). Madame Kielmansegg [Sophia Charlotte] writes here that she's very unwilling to give place to the new Duchess; therefore she will petition Parliament to be naturalized, that she may have a title equal to the other.[16]

Sophia Charlotte's 'petitions' were successful; George made her Countess of Leinster in 1721 and Countess of Darlington in 1722. But he made Melusine a duchess. Sophia Charlotte had to be content with a lesser title. Her behaviour can perhaps be attributed to the insecurity of being an illegitimate child in a royal family. Although George's mother had embraced her, we can see from Georg August's irreverent behaviour towards her, particularly his accusations of sexual promiscuity, that he did not treat her with the deference owed to an aunt. Perhaps Sophia Charlotte felt that Melusine was cherished by the king her brother, whereas she was forced to battle for his affection. She threw brilliant parties to entertain George, she was attentive to his intellectual and musical preferences and sought to bring the most dazzling minds to her soirees to divert him. In short, she loved him as a dear brother who was the source of much of her income, and was jealous of the attention he gave to Melusine. Like many of her contemporaries, she could not see why he was so enamoured of his mistress.

George was obviously fond of Sophia Charlotte, and it is in keeping with his loyal nature that he kept his half-sister so close to him for the rest of her life. He showed an equal concern for her children, though this must not lead us to deduce, as some contemporaries did, that he was their father. As far as circumstances allowed George was a family man; it would have been odd had he *not* looked after the interests of his nieces and nephews. Sophia Charlotte was his sister, she had many admirable qualities and he would not tolerate dissension, even from Melusine. His motto was, after all: 'Never desert a friend, strive to do justice to every person, fear no one.'[17]

George continued to prove a loving father to his illegitimate daughters. Trudchen, the youngest, was his favourite, perhaps because she was born in 1701 when he was divorced, more secure in his relationship with Melusine and enjoyed complete autonomy in Hanover as Elector. She had a happy, easy nature and adored her father as much as he did her. When her mother suffered bouts of ill health in the 1720s, it was Trudchen who accompanied her father on drives.[18]

She was the happiest in marriage. She made a love match at the age of twenty-one to Albrecht Wolfgang zu Schaumburg-Lippe, the son of Joanne Sophie, and the pair lived very happily together in England. To Joanne Sophie's evident delight, George paid a significant dowry. On 23 October 1721 the *Daily Journal* breathlessly reported: 'On Thursday night last the Count de Lippe . . . was married to Miss Inhousen, niece of the Duchess of Kendal, upon which occasion his Majesty, the Prince and Princess wore favours.'

Trudchen and Albrecht had two sons, George Augustus and William, born in 1722 and 1724. George delighted in them, and ordered their portraits painted by a fashionable artist, La Fontaine. It is testament to the gentle Trudchen's sunshine nature that even after the breakdown in their relationship with George, her half-brother and sister-in-law, Georg August and Caroline, accepted the couple's request that 'August' be included in their elder son's name, and the Prince and Princess of Wales happily graced the child's baptism. The *Evening Post* of 23 October 1722 told how on 'Monday night last the son of the Countess de Lippe, niece to the Duchess of Kendal, was christened by the Bishop of Winchester, the King and the Prince stood Godfathers, and the Princess Godmother.' Showing once again how Trudchen's goodness transcended family disharmony, both Sophia Charlotte and Melusine stood as godmothers to William.[19]

After the failure of his daughter Louise's marriage sometime before 1714, George attempted to give her financial and social independence. In 1722 he ensured that she was granted an Imperial title, Reichsgräfin von Delitz, and the following year he gave her some money from the Hanoverian treasury. There is evidence that George attempted to keep at least some of his gifts to Louise a secret from Melusine. With the money present of 1723 he specifically requested that it should be drawn 'without the knowledge of the Duchess of Kendal'.[20]

We only have Hervey's say-so for Louise's many lovers; but we know from Ernst August's letters however that she was headstrong, and that George, a besotted father, let her have her own way.

In 1726 she achieved further independence when her father gave her a small but perfect palace with a particularly beautiful fountain in its garden at Herrenhausen. It became known as the Delitzsche Palais when she took up residence there. But not all the members of his family had such warm relations with George.

Sophia had so wanted her eldest child George and her best-beloved Liselotte to be close, but in adulthood they had obviously grown apart. Despite Liselotte's move to France in 1671 with her marriage to the king's younger brother, her correspondence was so voluminous that she managed to maintain a close relationship with many of her relatives and friends. But George never wrote about her with any warmth, and it is apparent from his coolness towards her that he found her silly and irritating. Her correspondence is indeed peppered with childlike or vague statements, or the repetition of inane myths. It is easy to see why George preferred the company of the more serious Melusine. This is not to say that Melusine did not have a sense of fun. She was an excellent mimic, and created paper cut-out caricatures of the ministers George found infuriating, with which she entertained him in her apartments, and mocked them.

9.

A City out of Rubble

'The Contagion of the building influenza . . . has extended its virulence to the country where it rages with unabating violence . . . The metropolis is manifestly the centre of the disease . . . Mansions arise daily upon the marshes of Lambeth, the roads of Kensington, and the hills of Hampstead . . . The chain of buildings so closely unites the country with the town that the distinction is lost between Cheapside and St George's fields . . .'

Henry Kett[1]

London, Melusine's new home, was the most exciting city in the world, the capital of a burgeoning empire. Eighteenth-century Britain has been called 'a nation of shopkeepers', and it was trade and the strength of the rich mercantile classes that led London to develop independently of the whims of the monarch or according to any grand design. Successful wars, colonial possessions, and trade – particularly the slave trade – had made her rich. The boom towns of Manchester and Birmingham had grown fat on producing materials for the wars with France. And when Britain acquired the lucrative slave contract – the exclusive right to export Africans to the Americas as slaves – from Spain in 1713, growth in the ports on the western seaboard surged.

London was an incredibly noisy, crowded city. In 1791 Horace Walpole wrote: 'I have twice been going to stop my coach in Piccadilly, thinking there was a mob,' but, he continued, it was just Londoners 'sauntering or trudging' along.[2] It was a common enough sight. During the first half of the century ten thousand new people arrived every year, and by 1750 London was home to 10 per cent of the country's population, or roughly 600,000, equal to the entire population of Hanover. Public houses and coffee houses with their swinging, creaking signs were numerous. The accompanying chatter outside competed with the cries of tradesmen, soldiers, footmen and the fashionable promenaders. Livestock were driven through the streets, dogs roamed free, and the swarms of the populace were joined by horses and coaches. Puppet shows and theatre took place on street corners, as did gambling and fights at the cockpits, while the rich meandered in the city's gardens and down the Mall.

London's story is marked by purgings by fire; the most recent, the year before Melusine's birth in 1666 – the 'Great Fire of London' – destroyed seven-eighths of the city as thirteen thousand buildings burned. Sir Christopher Wren was appointed 'Principal Architect' for the rebuilding, but although his plan for a marvellous new metropolis with the broad streets typical of many European cities was grand – it was apparently sketched while the city still smouldered – it was never realized. London's ancient geography asserted itself and development of the devastated areas took place principally along the existing street plans. The year after the fire, Dryden glorified London in his poem *Annus Mirabilis: the Year of Wonders*:

> More great than human now, and more August,
> New deified she from her Fires does rise:
> Her widening Streets on new Foundations trust,
> And, opening, into larger parts she flies. (verse 295)

But Wren actually had little part in the rebuilding of the city as a whole. His most significant achievement was the reconstruction of St Paul's Cathedral, which the fire had reduced to rubble. Wren began work nine years after the fire; it was completed thirty-five years later, in 1710. Its stunning dome remains an icon of the London skyline.

The beginning of the eighteenth century saw a blossoming of architectural brilliance in London. In 1711 Queen Anne commissioned the building of 'fifty new churches' to mark the electoral victory of her last High Church Tory ministry. Although only twelve materialized, they were designed by the 'greats' of the English baroque – Wren, Nicholas Hawksmoor, James Gibbs, John James, Thomas Archer and Henry Flitcroft. Their beautiful white steeples and porticoes added to the elegance and grace of early Georgian London.

The first known portrait of Melusine, painted *c.*1691, soon after her arrival at the Hanoverian court, to mark her position as a lady-in-waiting to the Electress Sophia.

Portrait of Ehrengard Melusine von der Schulenburg, possibly painted soon after her arrival in England.

Johann Matthias von der Schulenburg, Melusine's eldest and favourite sibling, a brilliant and charismatic general and diplomat. He retired to the beautiful Palazzo Loredan in Venice.

Sophia of Hanover, George's mother. This image dates from 1714, the year of her death. Her relationship with Melusine was, at best, chilly.

George in his youth, depicted c.1680–81 during his visit to England, where he was greeted enthusiastically by his royal cousins.

George I, painted soon after his accession in 1714.

Sophia Charlotte, George's illegitimate half-sister. Contemporaries believed that both she *and* Melusine were George's mistresses.

Portrait of Melusine, painted during one of her and George's visits to Hanover, *c.*1720.

Klara Elisabeth von Platen, the beautiful, manipulative mistress of George's father, Ernst August.

Sophia Dorothea of Celle, George's wife and first cousin. Her elaborate dress reflects her desire to lead court fashion. Her children, Georg August and young Sophia Dorothea, are standing beside her.

Count Philipp Christoph von Königsmarck, Sophia Dorothea's lover. Thackeray said of him, 'one cannot imagine a more handsome, wicked, worthless reprobate.'

Georg August, son of George and Sophia Dorothea. Capricious and volatile, he hated his father but was always charming to Melusine.

Caroline of Ansbach, wife of Georg August. Entwined in her hair are some of Sophia's pearls – 'the Hanover pearls' – which George had brought with him to England.

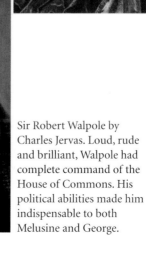

Sir Robert Walpole by Charles Jervas. Loud, rude and brilliant, Walpole had complete command of the House of Commons. His political abilities made him indispensable to both Melusine and George.

Young Sophia Dorothea, George's only legitimate daughter, who left Hanover in 1706 to marry her first cousin, Friedrich Wilhelm of Brandenburg-Prussia. Neglected by both her parents, she became a dreadful mother to her own children.

Portrait of Trudchen, aged eighteen or nineteen, painted during a holiday to Hanover, c.1720.

Sir Joshua Reynold's painting of Melusine's grandson, Frederick William, Count of Schaumburg-Lippe.

An anonymous satirical print of 1721, produced in the wake of the South-Sea Bubble. Melusine is shown hiding behind a screen in a richly decorated room, handing over money to Robert Knight, treasurer of the South Sea Company. He stands, whip in hand, poised to escape into exile. The table is inscribed with the words, 'Patience and Time and Money set everything to rights'.

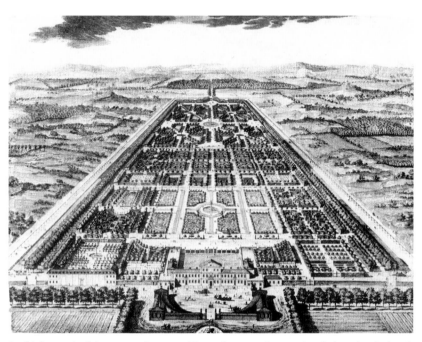

Sophia's wonderful summer home at Herrenhausen. Once a simple hunting lodge, it became one of the most beautiful, and most envied, palaces in Europe.

A Royal Hunting Party at Göhrde, a former hunting lodge and Melusine's favourite Hanoverian home. It was the place where she and George were at their most relaxed.

The grey marble chimney piece in Melusine's drawing room at Kensington Palace stands at nearly six feet high.

Melusine's magnificent staircase at Kensington Palace.

London was a city in which elegant villas and vile, foul-smelling slums coexisted side by side. It was a city of light and dark, with dingy alleys for the poor and smart, broad streets leading into stylish squares for the rich. Only one bridge spanned the Thames – London Bridge. The next crossing was some 30 miles away by river, at Kingston-upon-Thames. (London Bridge remained the only crossing until Westminster Bridge was completed in 1750.) The river and the docks were the financial lifeblood of the city. Numerous churches dotted the cityscape, one for each tiny parish. It was a city where Palladian, baroque and medieval architecture sat together. Throughout George's reign the city's surrounding fields were gradually developed, a continuation of the building boom that had exploded in the wake of the Peace of Utrecht and the ending of the war. Georgian London was very much the creation of independent master builders, property speculators and architects. George's reign was marked by constant building activity, particularly in the capital.

The grand Italianate Piazza of Covent Garden, built to designs by Inigo Jones between 1631 and 1637, was no longer fashionable and was already degenerating into seediness. It was only moments away from the newer houses favoured by the aristocracy and the recently wealthy. Building sites and the accompanying chaos and noise were everywhere; passers-by must tread carefully around them. The mass of building work added to the vitality and chaos of the city, bursting with an ever-expanding population.

Jonathan Swift beautifully described London's disorder at dawn:

> Now hardly here and there a hackney coach
> Appearing shows the ruddy morn's approach.
> Now Betty from her master's bed had flown,
> And softly stole to discompose her own.

The slipshod prentice from his master's door
Had pared the dirt, and sprinkled round the floor.
Now Moll had whirled her mop with dext'rous airs,
Prepared to scrub the entry and the stairs.
The youth with broomy stumps began to trace
The kennel-edge, where wheels had worn the place.
The small-coal man was heard with cadence deep,
Till drowned in shriller notes of chimney-sweep.
Duns at his lordship's gate began to meet,
And Brickdust Moll had screamed through half the street.
The turnkey now his flock returning sees,
Duly let out a-night to steal for fees.
The watchful bailiffs take their silent stands,
And schoolboys lag with satchels in their hands.[3]

But in spite of the dirt, the chaos and the din, London was a great and proud city where all desires could be satisfied, if you were lucky or wealthy enough. Otherwise you could find yourself homeless and poverty-stricken, or abandoned in the notorious debtors' prison, the Fleet.

In 1697 we find the Lord Mayor condemning the annual Bartholomew Fair at Smithfield market as the scene of 'obscene, lascivious and scandalous plays, comedies and farces, unlawful games and interludes, drunkenness etc'.[4] But Londoners loved the fairs. Screams of 'Show, Show, Show, Show!' rose from an excitable crowd until the players arrived to entertain them. Spectacles such as rope-dancing, acrobats, music booths, dwarfs and Siamese twins merged with strolling players who performed in plays such as the anonymously authored *The Creation of the World*, with its images of hellfire; the entertainments were accompanied by huge quantities of food and drink – coffee, tea, ale and sucking pigs.

The painter and satirist William Hogarth reveals the chaos and bawdiness of the fair in his *Southwark Fair* of 1734. An elaborate puppet show, 'The Siege of Troy', which was performed at Southwark in 1707, 1715 and 1716, had a huge impact on the young Hogarth. He depicted the show with an enormous picture of a wooden horse hoisted above the players. The actors are performing elaborate spectacles to entice the throng, with one swinging from the stage by a rope; but the crowd, with their grotesque and exaggerated features, have their backs to the stage, interested only in observing one another.

Gambling was ubiquitous among all classes, and the state lottery was a useful way of raising revenue. Even Melusine and Sophia Charlotte bought tickets, and Sophia Charlotte won £10,000 in 1719. Gambling took place either in the streets, adding to the noise and vitality of the city, or in private gaming dens. It was also loved by the aristocracy, and Melusine and George spent many evenings playing cards with their family, friends and courtiers.

Londoners could not get enough of gory spectacles; even public executions served as theatre. *The Chronicles of Newgate*, about London's notorious prison, records how: 'The upturned faces of the eager spectators resembled those of the "gods" at Drury Lane on Boxing Night.'

The aristocracy and the well-to-do preferred the pleasures of the stage. Theatres had been closed during the Puritanism of the Interregnum, and on their reopening with Charles II's restoration performances were sanitized to appeal to the monarch and the wealthy. New theatres were licensed in Drury Lane and Dorset Gardens, and Melusine, George and their daughters were frequent visitors; the theatre was one of the pleasures that reminded them of Hanover.

During George I's reign theatre remained a pleasant experience, reflecting the taste of the monarch and his mistress. Bonet complained that because George's understanding of English was poor, 'ingenious plays are neglected in order to present the spectacle, in the machines, in the dances, the decorations, the farces, and other things which entertain more the senses than the mind'.[5] England's commentators railed against the 'prodigal subscriptions for Squeaking Italians and capering Monsieurs' at the expense of the more highbrow English drama.[6]

But Melusine and George's greatest delight was the opera, in particular the music of George Frideric Handel, who thrived under the couple's patronage.

Opera had suffered in the wake of the Jacobite riots, and there were no performances at the King's Theatre between 1717 and 1719. But it was saved from oblivion by the founders of the Royal Academy of Music, a group of aristocrats and courtiers who established the institution specifically to revive opera on the London stage. George and Melusine were thrilled, with George committing to an annual grant of £1,000.

Opera at the Haymarket was under the direction of the Swiss impresario John James Heidegger. He created such a marvellous display that even sophisticated Londoners used to 'Show! Show!' were impressed. Heidegger scoured Italy for the best singers, securing them for astronomical sums; the castrato Francesco Bernard, known as Senesino, would only come for £2,000. His antics both on and off stage thrilled the crowd and filled the newspapers. Heidegger additionally made his theatre the setting of a sumptuous masquerade where the crowd would mingle in their finery and disguises in the glow of candlelight. This was the London that Melusine adored – music, spectacle and wealth. She and Heidegger became friends; in 1728 she leased his house at Barnes, near the river in Richmond, while he travelled to Italy in search of yet more operatic stars.[7]

The newly created Royal Academy of Music was financed by subscriptions of a minimum of £200, making it the province of the wealthy. The guidelines of its establishment reflected the contemporary mania for stocks and the resultant bubbles, and many contemporaries compared the fever for opera with the mania created by the catastrophic South Sea Bubble of 1720. Its excesses prompted commentators such as Bishop Berkeley to thunderous diatribes:

> Our gaming, our Operas, our Maskerades, are, in spite of our Debts and Poverty, become the Wonders of our Neighbours . . . The Plague dreadful as it is, is an Evil of short duration; Cities have often recovered and flourished after it; but when was it known that a People broken and corrupted by Luxury recovered themselves?[8]

But despite such ragings, the taste of Melusine and George triumphed. Many, such as Swift and Gay, were appalled. In the winter of 1723 Gay wrote:

> There is nobody allowed to say I sing but an Eunuch or an Italian Woman. Every body is grown now as great a judge of Music as they were in your time of Poetry, and folks that could not distinguish one tune from another now daily dispute about the different Styles of Handel, Bononcini and Attilio. People have now forgot Homer, and Virgil & Caesar, or at least they have lost their ranks, for in London and Westminster in all polite conversations, Senesino is daily voted to be the greatest man that ever liv'd.[9]

It was only in 1728, a year after George's death, that John Gay brought his irreverent *The Beggar's Opera* to the stage, with its vilification of the Whig oligarchy that served George and Melusine so well.

George Frideric Handel was the musician most closely associated with George and Melusine. Like most cultured Germans,

Handel's influences were primarily Italian. In 1706 he visited Italy and stayed for four years, developing his musical style. By the time he was appointed George's Kapellmeister in 1710 he was famous, not least for operas such as *Agrippina*, which had premiered in Venice in 1710. Handel spent the next four years in both Hanover and London, where his operas *Rinaldo*, *Il Pastor Fido* and *Teseo* were raging successes. He was reluctant to leave London for parochial Hanover, where one of his duties was teaching music to the royal grandchildren and Melusine's daughters; he was saved by the death of Queen Anne. He remained in England for the rest of his life (he was naturalized in 1726), enjoying the favour of the ruling house and the aristocracy. One of his most enduring pieces, the *Water Music* of 1717, written for string and wind instruments, was composed to accompany Melusine and George as they rowed down the Thames. In his biography of London, Peter Ackroyd puts a less romantic twist on this image of the companionship of love in middle age – Melusine and George snuggling to the sounds of Handel's exquisite composition as they wended their way along the river. Ackroyd suggests the music was performed not to accompany a romantic tryst but to drown out the sounds of the Thames's foul-mouthed boatmen.

In London Handel's operas were performed at Vanbrugh's King's Theatre on Haymarket. The premieres of the new operas that appeared almost every year were one of Melusine's chief delights. She enjoyed *Floridante* in 1721, *Ottone* in 1723, *Giulio Cesare* in 1724, *Rodelinda* in 1725 and *Scipione* in 1726.

Melusine and the girls all subscribed to music publications, particularly to Handel's.[10] It was a passion enjoyed by the extended family too. In 1721 we hear of an impromptu concert arranged for George by Sophia Charlotte, to George's evident delight:

Being one evening at the home of Mademoiselle Schulemburg [probably Louise], niece of the duchess of Kendal, the king sent for him [Bononcini – a musician] to look at the beginning of a pastorale, and he recognized its style [probably Steffani's]. When . . . [Sophia Charlotte] put on a very private concert of the king in his apartment, which was managed by her servant Brighella, that is, me, we decided to perform this pastorale and thus gave His Majesty a pleasant surprise . . .[11]

And in 1725 young Melusine interceded for a young Italian singer, Benedetta Sorosina, and managed to find her a small part in Handel's opera *Giulio Cesare*. By all accounts it was not a very good opera – or perhaps it was a case of professional jealousy – for in January 1725 Giuseppe Riva wrote to Agostino Steffani: 'Benedetta . . . could not make a great impact, because the arias are mediocre and stuck on, as they say, with spit . . .'[12]

One of the relatively new institutions that gave London such vibrancy – spreading the gossip and sparking political discourse – was the coffee and chocolate house, informal centres of both relaxation and fierce debate. Coffee-house culture exploded in the eighteenth century, but its beginnings can be found in the seventeenth. Originating in Venice, the first London coffee house was established in 1652 in St Michael's Alley, near Cornhill, and within five years two more opened nearby, in St Michael's Churchyard and in Fleet Street. The author of *The Topography of London* noted that 'theire ware also att this time a Turkish drink to be sould in eury street, called Coffee, and another kind of drink called Tee, and also a drink called Chacolate, which was a very hearty drink.'[13] Such was their popularity that they survived Charles II's attempts in 1675 to eradicate them – he feared that political discussion, so integral to coffee-house culture, would sow discord for his regime. By the time Melusine and George arrived in England there were roughly two thousand of them. They were cheap – Macaulay observed that you were 'able to pass evenings socially at a very small charge'. And they were everywhere.

The first edition of the *Spectator* in 1711 wrote of the variety of activities to be pursued in the coffee house:

> sometimes I am seen thrusting my Head into a Round of Politicians at Will's, and listening with great Attention to the Narratives that are made in those little Circular Audiences. Sometimes I smoak a Pipe at Child's, and whilst I seem attentive to nothing but the Post-Man [a newspaper commonly found in coffee houses] overhear the Conversation of every Table in the Room. I appear on Sunday Nights at St James's Coffee-House, and sometimes join the little Committee of Politicks in the Inner Room, as one who comes there to hear and to improve. My Face is likewise very well known at the Grecian, the Cocoa-Tree . . .[14]

Individual coffee houses became synonymous with different professions. Surgeons would congregate in one, lawyers in another, artists and writers in another, brokers in yet another. Some attracted Whigs, others Tories. One particular coffee house – The Chapter – even attracted members of the clergy. And the London Stock Exchange grew out of the coffee-house culture: brokers were accustomed to frequenting the coffee houses in Change Alley. When establishments such as Jonathan's became too noisy to effectively conduct business, they moved to New Jonathan's – renamed the Stock Exchange in 1773.[15] They were unofficial clubs without the fees, darting in and out of fashion. They were not particularly comfortable and they stank of tobacco, but they were excellent meeting places, profitable places of business, and they made London into a particularly sociable city. In the words of Macaulay, 'the coffee house was the Londoner's home, and . . . those who wished to find a gentleman commonly asked, not whether he lived in Fleet Street or Chancery Lane, but whether he frequented the Grecian or the Rainbow.'[16]

Coffee-house culture provided the perfect environment where Melusine and George could be mercilessly caricatured. In 1695 the Licensing Act, which demanded pre-publication censorship, had been allowed to lapse, leading to a flowering of the British press. (As England had relaxed its censorship laws, so autocratic Hanover increased its efforts to stifle a free press.) Britain's essayists and satirists were among the most talented in Europe, and Melusine's alleged crimes did not escape their pens. Swift, Pope and Gay did as much as anyone to destroy her reputation.

She and George were derided in publications such as the *Daily Courant* and the *Evening Post*, and Melusine was also a natural target for the hostile Jacobite press, as can be seen in a popular ballad entitled 'An Excellent New Ballad', dating sometime between 1716 and 1719 and referring to her as 'Munster' – Melusine was created Duchess of Munster in 1716. This particular ballad uses the popular anti-Hanoverian sentiment of comparing George to a turnip – the Hanoverians had introduced the turnip to Britain and they were often accused of eating nothing else. It also vilifies George for taking a throne he had no right to, for leaving Sophia Dorothea behind to rot in her lonely prison, and for surrounding himself with 'Turks and Germans'. His crimes are committed with 'Munster' (Melusine) on his knee:

An Excellent New Ballad
To the Tune of, 'A Begging we will go,' etc.

> I am a Turnip Ho-er,
> As good as ever ho'd;
> I have hoed from my Cradle,

And reap'd where I ne'er sow'd.
And a Ho-ing I will go, etc.
For my Turnips I must Hoe.

With a Hoe for myself,
And another for my Son;
A Third too for my Wife –
But Wives I've two, or None.
And a Ho-ing we will go, etc . . .

. . . I've pillag'd Town and Country round,
And no Man durst say, No;
I've lop'd off Heads, like Turnip-tops,
Made England cry, High! Ho!
And a Ho-ing I will go, etc . . .

. . . To Hannover I'll go, I'll go,
And there I'll mery be;
With a good Hoe in my right Hand,
And Munster on my Knee.
And a Ho-ing I will go, etc.

Come on, my Turks and Germans,
Pack up, pack up, and go,
Let J————s take his Scepter,
So I can have my Hoe.
And a Ho-ing we will go, etc . . .[17]

Melusine was also lampooned for the misconception that she
was part of George's 'harem', together with Sophia Charlotte and
Countess Platen. And another publication irreverently called Melusine and Sophia Charlotte 'two big blousy German women'.[18]

The *Weekly Journal* of May 1721 spat bile at her. Its editorial lamented that 'we are ruined by . . . parasites, bawds, whores, nay, what is more vexatious, old ugly whores! Such as could not find entertainment in the most hospitable hundreds of old Drury? . . .'[19]

In 1720, on the eve of George's departure for Hanover, Samuel Wesley, brother of John Wesley, penned a singularly unattractive sketch of Melusine. The poem was set against the background of George's appointments for his regency council while he was out of the country, and it imagines a conversation between George and Melusine:

As soon as the wind it came fairly about,
That kept the king in and his enemies out,
He determined no longer confinement to bear;
And thus to the Duchess his mind did declare:

Quoth he, my dear Kenny [Kendal], I've been tired a long while,
With living obscure in this poor little isle.
And now Spain and Pretender have no more enemies to spring
I'm resolved to go home and live like a king.

The Duchess approves of this, describes and laughs at all the persons nominated for the Council of Regency, and concludes:

'On the whole, I'll be hanged if all over the realm
There are thirteen such fools to be put to the helm!
So for this time be easy, nor have jealous thought,
They ha'n't sense to see you, nor are worth being bought.'

''Tis for that (quoth the King, in very bad French),
I chose them for my regents, and you for my wench.
And neither, I'm sure, will my trust e'er betray,
For the devil won't take you if I turn you away.'[20]

Melusine was vilified for her unattractiveness, George for his stupidity – he only speaks 'very bad French'. This is a complete falsehood. His French was as fluent as his German. The pair are portrayed mocking the kingdom they rule. If these damning reports from the Tory press hurt Melusine, we have no way of knowing. Nothing is recorded.

10.

Palaces

Nothing is more beautiful than the road from London to Kensington, crossing Hyde Park. It is perfectly straight and so wide that three or four coaches can drive abreast. It is bordered on either side by a wide ditch, and has posts put up at even distances, on the tops of which lanterns are hung and lamps placed in them, which are lighted every evening when the Court is at Kensington.

Saussure, *A Foreign View*[1]

For thirteen years Melusine enjoyed life in England's palaces, which were amongst the most sublime in Europe. St James's became much less crowded when Caroline, Georg August and their retinue were forcibly moved out and took up residence at Leicester House in 1717. The palace was enlarged and redecorated by Sir Christopher Wren and William Kent, an artist who enjoyed huge favour under both George and Georg August, but there was no grand scheme to redesign it, although St James's was their main London home. It was rather a policy of 'piecemeal alteration and adaptation'. A frustrated Vanbrugh submitted hopeful drawings for a grand new palace, but George was not keen, preferring to expend his time and imagination on redesigning Kensington.

George and Melusine saw no romance in St James's and the building work they carried out was mostly for practical purposes. According to the editor of *The History of the King's Works*, building was one of 'orders for new backstairs, laundries, wardrobes and dressing-rooms for members of the Court; alterations to guard-rooms, kitchens, stables and wine-cellars; of the gradual encroachment on the Tudor courtyards which is so apparent in the eighteenth-century surveys of the palace'.[2]

Melusine had the use of the best apartments in the palace, apartments that were, according to Sarah Duchess of Marlborough, later occupied by a mistress of George II, Henrietta Howard, Countess of Suffolk. They overlooked the garden and George insisted on their refurbishment, ordering a new parquet floor on his accession and authorizing works costing over £4,000 for the years between 1717 and 1723.

George also ensured that his other close confidantes were comfortable. Sophia Charlotte's lodgings were refurbished – she was noted in the accounts as 'Madame Kilmansack' and it is interesting that the accounts do not mention her husband, leaving us to wonder as to whether or not they cohabited. The apartments of the Turkish servants Mustapha and Mehemet were also improved, along with those that housed Baron Hattorf, George's Cabinet secretary, his tailor, and his fool Ulrich, of whom he was reportedly very fond. Money was exchanged for Ulrich when he arrived in England. Although he was ostensibly a gift from the Duke of Saxe Gotha, the duke's envoy was given £330 for him.

In keeping with the practical nature of the building works, Melusine had a large laundry 'with vaults beneath and rooms above' built in 1723, at a cost of over £2,000.[3] George indulged in a new library and a smoking room.

Tragically, in 1809 fire ripped through the palace, destroying nearly all of the building undertaken by George and Melusine. Today nothing remains of her lovely rooms facing the garden.

Hampton Court, their summer home, was the palace furthest from London, standing on the river about twelve miles from the capital. The writer César de Saussure was impressed. He wrote to his family: 'Had he [William III] lived longer, he would have made the palace of Hampton Court one of the most beautiful in Europe, for he was very fond of it and greatly embellished it.'[4]

Sir Christopher Wren as Master of the King's Works had been responsible for the extensive rebuilding programme initiated by William and Mary, demolishing much of the Tudor palace and replacing it with a large, modern mansion more in keeping with William's Dutch tastes. He was particularly fond of large, light spaces and indoor plumbing. Work more or less ceased with Mary's death in 1694 and by the time George and Melusine arrived Hampton Court was effectively two palaces. The remains of the magnificent Tudor building were at the front – a building so sublime that its beauty had compelled Henry VIII to steal it from Cardinal Wolsey – with the more modern and rather pedestrian structure, the work of Wren's dotage, welded to it, facing the river.

George commissioned Sir John Vanbrugh to complete the Queen's Apartments, designed by Wren for Mary, for Georg August and Caroline. Wren, a victim of political infighting, was dismissed from his post at the King's Works in 1718, at the age of eighty-six, and replaced by William Benson.

Melusine's detractors have accused her of having a hand in Wren's dismissal. One anti-Hanoverian historian of the early twentieth century argues that Wren was sacked because he 'refused to allow her to mutilate Hampton Court with her execrable taste, and in revenge she sold his place to William Benson'.[5] The historian goes on to claim that 'Frog Walk' at Hampton Court was actually a corruption of 'Frau' walk, so named because George used to walk there with Melusine and Sophia Charlotte.[6] I have found no evidence to substantiate either claim.

Wren's dismissal probably had far more to do with his age – he was eighty-two when George ascended the throne – and his close association with the Tories during Anne's reign. According to his biographer, Lisa Jardine, that he kept his position at the Board of Works during the early days of George's reign was 'something of a courtesy'.

Wren came to live on Hampton Court Green on his retirement. The nation that seemed to forget him with his dismissal honoured him in death. He was buried, very simply, in the crypt at St Paul's Cathedral beneath a black marble slab, with an inscription on a nearby wall reading: 'Si monumentum requiris, circumspice'– 'If you seek his monument, look around you.'

George held full court at Hampton Court in the summer of 1718, and the palace's partial Tudor backdrop created a fabulous theatre for the balls, masques, plays and games. But after 1720 Hampton Court was more or less abandoned by Melusine and George. Suburban Kensington, possibly because it reminded them of Herrenhausen, became the home they delighted in most. It was only when Georg August took the throne in 1727 as George II that Hampton Court enjoyed one last royal hurrah.

In a strange repetition of history, George II had a terrible relationship with his eldest son, Frederick. When Frederick's wife, Augusta of Saxe-Gotha-Altenburg, went into labour at Hampton Court, her husband dragged her away in the middle of the night to St James's, where she gave birth at once to a daughter, who died shortly afterwards. George II was furious at his son's negligence. Thereafter he and Caroline found the palace distasteful and full of unhappy memories. After Caroline died a few months later George never set foot there again.[7] Ten years later Hampton Court was abandoned by English monarchs for the last time.

According to the editor of *The King's Works*, little was done at Windsor during George's reign. George and Melusine rarely visited William the Conqueror's great fortress on the banks of the Thames; it was largely ignored. There was a brief flurry of activity in 1724 when they spent the summer there. The royal visit led to repairs and redecoration, but they did not stay in the castle itself, preferring, like Queen Anne before them, a small house in its grounds. There was one specific instruction regarding Melusine's accommodation: 'a new way to be made out of the Duchess of Kendall's apartment in Windsor Castle into the Terrass walk, and a new doore to be hung at the top of her stairs leading down to the Terrass; likewise a pair of stairs to be made to the great roome in the Devill's Tower, which is to be fitted up for the use of the Board of Green Cloth.'[8] Melusine, like George, loved to walk, and she required immediate access to open spaces.

It was at Kensington that Melusine and George expended most

of their creative efforts. The gardens, reminiscent of Herrenhausen, were particularly impressive. Saussure was enchanted. In the 1720s he wrote:

> Going north, about two miles from Chelsea you reach Kensington, a large and fine village situated on a slight elevation. The King has a palace at this spot . . . it was much enlarged and embellished by Queen Anne and by the present reigning King [George]. It contains some magnificent paintings by Titian, Correggio, Veronese, and other painters . . . This palace is not vast, but its apartments are convenient and in good taste. When the King does not go to Hanover, he spends his summer in this palace. The gardens are so immense that twenty or thirty gardeners work in them. One evening, being surprised at seeing so many of these men going home from work, I inquired how many there were. One of them answered there had been fifty or sixty at work for the last fortnight.

The house was bought by William III from the Earl of Nottingham as a way of escaping filthy London and relieving his asthma. William particularly liked it because the staircases were shallow, reducing exertion and the inevitable and often debilitating wheezing that accompanied it. Saussure noted in his diary that it was during George's reign that the old Nottingham House finally morphed into 'buildings of a more palatial character'. But with George's accession it was still a 'very sweet villa' and not the grandiose structure that we know today.

Melusine and George were eager to start work, but the upheaval of their first year in England meant that they could not seriously consider renovations until the beginning of 1716. Designs were submitted by Vanbrugh, and possibly by Wren in his capacity as Master of the King's Works. If Wren did submit plans he probably took them with him when he left his post in 1718. We have no trace of them today. Vanbrugh wanted to recreate unsurpassable

Blenheim in the suburbs of London, but neither Melusine nor George wanted anything that suggested pomp. His grand plans were rejected.

Instead, the architect of George and Melusine's Kensington was Colen Campbell, the architect favoured by William Benson, Wren's replacement at the Board of Works. Benson was well aware of George's taste. He accompanied the king to Hanover in 1716, and George was extremely impressed with his ideas for the fountain at Herrenhausen. Both Benson and Campbell shared George's love of simple Palladianism above the more exuberant English baroque of Wren and Vanbrugh, although the finished building was probably influenced by Vanbrugh. The plans were finally approved in the summer of 1718, when George required the renovations to be completed 'with all speed'.

The works conducted were on a huge scale, and saw the destruction of much of the old Nottingham House. The state apartments were sumptuously and expensively decorated by the artist William Kent. George uncharacteristically did not stint on cost – the colour he chose for the vaulted roof of the grand chamber, for example, was the expensive ultramarine at £350, over the Prussian blue at £300.

The most beautiful part of Kensington Palace was the Queen's Apartments, built for Mary II. The large windows frame sweeping views over the gardens and the rooms are light and airy. They are on a more intimate scale than English monarchs had traditionally enjoyed, influenced by Mary's years in the Netherlands and the Dutch predilection for a less formal monarchy. Her collection of pretty Chinese and Japanese porcelain, furniture and paintings can still be seen today. It was here that an often lonely and melancholy Mary would despair for the children so desired but never born, and imagine her adored husband's infidelity.

But despite their beauty, Mary's apartments were shut by

George I. They would not be used until Georg August came to the throne as George II. George may well have wanted Melusine to have the use of them, but propriety dictated that while Sophia Dorothea still lived in her Ahlden prison, not even Melusine could inhabit them. So he built her an exquisite house within Kensington Palace. It was the most beautiful of the non-state apartments.

It is generally very difficult to ascertain exactly who lived where at Kensington, as all we have is the information provided by the Board of Works, which is often patchy and incomplete. Much therefore is guesswork. But luckily in the case of Melusine we have the work of the art historian Christopher Hussey, who in 1928 wrote an article about the genesis of her accommodation at Kensington.[9]

We know from the accounts that Melusine's house was constructed between 1722 and 1726, at the northernmost end of the palace. We also know that it dates from that period, as plans of 1716–17 show a completely different structure on the site. The building work was a huge undertaking, and for much of that time Melusine probably made do in other apartments, living on a building site littered with rubble and scaffolding. From 1724 the old Kitchen Court – the western court – was demolished, and the eastern court, or Green Cloth Court, was rebuilt around the existing structure. It is in Kitchen Court that we find Melusine's house, occupying the north side. Today part of the house is occupied by Prince and Princess Michael of Kent.

Melusine's apartments were also decorated by William Kent, emulating his hero Inigo Jones's work at Burlington House. The stucco work is elaborate, the chimneypieces splendid and gorgeous – the grey marble example in the drawing room stands nearly 6 feet high – and the grand staircase, thought by earlier historians to have been the work of Inigo Jones himself, is magnificent. The apartment is just as stately as the newly refurbished public rooms

George commissioned, also decorated by William Kent. After all, much of the king's business was done in these rooms. Walpole, Townshend, Sunderland, Stanhope and the Prince and Princess of Wales were all regular visitors and the setting was appropriately magisterial.

With building completed, a pleased George let it be known that he was 'more at ease and tranquillity than ever before in England'.[10] To add a touch of excitement to the beautifully completed palace, a zoo was added, filled, rather incongruously, with a tiger and tortoises.

But Melusine only enjoyed her lovely rooms, where George visited her daily between five and eight o'clock, for a year, after which his death forced her into private accommodation. The next occupant was probably Frederick Prince of Wales, Georg August and Caroline's eldest child, who came over from Hanover soon after his grandfather's death. We know that he had apartments at Kensington, and as Kitchen Court is today known as Prince of Wales Court, it is probable that it took its name from Frederick.

Kensington took eight years to build. It was only completed in 1726 and the final touches – the hanging of the paintings and the drapes, and the positioning of the furniture – had yet to be decided. When Georg August and Caroline moved in to their grand chambers the following year, they found the rooms sparsely furnished. Many of the walls in the private apartments remained bare of paintings prior to George and Melusine's last trip to Hanover in the summer of 1727. They had expected to complete the final touches to the English home they were fondest of after their return.

11.

Politics and Players

*I will send you a general map of Courts; a region yet unexplored
. . . all the paths are slippery, and every slip is dangerous.*
  – The Earl of Chesterfield writing to his son, 1749[1]

After 1716 George never had fewer than twenty-five Hanoverian ministers in London.[2] He needed them with him because, although now king of Great Britain, he remained Elector of Hanover, with full responsibility for the principality. His Hanoverian ministers were vital to carrying out his business there. They had an office in St James's and their lodgings were either in the palace or nearby.

The Act of Settlement stated that no German could hold office or a title in England, and officially the Hanoverians were there solely to carry out George's Electoral business. But in reality they became his unofficial advisers, together with Melusine, and to a lesser extent Sophia Charlotte. Naturally this meant that the 'German cabal' had a huge influence over how George conducted the nation's business and who could rise at court.

The courtiers and George's English ministers quickly realized that if they wanted to get anything done – preferment for a friend or relative, a bill passed through parliament, a title – it was best to approach the Germans to smooth the path. They acted as inter-mediaries between George and his English Secretaries of State, in large part because George's English was, at least at first, extremely poor.[3] Chief amongst them was Melusine, and certainly for the last five years of George's reign, very little was done without her involvement. For example, in September 1723 Townshend, one of George's English ministers, wrote to his brother-in-law Robert Walpole about the relatively small matter of a post in the king's closet. Townshend wanted Sir William Irby to have the post but Melusine had a candidate of her own:

I must beg your pardon that I do not send you the King's commands in relation to Sir Wm. Irby this post . . . I must acquaint you that since my writing to you on this subject, the Duchess [of Kendal] pleads a prior promise made to one Willard. However I will certainly get it for Sir Wm. Irby if it can be done without disobliging her which I am sure you will not desire.[4]

Later in the month Townshend, obviously less assured of success after conversations with Melusine, went on to say: 'I hope Sir Wm. Irby's business will succeed and that I shall get the Duchess to desist . . .'[5] Although Townshend eventually triumphed and Irby was appointed at the beginning of 1724, it shows how integral Melusine's approval was to everything within the king's orbit.

Such was the importance of the Germans that in December 1714 Frederick Bonet, the Prussian Resident in London, told his master that the country was governed by Marlborough and Townshend, and also the Germans Bothmer and Bernstorff. In his opinion, he continued, the Germans were by far the most important of the four.[6]

Hans Kaspar von Bothmer had begun his service to the Hanoverians as Sophia Dorothea's chamberlain and had been George's envoy in England during the last years of Anne's reign. He was devoted to the house he served and was instrumental in proclaiming George King of Great Britain. On Anne's death he led a committee of the Council in burning her private papers – there could be no whiff of the suspicion that in her last days she might have preferred her Stuart brother as her successor – and appropriating her gold plate. Before George's actual arrival at the end of September Bothmer was the most important man in the kingdom, fielding requests from anyone 'with hopes of a job'.[7]

The most senior of George's ministers to accompany him to England was Baron Andreas von Bernstorff, often simply called 'the old Baron'. Bernstorff was a political veteran, having served George's Celle uncle from the 1690s. He was George's first minister in all but name, a wily operator with an encyclopedic knowledge of European affairs. George relied on him completely for foreign policy. In 1716 Lord Carnarvon's pointed remark that Bernstorff was 'the first and only minister the King relies on' was more or less the truth.[8] To the fury of George's English ministers, he interfered in foreign policy and had no qualms about trampling over the fuzzy lines of the British sphere of influence. He readily used British resources to promote Hanoverian interests, although in theory the two were meant to be entirely separate. He was also said to be madly in love with Lady Mary Cowper, a Lady of the Bedchamber to Caroline, although this was unrequited. Mary was helpful to the new regime, as she used her fluent French to act as a translator between the king and her husband, the Lord Chancellor.

It is Mary's extensive diaries of the beginning of Hanoverian rule that bring such life to the period. She was extremely beautiful and relatively young – she was twenty-eight on George's accession – and Bernstorff, in his late sixties, was enchanted. This great statesman ran to her apartments on any pretext, and Lady Essex Robartes chided Mary for not making more of his feelings for her: 'Mr Bernstorff, who never was in love in his life before and 'tis so considerable a conquest that you ought to be proud of it . . .'[9]

But Bernstorff's 'love' for Mary may have been a ruse to gain intelligence. Lord Cowper, a member of the Cabinet Council, was privy to information that Bernstorff was not. In October 1715 Mary recorded in her diary:

> There was at this time some misunderstandings in the Cabinet Council. B[aron] Bernstorff desired me to get information of it from my Lord Cowper who by me gave B. Bernstorff a faithful Account of every thing that was useful for him to know. It was an

employment I was not fond of, but as it was at the request of B. Bernstorff and that I thought he was right in getting all the information he could I consented to it and so did my Ld. Cowper.[10]

Bernstorff was assisted by the Huguenot refugee Jean Robethon, another political veteran, who had served Duke George William of Celle and William III before entering George's service. In England he was George's Councillor of the Embassy. Other members of the inner circle included Baron Görtz, George's treasurer, who had been in Hanoverian employ since 1686, and Friedrich Ernst von Fabrice, one of George's Gentlemen of the Bedchamber and an intimate friend of both Melusine and her brother Johann Matthias. Sophia Charlotte's husband, Johann Adolf Kielmansegg, was Master of the Horse – extremely important for George, considering how essential hunting was to his well-being – and young Frederick William Schulenburg, Melusine's half-brother, was another gentleman of the bedchamber and trusted adviser. There is evidence that he performed at least one sensitive diplomatic mission for George, and the confidence the king had in him further bolstered Melusine's position.

In October 1714 Peter Wentworth, brother of the Earl of Stafford, complained that although the Hanoverian courtiers and ministers who had accompanied George and Melusine 'pretend to have nothing to do with the English affairs . . . yet from the top to the Bottom they have a great stroak in recommend[ing] Persons that are fit to serve his Majesty. Most, nay All the Addresses are made to Mons. Bothmar he having been so long in England is suppos'd to know all the English.'[11] The English courtiers, more or less unanimously, resented the Hanoverian influence at court.

Hanoverians and English alike were open to bribes. At the English court in the early eighteenth century everybody, from the lowliest footman to the king himself, could be bribed. It was endemic and habitual. In April 1719 William Byrd, a Virginian who spent two years in London and was a regular visitor to court, wrote in his diary that Lord Islay 'advised me to bribe the German [Bernstorff] to get the governorship of Virginia and told me he would put me in the way'.[12]

Sarah Duchess of Marlborough, as mistress of the robes to Queen Anne, was quite open about the places that were in her gift:

> I gave the place of waiter in the Robes to Mr Curtis who married a woman that had served my children; I gave another place of the same kind to Mr Forster who was then in the service of the Duke of Marlborough and I made William Lovegrove coffer bearer who was also in the service of the Duke of Marlborough . . . I gave also a place of Coffer Bearer to Mr Woolrich and another place of Groom of the Wardrobe to Mr Hodges who were both servants in the family . . . Besides these I made Mrs Abrahal . . . the Queen's starcher and settled £100 a year upon her from the time of the Queens first allowing me to regulate the office of the Robes . . . I gave also the place of Sempstress, to Mrs Rhansford . . .[13]

We do not know whether money changed hands for these posts or if they were simply rewards for loyal servants. But elsewhere in her memoirs she admitted selling the place of a page of the backstairs for £400.[14]

Similarly James Brydges, Duke of Chandos, cultivated the German ministers, Melusine and Sophia Charlotte for preferment, and he oiled the wheels with bribes. In August 1714 he gave Bothmer 250 lottery tickets, and in September he sent 400 guineas to Robethon to gain a placement for an old friend.[15] He sent Sophia Charlotte £3,000, and a beautiful ring to her daughter. According to Beattie, between 1715 and 1720 he paid out at least £25,104 to the Germans at court. Amongst others, Melusine received £9,500, Sophia Charlotte £9,545, Bernstorff £2,909, and Bothmer £1,350.

Bonet, the Prussian envoy, has left us with a very telling description of the 'cloak and dagger' way in which George's business was conducted during the first year of his reign:

> It is at present a secret that the first knowledge of all affairs comes to the [English] ministers of State from Bernstorff and Bothmer, but it is uncertain how much longer this can be continued when this fact becomes known: to avoid causing embarrassment every evening the Duke of Marlborough and Lord Townshend go, under cover of night, to the house of the latter, and this quadrumvirate rules all . . .

On George's household, Bonet continues: 'he has not yet nominated a Keeper of the Privy Purse, where he has between £26,000 a year, in order that none can enter so easily into the secrets of his expenses and outlay; Baron Bothmer does the office in secret.'[16]

George was financially austere compared with his father, and the ministers he had inherited from Ernst August had amassed their fortunes before George became Elector. Bernstorff had grown rich through the generosity of George's uncle, Duke George William, and not through service to Hanover. All hoped to do well in England. Görtz even asked Sir John Vanbrugh for a house in his capacity as comptroller of the Office of Works. He was taken aback when Vanbrugh, a little shocked at his audacity, replied that there was none in George's gift.[17]

If the hard evidence for bribes is a little thin (Brydges provides us with the only solid report, verified by his account books), enough credible contemporaries – Walpole, Townshend, Craggs etc. – spoke of it for us to assume that there is truth in the claims. In 1716 Townshend accused Robethon of 'having nothing in his view but raising a vast estate for himself'. Townshend's accusations grew: the following year he circulated reports that Robethon had requested £40,000 from George's English ministers to be shared out amongst the members of the Hanoverian Chancery – £20,000 for Bernstorff, £10,000 for Bothmer, and £5,000 each for himself and Schütz.[18] Perhaps Townshend's tales were motivated by sour grapes, and his claim that Bothmer would not 'be satisfied till he has got the Ministry and Treasury into such hands that will satisfy his avarice'.[19]

It was not so much that bribes were being taken that offended the English ministers, but that they were being taken by Hanoverians. They preferred to keep the age-old system of patronage firmly within British hands. When Bothmer purchased an estate in Mecklenburg in 1723 its possible cost (some thought as much as £36,000) prompted feverish speculation amongst ministers who resented that the property had probably been paid for with British bribe money.[20] For the Germans it was an easy way of supplementing income in comparatively expensive England. Even the affable James Craggs the younger, a staunch Hanoverian who held several posts with both George and Georg August and who had joined the Whig Hanoverian Club before George's accession, found the Hanoverians gratuitously greedy – 'I have remarked that there is no distinction of person or circumstances. Jacobites, Tories, Papists, at the Exchange or in Church, by Land or Sea, during the Session or in the Recess, nothing is objected to provided there is money.'[21]

But although the Germans tried their utmost to exploit the system, they were not as successful as their detractors claimed. There was a political motive behind much of the criticism. The Germans were vilified by the Tory press and pamphleteers because they were foreign, and because they were not Stuarts. As much as anything, the taking of bribes provided an excellent excuse to attack them. But it must be admitted that in their satirizing of Melusine for her venality, they had a point. She was as willing as the next to take money for favours.

In July 1716 Mary Cowper recorded in her diary: 'Everybody believes that the Duchess of Munster [Melusine] had 5,000l. for making Lord St John [the father of the Tory Lord Bolingbroke, who had fled to France] a Lord.'[22] Melusine, together with young Melusine, was also suspected of using her influence, in return for hard cash, for obtaining the Order of the Garter for the dukes of Kent and Newcastle.

Although she was as assured as possible of George's affections, given that they were unmarried and their children illegitimate, Melusine was insecure about her finances all her life. Her parents had lifted themselves out of genteel poverty with a great deal of effort, and these actions defined her attitude to money. She spent a lot because she was extremely generous, particularly towards her family, and she gave a lot to charity. She and Johann Matthias were obliged to support their financially inept brother Daniel Bodo, with his obsessive alchemy experiments and his squandering of the family fortunes.

She gave presents of money to her sisters' husbands who had acknowledged the paternity of her daughters. But forever in her mind was the thought that George might cast her aside and that she and the girls would be destitute. That is not to say that George was not concerned for her financial future. An Imperial diplomat estimated that her pension from George was £7,500 per annum, paid from his Hanoverian and not his English resources. According to the same source she also had 'another secret pension, as also further perquisites ...'[23] Furthermore contemporaries gossiped that on Kielmansegg's death, Melusine received the salary of Master of the Horse, although this is unlikely as Sophia Charlotte's husband had received no salary from the post during the time that he had held it. In 1722

George granted her the patent for the Irish coinage, which she sold for £10,000 to William Wood – this would lead to one of the greatest scandals of George's reign. And in 1723 George wrote a will, witnessed by Walpole, leaving her £22,986.2s.2d. We have evidence that George told Melusine about the bequest.[24] But despite a generous annual allowance from George her fear of poverty led her to accept money and presents from often suspect individuals. It is unlikely that she betrayed her feelings to George, but they are evident in the surviving letter of Johann Matthias to their mutual friend Fabrice, as described above. Her lack of security made her unhappy, and it caused the sibling she was closest to to worry for her.

Sophia Charlotte was also ridiculed for accepting bribes and frittering away her money. She was said to have received £40,000 from her mother, Klara Platen, which quickly disappeared in a flurry of fripperies.

On arrival in England she and her husband Johann Adolf lived in grand style, as befitting his position as Master of the Horse, but because he was not English he was unable to draw the salary his post commanded. Lady Mary Wortley Montagu, Sophia Charlotte's regular correspondent, gossiped that the gorgeous jewellery she inherited from her mother was worth a fortune, but Hatton argues that it was not as valuable as has been suggested. When Johann Adolf died in 1717 her circumstances changed. George gave her a pension of £2,000 a year, but she was obliged to give up her official apartments to move to a house in Great George Street, near St James's Park.[25] Her staff was relatively small, and she must have been helped enormously by her £10,000 lottery win.[26] She had five children to support and obviously considered any cash that came her way in return for favours as a vital part of her income in her reduced circumstances.

Sophia Charlotte evidently enjoyed herself in England, and kept a lively salon. Despite her reputation for greed, she was liked by nearly everyone, with the notable exceptions of Melusine and Caroline. Lady Mary Wortley Montagu certainly preferred the more exuberant Sophia Charlotte to Melusine, and said of her:

> She had a greater vivacity in conversation than ever I knew in a German of either sex. She loved reading, and had a taste of all polite learning. Her humour was easy and sociable. Her constitution inclined her to gallantry. She was well bred and amusing in company. She knew how both to please and be pleased, and had experience enough to know it was hard to do either without money.

Liselotte remarked in a letter to Louise in 1716: 'Does Mme de Kielemansegg now speak English as well as she does French? Few Germans write French as well as she does . . .'[27]

Melusine's perceived venality quickly permeated the popular consciousness. A story exists, possibly apocryphal, of Melusine and Sophia Charlotte taking a carriage ride together soon after their arrival in England, and being confronted by an angry crowd. Evidently Melusine, in her heavily accented English, asked the mob: 'Good people, why do you plague us so? We have come for your own goods.' She meant for their benefit but the crowd replied: 'Yes, and for our chattels too.'[28]

As Melusine's reputation for corruption grew, so her detractors' pens grew sharper. The Duke of Wharton referred to her as 'the Concubine, who had hoarded up heaps of Treasure, while she was Mistress' to George.[29]

Alexander Pope attacked Melusine in his poem 'Phryne', which means 'Toad' in Greek. Here, she is seen as the conduit to power, accepting bribes from any who care to make use of her. The academic Kathleen Mahaffey notes that 'few of the court circle would have failed to recognise this character [Phryne] as belonging to . . .

Melusina . . . the chief port of entry for all who desired preferment and access to the King.' The poem is worth quoting in full:

Phryne had Talents for Mankind,
Open she was, and unconfin'd
Like some free Port of Trade.
Merchants unloaded here their Freight,
And Agents from each foreign State,
Here first their Entry made.

Her Learning and good Breeding such,
Whether th' Italian or the Dutch,
Spaniard or French came to her;
To all obliging she'd appear:
'Twas Si Signior, twas Yaw Mynheer,
'Twas S'il vous plait, Monsieur.

Obscure by Birth, renown'd by Crimes,
Still changing Names, Religions, Climes,
At length she turns a Bride:
In Di'monds, Pearls, and rich Brocades,
She shines the first of batter'd Jades,
And flutters in her Pride.

So have I known those Insects fair,
(Which curious Germans hold so rare,)
Still very Shapes and Dyes;
Still gain new Titles with new Forms;
First Grubs obscene, then wriggling Worms,
Then painted Butterflies.

The line 'At length she turns a Bride' reflects the court gossip that Melusine eventually married George, although whether Pope meant in Germany or later in England is not clear. Both rumours were given credence by contemporaries. Melusine is portrayed as extreme in her greed, the most corrupt in an age of tremendous corruptibility and bribery.

The poem probably dates from 1719 or shortly after, when Melusine was created Duchess of Kendal, as Pope satirizes her 'Still changing Names'. The image of Melusine as 'the first of batter'd Jades' is particularly harsh. It was not printed, probably deliberately, until after George's death. Pope was too wise to risk publishing something so disparaging during George's lifetime.

Sophia Charlotte did not escape Pope's pen either. He vilifies her in his poem, 'Artemisia', George's 'queen' who came with him to England. Here George is set in unflattering comparison with the Persian king Xerxes, whom Artemisia accompanied on his attempted invasion of Greece. In satirizing both Sophia Charlotte and Melusine, Pope was obviously influenced by the contemporary gossip that both were George's mistresses:

> Tho Artemisia talks, by Fits,
> Of Councils, Classicks, Fathers, Wits;
> Reads Malbranche, Boyle, and Locke;
> Yet in some Things methinks she fails,
> 'Twere well if she would pare her Nails,
> And wear a cleaner Smock.
>
> Haughty and huge as High-Dutch Bride,
> Such Nastiness and so much Pride
> Are oddly join'd by Fate:
> On her large Squab you find her spread,
> Like a fat Corpse upon a Bed,
> That lies and stinks in State.

She wears no Colours (sign of Grace)
On any Part except her Face;
All white and black beside:
Dauntless her Look, her Gesture proud,
Her Voice theatrically loud,
And masculine her Stride.

So have I seen, in black and white
A prating Thing, a Magpye hight,
Majestically stalk;
A stately, worthless Animal,
That plies the Tongue, and wags the Tail,
All Flutter, Pride, and Talk.[30]

Another writer who turned a disparaging eye on Melusine was the Tory Jonathan Swift, who despised her and attacked her in both poetry and pamphlets. Some contemporaries believed that she was the 'cushion' in his bestseller *Gulliver's Travels*, though literary critics today believe that Swift was using the allegory of *Gulliver's Travels* as a general indictment on the cabal of corrupt king's favourites and Whig ministers.

A century later the satirists' descriptions were swallowed whole and regurgitated as fact. The *Morning Chronicle* of February 1818, in its section entitled 'Political Questions', reported:

George the First, being a gallant person, and devoted to what was called the fair sex in Westphalia, where, among witches, fair is foul, and foul is fair, brought with him to England two ugly fiends to serve him for mistresses, and to make part of his official establishment. One of them was created Duchess of Kendal, the other, Countess of Darlington, to reward their merits in their respective departments, and to encourage the surrender of prudery in younger and handsomer subjects. All this is too notorious to be disputed ...[31]

The pseudonymous Captain Samuel Brunt's *A Voyage to Cacklogallinia: with a Description of the Religion, Policy, Customs and Manners of that Country* of 1727 also attacked the king's mistress. It portrayed Robert Walpole as a rooster, and Melusine as a hen.

The Hanoverian ministers in general and Melusine in particular were perceived to be 'sucking England dry' of money and titles. But if George turned a blind eye to bribery, he scrupulously adhered to the rule that no German could receive a British title. Titles were awarded to his close entourage, but only following their naturalization as British subjects, and then only for life. George's brother Ernst August became Duke of York in 1716 and young Melusine took the title Countess of Walsingham in 1722.

At the same time Louise was made a countess of the Empire – she received no English title – becoming the Gräfin von Delitz. Trudchen was felt too young to receive a title, but as she achieved one through her marriage to Albrecht Wolfgang zu Schaumburg-Lippe in 1722, it was not deemed necessary.

Unsurprisingly, given the rampant corruption in which the Hanoverians engaged so enthusiastically, George's first English ministry was rife with faction and discontent, as Whig intrigued against Whig. There were at least two very unhappy members. The most coveted roles of Secretary of State for the North and for the South had gone to Charles Townshend and James Stanhope respectively. One Secretary of State, or 'Foreign Minister', was responsible for Northern Europe – the Dutch Republic, Sweden, Denmark-Norway, Poland, Russia, the German states. The other was responsible for Southern Europe – France, Spain, Portugal, the Italian states and the Ottoman Empire. Charles Montagu, Lord Halifax, was appointed First Lord of the Treasury and the Tory

Lord Nottingham became Lord President. Robert Walpole, Townshend's brother-in-law, became Paymaster (until 1715) and the Duke of Argyll Groom of the Stool to the Prince of Wales.

But George, largely because he disliked their arrogance and self-obsession, sidelined both the great war hero Marlborough and his son-in-law Charles Spencer, third Earl of Sunderland, who had been a secretary of state under Anne. Marlborough, who irritated George with his vaunting of his great victories, was given the relatively lowly post of Captain-General and Sunderland got Lord Lieutenant of Ireland, which was also a demotion.

In his description of the English court after George's accession the Prussian envoy Bonet writes to his master of Marlborough's greed:

> The man who has been most ardent in his [the king's] growing displeasure is the duke of Marlborough, who has but his personal merit, and little credit throughout the country due to his insatiable avarice, which renders his riches, and even his friendship and faithful duties useless to society, since the former are buried, and the latter dispensed only for money.[32]

Both Stanhope and Marlborough were extremely bitter at their marginalization. Stanhope believed he should be Secretary of State in Townshend's place and he and Marlborough formed a cabal to oust Townshend.

As early as November 1714 Oxford gleefully wrote: 'Germans and Whigs divided amongst themselves . . . two parties . . . now hang out their colours in battle array. Nothing but the fear of the Tories keeps them from outraging each other.'[33] Townshend and Walpole, who disliked the German ministers' intervention in English affairs, led one faction, and Sunderland, Marlborough and their good friend William Cadogan another. They attempted to discredit Townshend in the eyes of the king and to replace him with Sunderland as Secretary of State.

By the summer of 1716 Walpole feared that the machinations against them had reached a crisis. Some of the Germans had made it clear that they favoured the Sunderland faction, and when George went on the first of his visits to Hanover in July – George and Melusine made five visits to Hanover throughout the reign, in 1716, 1719, 1720, 1723 and 1725 – taking Melusine, Bernstorff, Robethon and secretary Stanhope with him, Walpole and Townshend were dismayed. Once Sunderland managed to join the king later in the summer the pair knew they were doomed. Mary Countess Cowper suggested in her diary that everything had been decided even before George and Melusine left London. On July 16 1716 she wrote: 'A new scheme was let out by the Duke of Marlborough's friends for the State of the Nation in the next sessions of parliament. By that it was resolved, first, that my Lord Townshend should be turned out (the Duchess of Munster had given me a hint that that was resolved upon before she left London) . . .'[34]

Townshend was stripped of his post and offered the relatively lowly position of Lord Lieutenant of Ireland. He reluctantly accepted, as he and Walpole were determined to maintain the veneer of Whig unity. However he only lasted four months. George, exasperated by his obvious antagonism, dismissed him in the spring. Walpole and many of their colleagues resigned in protest, creating a political schism.

Townshend, one of the ablest politicians of his generation, was not lightly demoted or dismissed by George. Why then did he fall? He was demoted in the first instance because he disagreed with the king on foreign policy and was vocal in his belief that British resources should not be used to aid Hanoverian foreign policy. Bernstorff, for instance, in 1716 had no compunction in advising George to order the English fleet in the Baltic to fight against the

Russian Tsar's forces to oust the Russians from Mecklenburg, a territory next to Hanover – an action that infuriated Townshend. This was very obviously a Hanoverian and not a British problem. But Stanhope and Sunderland were more amenable to enabling the king and his German advisers to use British resources in Hanoverian matters.

Secondly, George, already on poor terms with his son, perceived the beginning of an alliance between Townshend, Walpole and Georg August. As we shall see in the next chapter, it was not something that they deliberately set out to achieve, but even so it allowed the personal antagonism between the king and the Prince of Wales to explode into the political sphere.

Most importantly, Townshend had earned the loathing of Melusine. It was only with his dismissal that he belatedly realized the extent of her power. In the summer of 1716 he wrote to a Dutch friend: 'I believe the duchess of Munster [Melusine], Mr Bernstorff, and Mr Robethon could give a much more exact and authentic account of the real causes that produced this event [his demotion and dismissal].'

In 1716 George, wanting to honour Melusine, had created her Duchess of Munster following her naturalization. As such she was elevated to the Irish peerage. She had obviously lobbied for it: her need for security made itself far more apparent in England than it had in Hanover. On 12 June Mary Countess Cowper recorded in her diary: 'Mademoiselle Schulenberg here about her title . . .' and on 26 June she wrote: 'At night I go out with my Lord to take the air, then to Mademoiselle Schulenberg to wish her joy.'[35] But Melusine soon discovered that Irish peerages were distinctly inferior to English ones, and she was furious. She blamed Townshend for her meagre title; he had suggested it to the king.

Historians have condemned her for being petty over her Irish peerage. Though this attitude does not seem consistent with the image we have of her in Hanover – calm, collected, self-assured – England was a very different environment. In Germany she was used to getting her own way – in Walpole's words she had become a 'queen'. The only person who had challenged her authority there was George's mother, Sophia, and the pair had learned to avoid one another. Whilst in the principality, Melusine had utter confidence in George's loyalty to her, and any dealings with the Hanoverian courtiers – she had been on intimate terms with most of them since her early twenties – were smooth. All knew the state of affairs and were sensible enough to treat her with respect. There was little opportunity for Melusine to 'meddle' in politics, even if she had been inclined to. George and his mother each had very defined areas of interest, leaving no room for Melusine.

By contrast, in England Melusine's fluent English and easy, diplomatic manner were of enormous use to George. She had a great deal more scope for exerting influence, but this greater freedom brought with it a correspondingly higher chance of failure and disgrace. Less secure, she sought titles and wealth.

It is telling that the English politicians whom both Melusine and George initially favoured were Stanhope and Sunderland, both of whom were charming, urbane, and showed the new monarch and his favourite much respect. Walpole and less markedly Townshend, although both brilliant politicians, were gruff and plain-spoken, Walpole to the point of using gratuitously filthy language. Melusine, a stickler for good manners, and used to the benign dictatorship that was Hanover, was not impressed. Already poorly disposed towards the pair, she used the excuse of her second-rate title to bring Townshend down.

In the late summer Walpole, furious, wrote to Stanhope:

> We conceive that there is reason to believe that the designs of Lord
> Sunderland, Cadogan etc were carried further, and better supported

than we did imagine whilst you were here, and that all the foreigners were engaged on their side of the question; and in chief that
the Duchess of Munster enter'd into the dispute with a more than
ordinary zeal and resentment against us, insomuch that by an
account we have of a conversation with the King at the Duchess of
Munster's, they flatter themselves that nothing but the want of time
and the hurry the king was in upon his going away [to Hanover]
prevented a thorough change of the ministry . . . That the Duchesse
of Munster was very angry at her not being an English Dutchesse
is most certain, and that she imputes the whole to my Lord Townshend, and has express'd a particular resentment against him . . .[36]

Townshend and Walpole, at Melusine's instigation, were out. It
would take a crisis to bring them back.

Melusine was instrumental in the rise and fall of George's English ministers. She promoted one over the other with great success,
depending on where her interest took her. Townshend fell through
her contrivance, and later she championed Stanhope against Bernstorff, again with success.

One of the reasons behind her new influence was that George
liked to garner his information from 'other hands than by his
ministers',[37] and here Melusine played a crucial role, not previously available to her. Whilst they were still in Hanover she had
already familiarized herself with the major British courtiers and
their wives, who had flooded into the principality to secure
favour with the putative new regime. Melusine's surviving letters
show that she was charming and gracious. She had established a
friendly correspondence with many of the court ladies and was
on good terms with the venomous gossip Lady Mary Wortley
Montagu, who had learned German and spent time in Hanover
in the 1710s to ingratiate herself with the new monarch and his
entourage. Montagu was a regular correspondent of Melusine's,

although she was vicious about her behind her back. In 1715 Melusine replied to her:

> I fear I have no words strong enough to assure you of the joy I felt
> ... that you (have done me) the honour of writing to me, assuring
> you that no one could be more grateful than I am for the goodness
> you show me, and that you will do me great pleasure and honour
> by coming here when you please. You can be well persuaded that the
> soonest will be the most agreeable to me; I thus flatter myself with
> having the honour very soon of being able to tell you in person how
> much I love you and how much I am, my dear madam, Your very
> humble and very obedient Servant,
> M. de Schoulenbourg
> It is up to me to make many apologies for such a scribble, but as
> I am very busy I hope you will not look at it too closely.[38]

On arrival in England, once Melusine had fully acquainted herself with the workings of English government, little was done without her knowledge and, often, approval. She and George had supper together most nights, and it was at supper that Melusine, in her quiet and gentle way, would put the requests of George's ministers to him. In the summer of 1719 Sunderland wished to journey to Hanover to see the king while he was there. Stanhope wrote to him from Hanover: 'I have mentioned to the Dutchess your lordships coming over and she has promised and judges it most proper to open it herself first to the king.'[39] And the Prussian envoy reported that Melusine frequently 'broke the first ice' with George.[40] As we shall see, after the catastrophic South Sea Bubble Melusine was instrumental in maintaining Walpole in power, and in 1723 she lent her support to Townshend to prevent his fall. In an amazing volte-face, Townshend was able to write to Walpole in that year that Melusine is 'the good duchess and ... fast friend' to whom 'we have sworn an eternal and inviolable attachment'.[41] Although she could never bring herself to like him, they had become useful to one another.

In 1716 Walpole said: 'Nobody can carry on the king's business if he is not supported at Court.'[42] It was Melusine's intercession on Walpole and Townshend's behalf during the last five years of George's reign that was so vital to their political health, and earlier in his reign, it was only because of Melusine's intercession that Sarah Duchess of Marlborough, whose husband had so fallen in George's esteem, was granted a private interview with the new monarch.

However, Melusine's unique access to the king was resented. Lady Mary Wortley Montagu wrote bitchily that Melusine 'was so much of his temper that I do not wonder at the engagement between them. She was duller than himself, and consequently did not find out that he was so; and had lived in that figure at Hanover almost forty years (for she came hither threescore) without meddling in any affairs of the Electorate.'[43]

But this kind of petty gossip would pale in comparison with what was to follow. The summer of 1716 saw the beginnings of a terrible quarrel between George and his son. It led to Georg August and Caroline being forced from St James's, to the removal of their children from their care and, most importantly for political life in Britain, to the establishment of a separate court of the Prince of Wales in direct opposition to that of his father the king.

12.

A Battle

God prosper long our noble King
His Turks and Germans all
A woeful christ'ning late there did
In James's house befall.

– 'An Excellent New Ballad'

The mores that governed royal family life were very different from those of families further down the social scale. We may be tempted from our vantage point of the twenty-first century to see George's familial relationships as extremely dysfunctional. His father had paraded his mistresses in front of his mother, George had broken with all but two of his siblings over the issue of primogeniture, and one of his brothers may have tried to poison their father because he felt cheated of his inheritance. George and his eldest legitimate son could not stand one another, and by all accounts he was awkward in the company of his daughter Sophia Dorothea when she was a child, only opening up to her when she was safely married into the Prussian royal family and he could hide behind his letters.

This 'dysfunction' crossed the generations, with rumours of incest abounding in connection to both George and his mother. And when George argued with his son and threw him out of St James's Palace without his children, Caroline, who was given the choice to stay, abandoned them to be with her husband. George's children were similarly unfeeling towards their own children. Georg August's relations with his eldest son, never easy (the boy had been left behind in Hanover when the royal family came to England in 1714), suffered a comparable rupture to George's split with Georg August in 1717; and Wilhelmine's memoirs are peppered with beatings and verbal abuse from her mother.

The explanation for the dislike bordering on hatred often found between kings and their sons is very simple: the son, who desires autonomy in his father's lifetime and is never given it, resents the very air his father breathes. Crudely, he wishes him dead. It was this longing for power that would never be granted while both generations were alive that also poisoned all peripheral familial relationships.[1] Melusine managed to an extent to soothe the ever-bickering Hanoverians, but in this case she was powerless.

Georg August's personality was very different to George's; he was volatile, outspoken, exuberant, a man who showed his passions to all. Lady Mary Wortley Montagu noted: 'The fire of his temper appear'd in every look and Gesture, which being unhappily under the Direction of a small understanding was every day throwing him upon some indiscretion.'[2] He craved power during his father's lifetime and George was reluctant to grant it.

The origins of the specific breach between George and his only legitimate son that began in the summer of 1716 and would last for nearly four years can arguably be found twenty-two years earlier in 1694, when George divorced the disgraced Sophia Dorothea and ordered her incarcerated with no hope of release. Georg August was only eleven years old when he saw his mother for the last time, and although George would have argued passionately that her removal was vital to the security of their house – to which Georg August was the heir – it is unlikely that her bemused young son would have cared for such justifications.

George probably remained silent on the matter and offered no explanation to his children. Georg August never forgave his father. Although Sophia Dorothea, as with most women of her class, probably had little to do with his day-to-day care or upbringing – evidence from George's mother's correspondence suggests that the young prince was closer to his paternal grand-parents than to his parents – she was after all his mother, and he retained a frustrated devotion to her until just after George's death.[3] The often unreliable chatterer Horace Walpole tells us that when George died in 1727, the new king at once hung two portraits of his mother in prominent positions.[4] In 1732 he made enormous efforts to suppress the publication of a scandalous book about her life, the anonymous *Histoire secrète de la duchesse d'Hanover*.[5] Horace Walpole also tells us that the prince made at least one failed attempt to see his mother in her Ahlden prison, running away from a hunting trip nearby in a desperate dash to reach her. But he was caught and brought back to his father. And Walpole again tells us that he had it from the lips of Henrietta Howard, the prince's mistress, that should his father predecease his mother he would give her all honours, bringing her to England in state or possibly making her regent of Hanover.[6]

Even before the family reached England, relations between George and his son, the newly fashioned Prince of Wales, were cool. Melusine's friendship with Caroline helped, and George obviously liked his daughter-in-law enormously – the king was always beguiled by a pretty face, and the canny Caroline went out of her way to charm him – but all the court noticed that the king and his son could barely tolerate one another. Bonet reported to his Prussian master and mistress:

> It is true that there is a manifest coolness between the King and the Prince; they do not speak to one another; they have never gone to one another's apartments; they have never eaten together; they have never been together in the Royal or private houses, nor in the promenades, nor at the hunt, but only in Council, at Chapel, and in the evening in the circle of the Princess, without speaking: But this coolness must be anterior to their arrival in this Kingdom, nothing having occurred here that could have caused it.[7]

Bonet commented on the prince's lack of freedom, either of thought or action:

He [Georg August] has not the liberty, because he must be obedient to the King, and report everything to him as the centre: that his conduct is considered more closely than that of a subject of inferior rank: And if he may not have even a footman who is not in agreement with His Majesty: he is permitted still less to take a part contrary to the measures of the King.[8]

George made himself amenable to everyone in his family and close circle except Georg August. He allowed his daughters by Melusine great freedom, and there is real affection in his letters to the young Sophia Dorothea and obvious warmth between them in their occasional meetings in Hanover, and once at her home in Berlin. His closest friends, particularly Melusine's brother Frederick William, who was one of George's intimates, bore witness to his good character – his loyalty, his diligence, his dry humour – and Melusine's other brothers and sisters seemed to have genuinely liked him. But he showed no softness towards his son, despite the total fidelity that Georg August displayed towards his father both in Hanover and, at first, in England, and his willingness to take the lead socially, letting the more reticent George and Melusine off the hook. Georg August had excelled himself in the battle of Oudenarde in 1708 – where he was part of Marlborough's forces – and it is possible that George was jealous of the success of a son he did not care for.

The row began in the summer of 1716 when George and Melusine returned to Hanover for their first holiday since their arrival in England. George was reluctant to leave his son as regent in his absence. Georg August was devastated; he believed it showed how little his father valued his abilities and exposed his total lack of trust in him. But George's biographer Ragnhild Hatton argues convincingly that the king was actually following the same pattern his own father assumed regarding his training for leadership.

George, like Ernst August, adopted a 'slowly, slowly' approach, including his son in Cabinet meetings and gradually preparing him to rule while not giving him any genuine autonomy. George believed in Ernst August's methods and reproduced them with his own son. But it is feasible that George, less voluble than his father, failed to communicate his rationale to Georg August.

George did give Georg August some responsibility in his absence. His son was created 'guardian and lieutenant of the realm' and George left him a warm letter of instructions. Phrases such as 'all imaginable regard' for his advice during the king's absence abound, but, as George explained, he could not entrust him with full powers because he was concerned for precedent, 'lest in the future great inconveniences to our posterity should follow'.[9]

Georg August railed against his limited powers. He could not appoint anyone to a position worth more than £50 a year, could not summon or dissolve parliament. George entrusted his son with no more responsibility than his council in Hanover enjoyed in his absences in England.

But the prince had another grievance against his father. Just before his departure George, fearing his influence over the prince, insisted on the dismissal of his son's friend and groom of the stole, Archibald Campbell, third Duke of Argyll. It was also for the sake of political stability in his absence – Argyll was the enemy of Walpole and Townshend. Argyll was generally disliked, motivated in everything he did by his intense jealousy of Marlborough. According to the historian of the Georgian era, J. H. Plumb: 'Few liked him, few trusted him . . . he could be relied upon to create the maximum trouble given half an opportunity. His power was far from negligible, for he and his brother controlled a great deal of the political world of Scotland. Their family had a long history of treason.'[10] But this quarrelsome duke had made himself very amenable to the prince. Georg August was furious at Argyll's dismissal, and George was forced to threaten to bring his own brother, Ernst August, over from Hanover to act as 'regent' in Georg August's place unless he calmed down.

Melusine, ever trying to maintain a tranquil atmosphere, was against Argyll's removal. She had known Georg August most of his life and was well aware of his volatility. She feared there would be trouble. Mary Cowper recorded in her diary on 8 July 1716: 'Lady St John here [wife of Sir Henry, created in 1716 viscount St John, father of Lord Bolingbroke] . . . She says that the Duchess of Munster [Melusine] had told her that she was against turning out Argyll at this juncture, and that she believed it was the ministers had put the king upon it . . .'

Although Georg August declared himself 'resolved to sacrifice everything to please and live well with the king', he spent the summer and autumn of George's absence behaving in a way that, if not in open opposition, was not entirely loyal. He headed a splendid court at Hampton Court and kept Argyll with him, although not in his official position. Townshend and Walpole found it prudent not to complain and went to see the prince regularly, where they found him charming and willing to conduct ministerial business. But they sent to Hanover their fears of the prince's design, encouraged by Argyll, 'to keep up an interest of his own in Parliament independent of the King's'.[11] Georg August was determined to create his own prince's party in parliament. One of George's greatest attributes was his loyalty. He was bewildered and miserable at what he saw as the prince's treachery.

Georg August, ever prone to sulks and tantrums, stayed pointedly away from Cabinet meetings despite the pleas of the king and his ministers, and encouraged his supporters in the Commons and the Lords to vote against his father's ministry. But Sunderland refused to be held captive to the prince's ill temper. He sought to persuade George to drastic measures. He recommended banning

Georg August from the royal palaces, and in his wilder moments he even postulated deportation to the colonies.

The loathing between Walpole and Townshend on the one hand and Sunderland on the other possibly precipitated such outlandish suggestions. Melusine's youngest brother Schulenburg's letters tell us that Walpole and Townshend 'hated' Sunderland and the feeling was no doubt reciprocated.[12] They enjoyed fanning the flames of acrimony between George and his son.

But George refused to consider these ridiculous ideas. He did everything he could to appease Georg August for the sake of familial and parliamentary unity, despite his son's provocative actions. Melusine, worried for George's health, strove to keep him calm. She encouraged him to approach Caroline to smooth things over, and the diplomatic Stanhope was duly dispatched on George's behalf.

But the situation worsened throughout the summer of 1717 after George and Melusine's return from Hanover, despite Melusine's best efforts to bring Caroline on side. The two women continued their friendly relations, but the princess steadfastly refused to ask her husband to step into line. Georg August deliberately distanced himself from Melusine, probably from a desire not to embarrass her with his temper. He always showed her the greatest respect, even after his father's death.

Georg August's recalcitrance thrust George and Melusine into the limelight. Rather than returning to Hanover for the summer as planned, they were forced to make a splendid show at Hampton Court. Melusine was disappointed; the trip to Hanover included a spa cure for George at Bad Pyrmont, and she was increasingly worried about his health. It was at this time that George showed all the symptoms of an anal fistula, and family and friends panicked. Louis XIV, suffering from the condition in 1686, had been obliged to undergo surgery, and this option was viewed with horror by

George, Melusine and their immediate circle. Operations in the days before general anaesthetic were extremely risky, and George was never comfortable with doctors. It was Mehemet who was nominated to persuade him to undergo an examination, and to the delight of Melusine and the king's friends and family, no fistula was found.

But despite George's medical scare, he and Melusine felt compelled to host receptions, balls, card games, shoots and festivals. Public days were held on Sundays and Thursdays, George dined in public and, against his natural inclinations, held levees and couchers. He mixed freely with his visitors. He had card tables and a billiard table set up in the Gallery at Hampton Court and he attended these parties every night, staying until past midnight. George also made a point of spending far more time with his English staff and courtiers. His ministers and subjects were thrilled at this 'royal' behaviour.

Much of our information about this period comes from the letters that Melusine's brother, Frederick William Schulenburg, sent to Görtz. He was part of the inner sanctum, almost on a par in George's affections with the beloved Mehemet and Mustapha. He tells us of a 'rupture' between father and son, and the weakening of the king's party of parliament. Georg August was now openly acting with the rebel Whigs (led by Walpole, and often called the Walpolian Whigs) against his father. Melusine's brother, in another letter to Görtz, listed the group of those dissenting Whigs – chiefly Walpole and Townshend – under the heading 'Le Prince'.[13] Walpole's enormous skill in managing the Commons was proved as he held up bill after bill.

The breach was not yet irrevocable. To George and Melusine's surprise and delight the Prince and Princess of Wales came to Hampton Court for the summer, although the prince could barely tolerate his father's company. Caroline was pregnant once more;

her last child, a boy, had been stillborn and George wanted nothing to jeopardize the safe delivery of a hoped-for prince. The summer passed without incident between father and son, although both were sulking.

The prince and princess returned to St James's to await the birth while George and Melusine took the opportunity to embark on a mini-progress to visit nearby estates and to go to the races at Newmarket. By showing himself to his subjects, his ministers agreed, the king had done 'great good'. But Addison, George's Secretary of the South at the time, tells us that George only 'took the sudden resolution of being present at the diversion of that place [Newmarket]' because he thought the prince would be there and now, in the midst of a conflict, he did not want Georg August to outshine him.[14]

George's enforced sociability continued after the court returned to St James's in November, when he held an evening drawing room three times a week.[15] George tried to make the court, and therefore his ministry, more desirable than the opposition of Townshend, Walpole and his son. A contemporary, Arthur Onslow, notes: 'Among other methods used by the Court to secure a majority, chiefly in the House of Commons, a magnificent public table, at vast expense to the King, was kept at St James's House in Parliament time, for the entertainment of the members.'[16] George spent the formidable sum of £700 a month on this merry-making, a sign that he was conducting, in Beattie's words, 'a competition for popularity'.

It was the birth of a healthy boy on 20 October that precipitated the final rupture.[17] The events that led to George and his son not speaking for nearly three years were almost comical. They began when the parents set about searching for a name. Caroline wanted to call her son William. George's ministers insisted that, as George was to be one of the godfathers, he should be called George. A compromise, 'George William', was agreed upon.

The couple naturally expected to choose a second godfather for the boy, and they decided on Georg August's uncle, Ernst August. This choice should have pleased George, but Sunderland and Stanhope took a hand. Hoping to break the prince's dangerous links with Walpole and Townshend so that the king's business could be carried out without hindrance once more, they insisted on the lord chamberlain, the Duke of Newcastle, as the other godfather.

George, seemingly wishing to accommodate his son and daughter-in-law, suggested that Newcastle instead act as proxy for Ernst August at the ceremony. But Georg August loathed Newcastle and refused. The more diplomatic Caroline suggested a postponement, but no one was willing; the ministry was furious with the disobedient prince, and Melusine and the king's closest friends wanted the matter dealt with as quickly as possible so that the king could finally have his holiday in Hanover in the spring.

The christening went ahead on 28 November, but as soon as his father was out of the room Georg August turned the full force of his infamous temper on Newcastle and verbally abused him. He accused him of dishonourable behaviour and evidently used other 'strong, injurious expressions'.[18] During this rant he probably said, in his thick German accent: 'I'll find you.' But Newcastle, in shock and frightened of this princely tornado, misheard and thought that Georg August had challenged him to a duel with the words 'I'll fight you.' He was, he believed, in peril of his life. He ran to the king for protection.

George, furious, took drastic measures. He placed his son under house arrest at St James's before expelling him from the palace on 2 December, to Georg August's enormous surprise. Caroline, he made clear, was welcome to stay at the palace with her children, but the princess insisted on leaving with her husband. Under English law the royal children belonged to the Crown, and as such they were obliged to stay. Georg August took his father to court in an attempt to get them back, but the court found for the king. Georg August was further incensed when his father insisted the prince give him £40,000 a year for the children's upkeep. Although the king's demands came to nothing, they succeeded in worsening the breach.

Liselotte, despite having never met Caroline – their correspondence was a method devised by Liselotte's son the Regent for shoring up relations with Britain – sent a flurry of letters to her correspondents and wrote to Louise on 23 December 1717:

> I am so sorry for our dear Princess of Wales that I shed tears for her yesterday. It is so pitiful, the way the Countess of Bückeburg [Joanne Sophie zu Schaumburg-Lippe] described her departure from St James's. The poor Princess went into one faint after another when her weeping little Princesses said goodbye.

She continued: 'The King of England is really cruel to the Princess of Wales. Although she has done nothing, he has taken her children away from her.'[19]

Mary Cowper wrote in her diary: 'The Princess is all in a flame, the Prince in an agony. They are all mad, and for their own private ends will destroy all.'[20]

The spat, so public, was devastating for the entire family. Londoners deplored what they saw as the snatching away of the children and public sympathy rested with the prince and princess. The Jacobite press was overjoyed, as were the Tories who crowded to George's court.[21]

Frederick William Schulenburg reported that the king, so saddened, was 'quite altered'. And it is from this period that George's health went into gradual decline. His sadness was compounded by Sophia Charlotte's intense grief at the death of her husband Johann Adolf von Kielmansegg. George also mourned the loss of a close friend.

The prince and princess rented a fine seventeenth-century house in Leicester Square, on the edge of Leicester fields – it was the house in which Sophia's mother, Elizabeth of Bohemia, had died. Here they established a rival court, attracting a younger and livelier crowd of politicians and courtiers than George's 'official' court. George, incensed, made it clear that anyone who had been received at Leicester House would not be welcome at court. Friendships suffered, with Mary Cowper forced to leave Caroline's service because of her husband's position in George's ministry. But cloak-and-dagger ways were found of communicating, at masked balls and with secret notes, all heightening the sense of intrigue.

The critical ramification of the rupture between the king and the Prince of Wales was the solidifying of the opposition of Walpole and Townshend around the prince at Leicester House. Father and son effectively led rival factions. George and his ministers experienced a 'painful session' when parliament reconvened in October, with Walpole continuing to consistently block the progress of the king's bills.

And with the removal of the most sociable elements of the royal family, the Prince and Princess of Wales, George's court had to glitter more than ever. In April 1718 the court moved to Kensington Palace, where the king continued his evening parties. Mrs Allanson wrote to Lady Cowper in May: 'the ladies say they [have] never see[n] so much company and every body fine, the King very obliging and in great good humour ... [at night] all the garden illuminated and music in it and dancing in the Green House and the long Gallery'.[22]

George kept up his extravagant hospitality when the court moved to Hampton Court for the summer, with assemblies every evening in the Cartoon Gallery or the Tennis Court. He kept twenty musicians and held a ball at least twice a week. Plays were regularly put on throughout the summer, reminiscent of the glory days of Herrenhausen. He even brought Steel's Company, the group of players based at the theatre in Drury Lane, to Hampton Court to entertain, at enormous expense. Melusine appeared nightly with George, socializing and entertaining.

The parties continued at St James's when the court returned there for the winter. Beattie points out that they were often boisterous affairs. On one occasion 'the room where the Side Board was kept' was so 'stained with claret [that] it was necessary to provide Sayl cloth against another Ball to prevent the like damage'.[23]

Years later, when Georg August's son Frederick contemplated setting up a rival court to his father, Lord Hervey was emphatically against it. He told him how opposition had impacted on his father:

> I can remember when your father had the misfortune to quarrel with your grandfather, and notwithstanding he had many people of the first rank, quality, understanding, character, and consideration of this kingdom in his party; notwithstanding one of his own servants was in the chair of the House of Commons; and notwithstanding he had a revenue of £120,000 a year independent of the King, I can remember in a little time how poor a figure his opposition to the Court made, how weary both he and his adherents were of it . . . and how little it availed him in any one article.[24]

As a result of the split in the family Melusine fretted not only for George's health – she was relieved when they went to Hanover during the summers of 1719 and 1720 – but for her own future. Evidence suggests that she may have sanctioned overtures to the Pretender; if so, the breach must have made Melusine very fearful indeed. Beneath the cool public face, she experienced dread bordering on hysteria.

According to the Duke of Hamilton, Melusine had conversations with his mother, Elizabeth Gerard, Duchess of Hamilton, that were tantamount to treason. The duchess reported back to her son, who duly wrote to the Pretender, that 'the irreconcilable difference' between the king and his son made Kendal fearful for her future position should the Prince of Wales succeed. Thus for an allowance for life from the Pretender, Kendal would use her power with the king to 'have his son laid aside' and to 'enter into measures for your majesty [the Pretender] to succeed'.[25]

Elizabeth, disliked by many, seems to have been in the habit of speaking her mind. In 1711 Swift said of her: 'she talks too much, is a plaguey detractor, and I believe I shall not much like her . . .' The following year he changed his opinion: 'she has abundance of wit and spirit . . . handsome and airy, and seldom spared anybody that gave her the least provocation, by which she had many enemies and few friends.' But was the duchess telling the truth? Jacobite supporters in England – the Hamiltons were fervent supporters of James's cause – felt obliged to give the Pretender some good news, and repeated any favourable gossip or hearsay as fact.

There are rumours elsewhere that George wanted to put his son aside. In March 1718, at the height of the crisis between the king and the prince, Liselotte wrote in a panic to her half-sister Louise:

Everything goes from bad to worse in England. It is not safe to write anything about it. All Paris says that King George wants to declare publicly that the Prince of Wales is not his son, and that, in order to spite him still further, he wants to marry the Schulenberg woman who is now Duchess of Munster. I told Lord Stair all this, and he replied that nothing of the sort would happen, and that I had no need to alarm myself.[26]

It is probable that George and Melusine, tired from the unceasing round of social engagements, both intermittently unwell, missing Hanover and resentful that they could not return in 1718, as well as facing the additional strain of bringing up Georg August's and Caroline's young family, did contemplate drastic measures. It would have been easy for George to resurrect the myth that Georg August was Königsmarck's son because many of George's subjects already believed it to be true. In 1716 Caroline received an alarming Jacobite letter, 'asking her to consider, just and God-fearing as she is known to be, that the only rightful heir to the kingdom is the one known as the Pretender, as he was King James II's son as surely as her husband was Count Königsmarck's'.[27] But it is extremely unlikely that the cautious George would have considered such a move seriously.

The Duchess of Hamilton's claims are more serious. If they were true, they show Melusine as uncharacteristically desperate, and may explain why she was amenable to ever-increasing presents of money for favours and access, as with her involvement in the catastrophic South Sea Bubble, and why she took an £11,000 bribe from Bolingbroke in 1725 for aiding his return to England.

Meanwhile it was imperative that the royal children be well cared for with as little disruption as possible. Melusine's hand can be seen here. They were entrusted to her great friend Joanne Sophie zu Schaumburg-Lippe, and it is possible that familial links were maintained with the presence of Trudchen, their aunt, now sixteen years old. At least one historian believes that Melusine's youngest daughter, who was renowned for her kindness and her gentle nature, was involved in the day-to-day care of the children. The German historian Mijndert Bertram claims that Trudchen received custody of the children, but it may be that he has confused her with her future mother-in-law; in 1722 Trudchen married Joanne Sophie's son, Albrecht Wolfgang zu Schaumburg-Lippe. But it is entirely feasible that Trudchen, not much older than the eldest princess, had a hand in caring for her young nieces and nephew. In 1717 Anne was twelve, Amalie ten, and Caroline only four years old; George William, of course, was only a baby.

Melusine ensured that she was physically close to the princesses in order to supervise their upbringing. In May 1719 Kensington Palace became their main home. Melusine and George had great plans for Kensington, as witnessed by the extensive rebuilding that took place between 1718 and 1726. Even after the reconciliation between father and son, the princesses' main home remained the palace best beloved of their grandfather and his mistress.

Two specific entries relating to Melusine's accommodation at Kensington occur in the minutes of the Board of Works. The first, from January 1724, tells us: 'The young Princesses' Gallery to be paneled. For making a colonnaded way from the Duchess of Kendall's to the young Princesses' lodging.' This entrance was not in the architect's original plans, and shows how much interaction there was between the two households. Although Joanne Sophie zu Schaumburg-Lippe was officially in charge of the young princesses, the fact that she and Melusine were close friends, and that Melusine's apartments were linked to the princesses', makes it likely that Melusine had overall responsibility for the children.

The second entry, dating from May 1725, gives the commission 'to build two rooms over the new arcade in Green Cloth Court for the Duchess of Kendall and two closets for the young princesses, and one for the Countess of Portland'. Jane, Countess of Portland, was governess to the princesses from 1718, and both entries show how imperative Melusine was to the girls' lives, living on such intimate terms with them and their governess.

The Countess of Portland had been carefully chosen for her intelligence and the fact that she had already raised a large family. In December 1714 Mary Cowper wrote of the princesses: 'After dinner, I went to wait upon the little princesses, who are miracles of their ages, especially princess Anne, who at five years old speaks, reads, and writes both German and French to perfection, knows a great deal of history and geography, speaks English very prettily, and dances very well.'[28]

Melusine and Joanne Sophie were keen to continue the development of their education, particularly dancing, which they loved. The girls enjoyed showing off their skills, to the delight of family and court at George's elaborate birthday parties, where they would dance 'till 11'. All was certainly not doom and gloom without their parents. They saw their mother nearly every day – Caroline was in the habit of coming to Kensington to bathe them and put them to bed – and their father often, and Melusine did her best to create a warm family home. Continuity was ensured with their music master, Handel. With Melusine, the Countess of Portland, Joanne Sophie and their grandfather visiting often, they perhaps did not suffer as much as George and Melusine's detractors claimed.

William Nicolson, Bishop of Carlisle, was in love with the German governess to the princesses, Madame Gemmingen. He called her Pallas for her intelligence and her inquisitiveness – he was impressed that she read the *Spectator* – and records her delight in Melusine's and George's kindness. His diary entry for 28 January 1718 reads: '[Jan] 28. M[adame] Gem[mingen]'s grateful account of the K[ing]'s goodness to her; and the D[uchess] of M[unster]'s, etc', and the entry for 4 February 1718 reports: 'G[emmingen] in new joy on the king's repeated goodness to her and the children. Esto!'[29] Her chatter to the bishop shows a household full of warmth, and the central role of Melusine.[30]

But despite George and Melusine's best efforts, the princesses naturally missed their parents, particularly as they grew older. They were often rude to Lady Portland, their governess. Liselotte, who always seemed particularly animated whenever she reported on her dysfunctional cousins in England, happily wrote that 'the poor little things sent a basket of cherries to their father, with a message that though they were not allowed to go to him, their hearts, souls and thoughts were with their dear parents always'.

The family's tragedy was compounded when the young prince died in February 1718. He was only four months old and had been deprived of a mother's constant care for most of his life. Liselotte wrote to Frederick von Harling, the Hanoverian Master of the Horse – she had known him well during her days in Osnabrück and Hanover – in great distress:

> I pity the princess [Caroline] with all my heart; on the seventeenth of this month her newborn little prince died of convulsions and cough at Kensington. The princess is said to be dreadfully distressed about this loss. In her last letter her Grace tells me that she and her husband have begged the king's forgiveness three times, but to no avail. I do not understand anything about this matter, but I am afraid that the prince shares in his mother's misfortune and therefore cannot ever be loved, and that is a hopeless situation. However, it seems to me that since the king has acknowledged this prince as his son, he should also treat him as his son; nor should he be so severe with the princess, who has never done anything against him and has always honoured, respected and indeed loved him as if he were her own father. As I see it, I do not think anything good will ever come of this, the bitterness has grown too great; yet the king would be well advised to put an end to this matter, for it only gives rise to a lot of impertinent talk and brings up ugly old stories that had much better be entirely forgotten.[31]

But despite the horror of their baby's death, Caroline and Georg August were still unable to claim back their daughters. They remained the Crown's responsibility. George allowed Caroline secret but regular visits and Joanne Sophie zu Schaumburg-Lippe went to Leicester House every day to report on the children's progress. This countess, so trusted by George and Melusine, had cared for the baby prince 'day and night' during his illness at Kensington, to make it easier for his parents to visit him. When George and Melusine went to Hanover in 1719 the king was very specific that the Prince and Princess of Wales could see the girls as often as they liked, but only in the princesses' apartments. But generous visiting rights did not make up for the fact that Georg August and Caroline had no say in their daughter's upbringing. George was very clear that the Prince and Princess of Wales could not use St James's in his absence, and that any official functions should be hosted by his granddaughters, and not by his son and daughter-in-law.

Meanwhile the political rift amongst the Whigs worsened, with Walpole and Townshend hindering the king's business, and George's Whig ministers (chief amongst them Sunderland and Stanhope, with the young and ambitious James Craggs as Secretary of the South from April 1717) frustrated. And the division within the party was not only ideological; it had much to do with personal enmity, particularly between Walpole and Stanhope. The king's ministers sought to shore up their positions with George. Naturally, given her importance to the king, the competing ministers strove to court Melusine, and evidence of this can be found in her brother Frederick William's letters of April 1717, where he claims that Sunderland hoped to marry one of her daughters.[32] He did not say which one, but it was probably young Melusine. Louise, now divorced, enjoyed her independent lifestyle and her lovers, while George did his best to shield Melusine from the rumours that surrounded her. Trudchen was still very young and she may have already told her parents of her preference for Joanne Sophie's handsome son. Sunderland's hopes however went unrealized. Young Melusine remained unmarried until 1733, despite reports of her beauty and charm, and when she did eventually marry the Earl of Chesterfield, she lived next door to her mother.

By early 1718 Melusine was in a unique position, probably the only person who had a full picture of the schemes of both the English and the German cabals, across all factions. In the spring of 1718 her brother Schulenburg observed how George's English ministers were deliberately excluding Bernstorff and Bothmer from 'secret matters', whereupon the Germans found comfort in 'seeking refuge' with Melusine, who was naturally aware of all developments through both George and his ministers.[33] Throughout the crisis Melusine kept open a channel of communication between George, Walpole and Townshend. In one instance she arranged for one of her intimates – we do not know their name – to approach Walpole on George's behalf. On another occasion she used the services of the Hanoverian major-general Alexander von Hammerstein, a member of the inner circle and a trusted confidant of George's, not least because he had saved his life at the Battle of Neerwinden in 1693. For that reason alone, together with his devoted friendship, Melusine had reason to trust him.

The reunion came about not through any inclination on the part of Georg August or his father, but through the machinations and singular might of Robert Walpole's personality. As Hatton so aptly puts it: 'Robert Walpole opposed the king and his ministry in order to demonstrate his political power in the House of Commons and force George to restore him to office and the inner cabinet.' By 1720 a rift within the royal family was no longer convenient, and he determined to bring the row to a close.

Walpole completely dominated the House of Commons. A contemporary noted that his speeches had 'as much of natural eloquence and of genius ... as had been heard by any of the audience within those walls . . . whatever he proposes seldom fails to being pass'd'.[34] Mary Cowper recorded in her diary how Walpole courted Melusine with a view to ending the rift. He used a pragmatic and willing Melusine and a reluctant Caroline to bring pressure to bear on the king and the prince – Caroline, deeply upset, felt Georg August had been bribed. In April 1720 Walpole effectively forced a reluctant Georg August to go down on his knees before his father.

A reconciliation within the family and an end, at least formally, to the split within the Whigs was equally beneficial to the ministry. In December 1719 Walpole had almost single-handedly ensured that George's Peerage Bill (an attempt to restrict the power of the king to increase the size of the House of Lords), engineered by Stanhope and Sunderland, was thrown out, to the fury of the king's English ministers. In what was widely reputed to be the most brilliant speech of his parliamentary career, he argued that the bill would 'subvert the whole constitution' by destroying the 'due balance between the three branches of the legislature'.[35] The longer Walpole stayed in opposition, the harder George would find it to pass any kind of legislation.

Walpole was tempted back to office, chiefly because he needed the money. In turn, the return to power of Walpole and Townsend was sweetened for George and his ministers by an undertaking to pay off the debt of the civil list, which stood at an astounding £600,000 at the beginning of 1720. Walpole drafted the prince's letter of apology to his father, and as arranged, George immediately agreed to see him. In his father's private closet he declared that:

> it had been a great grief to him to have been in his displeasure so long; that he was infinitely obliged to His Majesty for this permission of waiting upon him, and that he hoped the rest of his life would be such as the king would never have cause to complain of.

A visibly distressed George 'was much dismayed, pale, and could not speak to be heard but by broken sentences, and said several times, "Votre conduite, votre conduite [Your conduct, your conduct]," but the Prince said he could not hear distinctly anything but those words. The prince went after he had stayed about five minutes in the closet.'[36] Following the uncomfortable meeting, father and son, bowing to the demands of public relations, attended the premiere of Handel's *Radamisto* a week later.

It was a reconciliation of sorts, but emotionally stunted as it was, it was more than enough for Walpole. The courtiers, almost as one, breathed a deep sigh of relief. The days of attempting to please two rival courts were finally over. Mary Cowper recorded the reaction at Leicester House. She 'found the guards before the door, and the square full of coaches; the rooms full of company, everything gay and laughing; nothing but kissing and wishing of joy'.

But Caroline could not share the joy, for George refused to relinquish her children. She blamed Walpole, and spat at him: 'Mr Walpole . . . this be no jesting matter for me; you will hear of me and my complaints every day and hour, in every place, if I have not my children again.'[37] Caroline was forced to endure a life without her children's daily presence for seven years. Only after George's death was she reunited with them.

13.

A Bubble

As fishes on each other prey,
The great ones swallowing up the small,
So fares it in the Southern Sea,
The whale directors eat up all.
   – Jonathan Swift, *The South Sea Project,* 1721

Although 1720 marked the year when all was harmony once more in the family – at least superficially – it was also a year of devastating loss for Melusine. In January her youngest brother, Frederick William, died, possibly of a stroke. The newspapers reported that he went to bed well, yet died in his sleep of an 'apoplexie'. He was buried, because of his high standing with Melusine and George, at Westminster Abbey.

He was only forty years old. He and Melusine were extraordinarily close, not least because he was the only one of her siblings to live with her in London. We know from his letters to Görtz that he was clever, intuitive and observant, and one of the few the discerning George trusted implicitly. Melusine relished his company amidst the often viperous court. They even took holidays together – a newsletter of November 1718 reported that 'Baron Schulemburg with the Duchess of Munster, his sisters and his niece is returned from drinking the waters beyond the sea [probably at Bad Pyrmont] . . .'

It was also the year that Melusine's actions did much to tarnish the image of the monarchy. The summer of 1720 saw thousands impoverished and many taking their lives in despair as England suffered the greatest financial crisis in its history – the South Sea Bubble. Melusine was at its heart.

Two other figures who would play a central part in the dramatic events that would soon unfold were Robert Walpole and Charles Townshend. They had re-entered government very much the junior partners to their adversaries Stanhope and Sunderland, despite the camaraderie that seemed to prevail. In a show of political hypocrisy the old enemies were often seen laughing and joking with their arms around one another. Mary Cowper recorded that there was 'great hugging and kissing between the two old & two new Ministers' and they were observed walking 'all four with their Arms round each other to show they are now all one'.

Walpole had the post of Paymaster General, with a promise of the Treasury when a position next arose, and Townshend became Lord President of the Council. They might have continued in these secondary positions had it not been for some timely deaths and a financial catastrophe that many believed brought England to the brink of revolution. It was in large part the madness of the fever of speculation – the South Sea Bubble – that gripped England in 1720 that cemented Walpole's political dominance for the next two decades. He appeared – not entirely correctly – as the country's saviour from financial ruin, and in saving England and George's monarchy, he also saved Melusine.

We know from our own times how intoxicating financial bubbles can be, irresistible 'get rich quick' schemes that promise fabled riches. Entire populations seem to succumb to lunacy in the single-minded pursuit of wealth. As Charles Mackay puts it: 'We find whole communities suddenly fix their minds upon one object, and go mad in its pursuit; that millions of people become simultaneously impressed with one delusion, and run after it . . .'[1] Tulip Mania in the Netherlands in the seventeenth century, where a single bulb could sell for lunatic amounts, was one such madness, and John Law's Mississippi Scheme in France in 1720 was another. England's own peculiar brand of collective insanity was the South Sea Bubble. We have seen how addicted eighteenth-century Englishmen were to betting – on anything from horse racing and cockfights, to the date of resolution of conflicts and the tamer games of cards. The South Sea Scheme was just another form of gambling, but one – so its dupes were persuaded – with far better odds. Greed sucked in many, high- and low-born, men and women, politicians, clergymen, courtiers, the royal family, including the king – and Melusine.

Alexander Pope was hardly unique amongst contemporary commentators in writing about it, lamenting that:

> At length corruption, like a general flood,
> Did deluge all; and avarice creeping on,
> Spread, like a low-born mist, and hid the sun.
> Statesmen and patriots plied alike the stocks,
> Peeress and butler shared alike the box;
> And judges jobbed, and bishops bit the town.
> And mighty dukes packed cards for half-a-crown:
> Britain was sunk in lucre's sordid charms.[2]

It was the country's first – and, to date, largest – stock-market crash. Melusine was so integral to the events that brought so many to ruin and suicide, that it is hard to believe that she survived them.

The origins of the Bubble can be found in 1711, with the rather innocuous establishment of a joint-stock company, the South Sea Company. As a part of the Peace of Utrecht of 1713 with Spain, the company was granted exclusive trading rights to Spanish South America – 'the South Seas'. The Company had been formed out of the imagination of the Tory Robert Harley to offset the power of the Whiggish Bank of England. It was fundamentally a finance company and by 1714 it had acquired absolute respectability.

The heart of the operation was South Sea House, in the City, at the corner of Bishopsgate and Threadneedle Street. The directors had given Queen Anne substantial shares, which became George's property when he succeeded her. It was Georg August who took over the governorship of the company in 1714, with George only taking the position in 1718 after the breach between father and son. The Duchess of Ormond wrote pointedly to Jonathan Swift: 'You remember how the South Sea was said to be Lord Oxford's brat, now the King has adopted it and called it his beloved child.'[3]

It was, in Hatton's words, 'one of the three pillars, with the Bank of England and the East India Company, of the credit structure of Britain'. But in reality the company was trading in futures, everything nebulous and nothing tangible, betting on finding gold and establishing trade in the New World.

Since Columbus's 'discovery' of America in the fifteenth century, that continent had become linked in the minds of Europeans with an abundance of riches as they saw gold and jewels travelling back to the Old World. Even the most cautious of early eighteenth-century speculators believed they could grab a share of the wealth, and astonishing numbers bought into the scheme. In return for their monopoly, the South Sea Company undertook, in April 1720, to pay off a large portion of the national debt – £31 million – which proved irresistible to the ministry, not least because the company agreed to charge only a modest interest rate of 5 per cent. John Aislabie, the Chancellor of the Exchequer, had such confidence in the scheme that he guaranteed that the national debt would be paid off within twenty-five years.

The company did not deal only in the promise of riches in gold. It also dealt in human traffic, and transported Africans to the Americas through the notorious 'middle passage', a route westwards across the Atlantic that claimed the lives of thousands of people. As early as 1712 Queen Anne told parliament: 'I have insisted and obtained that the *asiento* or contract for furnishing the Spanish West Indies with negroes shall be made with us for thirty years.'[4] The South Sea Company undertook to deliver 4,800 slaves every year for thirty years. The historian Hugh Thomas describes the company's complicity:

The South Sea Company agreed to buy in Africa the slaves required from the old RAC [Royal Africa Company]; take them to Jamaica, where the weakest, the 'refuse' slaves, would be eliminated (left to die uncared for on the dock, in many cases); and then carry the prime slaves to Spanish markets.

The ministers had been influenced by contemporary events in France, by the huge and similar success of John Law's Mississippi Scheme. As Charles Mackay eloquently put it:

> It was while Law's plan was at its greatest height of popularity, while people were crowding in thousands to the Rue Quincampoix, and ruining themselves with frantic eagerness, that the South-Sea directors laid before parliament their famous plan for paying off the national debt . . . The English commenced their career of extravagance somewhat later than the French; but as soon as the delirium seized upon them, they were determined not to be outdone . . .[5]

To obtain their monopoly the Company had bribed heavily, encouraged by James Craggs, Secretary of State for the South. Melusine and Sophia Charlotte, both perceived by the Company's directors to be highly influential with the king, each received £15,000 worth of stock, for which £120 would be paid for each point the stock price rose above £154. Contemporaries believed that Craggs was Sophia Charlotte's lover, and if it is true, this may be why she received the stock. She had not nearly as much influence with George as Melusine, but Craggs may have exaggerated to get her a cash gift. Young Melusine and Trudchen received £5,000 each, and George was elected governor of the Company in 1718. Contemporaries believed that he too had received a cash bribe, but his biographer, Ragnhild Hatton, has disproved this. The politicians also received enormous gifts of stock. Stanhope got £60,000,

Sunderland £50,000, James Craggs the elder, the Postmaster
General and father of James Craggs, £30,000, and Aislabie £20,000.

The extravagance of the heady days of early summer before the
Bubble burst was reflected in an especially profligate London
season. Ridiculous amounts of money were spent; the governors of
the South Sea Company were socially the most sought-after guests
in London, more so than the king's ministers. One director was
reputed to have made £3 million in three months and Georg
August presented another director, said to be worth half a million,
with a diamond ring.[6] And the South Sea was the major topic of
conversation amongst the cognoscenti. At the end of March
Oxford's daughter Abigail, Countess of Kinnoull, wrote to her
father: 'The town [London] is quite mad about the South Sea . . .
one can hear nothing else talked of . . . It is very unfashionable not
to be in the South Sea.'[7] Edward Harley junior reported to his sister:
'I find that there are few in London that mind anything but the
rising and falling of the stocks, upon which all the news and talk of
the town turns, so that unless I bring South Sea, African Bank, cert.
per cent., par, etc, and such stuff into my letter I shall neither be
fashionable nor fill it up . . .'[8]

In July, at the height of the craze, Craggs wrote to Stanhope of
the mania that had overtaken everyday life: 'It is impossible to tell
you, what a rage prevails here for South Sea subscriptions at any
price. The crowd of those that possess the redeemable annuitys is
so great, that the bank, who are obliged to take them in, has been
forced to set tables with clerks in the streets.'[9]

The ubiquitous lavishness was also reflected at court. George's
birthday party that year was the most fabulous to date. Melusine
spent a fortune on a 'hundred dozen' bottles of claret. Mary
Cowper claimed the crowd was the largest she had ever seen at a
royal birthday celebration, which took place at St James's at the end
of May. Melusine delivered the *coup de grâce* by appearing in a dress

studded with jewels valued at £5,000 and her extravagance was reported in the newspapers.[10]

The Reverend Laurence Eusden read his congratulatory ode to the king, rejoicing in the riches the South Seas had brought:

> Hence (for in his peculiar reign were laid
> Schemes, that produc'd the sure increase of trade)
> Shall generations, yet unborn, be told,
> Who gifted them with silver mines and gold;
> Who gave them all the commerce of the Main,
> And made South Seas send home the wealth of Spain.[11]

Few had any idea that they were just days away from ruin.

When Melusine and George went to Hanover for their summer holiday they left the management of their stock in John Aislabie's hands – after all, who better than the Chancellor of the Exchequer? The holiday was desperately needed. Melusine had been very ill in April. One newspaper reported: 'The Duchess of Kendal has been so ill for this week past, that her life was once thought to be in danger . . .'[12] Furthermore George's granddaughter Princess Anne had contracted smallpox in the same month. It had been a stressful time for the family and they looked forward to leaving for Hanover. Melusine was particularly pleased that Johann Matthias was to join them, and in July *The Weekly Packet* reported: 'The King of Great Britain set out for Pyrmont on the 10th instant; [accompanied by] . . . the Duchess of Kendal, Lieutenant-General Schulenburg, with his Lady; but none of the ministers are gone thither, because his Majesty hath no mind to be troubled with matters of state, while he is drinking the waters . . .'

But while Melusine and George embarked for Germany, the Bubble began to deflate. As the South Sea furore had swelled in Britain during the early summer, the similar bubble in France –

John Law's Mississippi bubble – had burst in May. Liselotte wrote to Caroline from St Cloud on 31 May 1720: 'Law, whom people here have worshipped like a god, had to be removed from his post by my son. It is necessary to guard him, for his life is not safe, and the man is terribly frightened.' In Britain the stock reached its peak at the end of June, when stock was valued at just over £1,000, and then it gradually began to come down. But its fall was so slow at first that few seemed to notice.

Melusine and George, buoyed by the Bubble delirium and the recovery of Princess Anne, made a merry party in Hanover that summer. Young Sophia Dorothea and her husband joined them at Ghörde, as did George's brother Ernst-August (he had been prince-bishop of Osnabrück since the death of the Catholic incumbent Charles Joseph of Lorraine in 1715 and resided in its palace) and his grandson Frederick, who had remained behind in Hanover in 1714. At least one of Melusine's sisters came too, and the girls of course were there. Trudchen's courtship with Joanne Sophie's son continued during the heady sunny days at the family's holiday home. After hunting at Ghörde, the party went to Herrenhausen for balls, plays and celebrations. But the happy family holiday was a brief hiatus before catastrophe broke their idyll.

Stanhope and Sunderland joined them later in the summer. Sunderland arrived in early September but amazingly, considering that he was First Lord of the Treasury, with a large financial stake in the South Sea Company, he failed to communicate to George or to Melusine the looming crisis; for by the time he arrived at Herrenhausen, the stock had sunk alarmingly from £775 to £500. The bankruptcy listings in the *London Gazette* of mid-August were through the roof and people began to lose their fortunes. By the end of September the stock had fallen to a dismal £135.

The historian of the South Sea Bubble, John Carswell, is incredulous at Sunderland's failure to inform the king:

His sublime indifference and exuberant confidence cannot be excused, like the King's, by lack of information. He was receiving regular reports and even his wife . . . wrote anxiously about the family investments asking if there was anything she ought to do. 'The stock will mend', he assured her, 'the stock will rise again' . . .[13]

So he said nothing.

And neither did George's Regency Council in London, who only notified the king of 'the very extraordinary case which hath happened in the last fortnight' on 21 September. They asked George to set out for London straight away. But it was too late. Even had he left immediately, it was impossible that he could arrive in London before the end of October, so large was his household and so feckless the winds demanded for a successful crossing.

George and Stanhope, absorbed in foreign policy, failed to appreciate the gravity of the looming crisis and asked the ministers in London to 'Give us a week to settle the most urgent matters . . .' despite Bothmer's pleas that unless the king return, the English might revolt.[14]

Meanwhile Melusine, keeping an eye on George's interests as well as on her own, trusted Aislabie to sell their stock at the most advantageous price possible. But the Chancellor, wishing not to antagonize the king and his mistress, was overly cautious, to Melusine's annoyance. She wrote him a barbed letter from Herrenhausen on 27 September. She was incensed that he had wasted time in writing to Hanover for further instructions, and reminded him that he had been entrusted to act on his own initiative. She told him to stop wasting time and 'to sell or buy as you would think it the most profitable and convenient . . . if the best occasion is missed you will be pleased to make use of those that shall offer themselves for the future without expecting any new advices'. She went on to chide him with the quietly devastating words:

> I and my two nieces give you many thanks for what you have been pleased to subscribe and pay on our account at the third subscription. If we had been present in England, we would not have failed to sell them out, when they were at such an advantageous Price, and I wish you had been so kind as to do it for us, the more when you judged and saw they was [*sic*] not to rise but fall as they have done. I am sorry our Absence made us miss that good Opportunity; and I hope you will be so kind as to take a little Care of our Interest if it is not to[o] great a disadvantage in your other Affairs.[15]

But Melusine's reprimand reached England too late, at the end of September. Aislabie did not sell the stock, as he felt he could not do so 'without increasing the public clamour upon myself, or without prejudice to the king's affairs'.[16] Contrary to public opinion, and despite her detractors' claims that she made a fortune out of the Bubble, Melusine and George actually made substantial losses with the crash. George believed that through Aislabie's inertia he had lost £35,704. But Melusine, ever discreet, did not even hint at her financial fears to Johann Matthias, saying that she was 'well content' with what she had, considering she had thought at one stage that she would lose everything.[17]

Subsidiary bubbles which had formed on the back of the success of the South Sea began to deflate at the same time. Some of the companies were legitimate; most were not. Amazingly, such was the mania for financial speculation, a company that had established itself in the summer of 1720 'for carrying on an undertaking of great advantage, but nobody to know what it is' attracted numerous investors.[18] Mackay tells us that according to this company's prospectus:

the required capital was half a million, in five thousand shares of 100 pounds each, deposit 2 pounds per share. Each subscriber, paying his [or her] deposit, was entitled to condescend to inform [the buyers] at that time, but promised that in a month full particulars should be duly announced, and a call made for the remaining 98 pounds of the subscription. Next morning, at nine o'clock, this great man opened an office in Cornhill. Crowds of people beset his door, and when he shut up at three o'clock, he found that no less than one thousand shares had been subscribed for, and the deposits paid. He was thus, in five hours, the winner of 2000 pounds. He was philosophical enough to be contented with his venture, and set off the same evening for the Continent. He was never heard of again.[19]

The real beneficiaries of the summer of madness of 1720 were characters such as this.

In France the economic devastation was compounded by an outbreak of plague in Marseille, adding to the general panic throughout France. And eighteen months later, when many were still left shattered after the crisis both in France and England, Liselotte wrote to von Harling: 'Monsieur Law will probably leave for Holland, but I do not believe that he will be permitted to go to England, because his name is mud there.' Melusine and George had departed for Hanover while England was riding on an economic high, but they came back to desolation and chaos.

Swift parodied the misery of those suffering financial chaos at Garraway's coffee house, which became 'on Garraway's cliffs', as 'A savage race by shipwrecks fed'.[20] Families lost fortunes, and William Windham noted: 'You can't imagine the number of families undone . . . many a £100,000 man not worth a groat, and it grieves me to think of some of them.'[21] In November 1720 William Pulteney wrote to his son Daniel: 'I assure you, that I have done nothing, nor thought of nothing, for these last two months, but South Sea stock, and yet I am not myself any great sufferer by it; but so many of my acquaintance are ruined and undone, that I am under as much anxiety and uneasiness of mind, as if I was so myself.' And Daniel in turn received a letter lamenting that: 'There are many and considerable familys reduced by extravagant bargains . . . The dukes of Wharton and Bolton are great sufferers; and indeed even the South Sea directors included, hardly one in 20 are gainers.'[22]

For many families the distress of bankruptcy through the failure of the scheme, and the cries for scapegoats, were enough to raise the spectre of revolution. In September one Thomas Broderick wrote to his friend Middleton: 'Thousands of families will be reduced to beggary, what the consequences of that will bee, time must shew . . . The consternation is inexpressible, the rage beyond expression, and the case so desperate that I doe nott see any plan or scheme . . . for averting the blow, soe that I can't pretend to guese att what is next to be done.'[23]

George and Melusine stayed calm on their return, and united with Walpole to brave it out. A Select Committee was formed to establish and assign blame. But when Robert Knight, the Treasurer of the South Sea Company, appeared before the Committee on 21 January, he revealed the extent of the bribes with which the Company had bought the good will of the great and the good. He further disclosed that he had 'cooked the books' by entering false names and fabricated amounts. Knight, charming and discreet, had wooed the glitterati during the heady days before the Bubble burst, and a contemporary recorded that: 'Whigs and Tories made their court to Robert Knight . . . with more assiduity and complacence than we see at the levees of Prime Ministers.'[24] When Knight emphatically refused to give the names of those the Company had bribed, the Committee, frustrated, agreed to adjourn for the weekend. Melusine shuddered; she knew she would be on the list.

The events that followed were astonishing and read like a crime caper. Knight fled the country to Calais, taking his list of names with him. There he was met by the son of John Law, the Mississippi bubble swindler. Carswell speculates, intriguingly, that 'some further great scheme in partnership was being contemplated' and we can only wonder at what the brains behind two of the greatest European financial swindles in history would have devised together had such a plan materialized.

Contemporaries blamed Melusine for his flight, and even speculated that she gave him the use of one of her properties in Germany, but these claims were untrue. She was, as ever, parodied in the press. The Brabant Screen, a satirical print drawn in the wake of the crisis, puts the blame squarely on Melusine. It shows her hiding behind a screen in a richly decorated and beautifully opulent room – she was certainly not suffering financially, as so many thousands were! – handing over money to Knight. The Company's treasurer stands expectantly, riding-whip in hand, poised to escape into exile. The table is inscribed with the words: 'Patience and Time and Money set everything to rights'.

Knight had obviously been planning his flight for some time, and had moved sizeable assets out of the country in preparation. But once he had gone, Melusine was determined that he would never be called to testify again before the Committee. It was impossible that he could return to England without implicating her and George in the Bubble. Panicked calls for a return of the Pretender, the threat of revolution, and thousands on the streets decrying the loss of their fortunes all unnerved her. Parliament and country demanded a reckoning. Lord Molesworth went so far as to demand the reinstatement for the South Sea directors of the ancient Roman punishment for parricide – to be sewn into a sack with a monkey and a snake and drowned, in this case in the Thames and not the Tiber.[25]

Meanwhile John Blunt, one of the founders of the South Sea Company, had been taken into custody on 23 January. When the Committee reconvened after the weekend and Knight's flight was established, Blunt, alarmingly, began to tell all. He made known the full extent of the bribe list, probably believing that the Commons Committee would give him a lesser punishment if he cooperated. He revealed that Knight had kept two books of accounts; he had taken the real book, 'the green book', with him into exile. This green book held the true names of those who had received bribes, whereas the false book listed pseudonyms. He stunningly revealed that: 'More than £1 million had been spent on bribes . . . Blunt could not remember all the recipients; but certainly he said, he had followed the instructions of Craggs the younger by paying the Duchess of Kendal £10,000 in return for her "good offices" in bending the King's ear when the Company launches its scheme . . .'[26] Carswell notes:

> he named Aislabie, Postmaster Craggs, Sunderland, Charles Stanhope [the minister James Stanhope's cousin], the Duchess of Kendal, and Countess von Platen [Sophia Charlotte] . . . 'What!' exclaimed the bewildered Deputy Governor [Charles Joye, Deputy Governor of the South Sea Company]. 'Royal ladies and all?' Blunt was at his sanctimonious best. 'Yes', he replied; 'the examination is very strict and nothing but the whole truth will do.'[27]

In February the crisis took a turn for the worse for Melusine, amongst others. The Tory Edward Harley rather gleefully reported to his father the Earl of Oxford:

This day Mr Brodrick, chairman of the Secret [Select] Committee, made his report, which took up four hours in the reading at the bar and the table. It discloses the greatest scene of corruption and villainy that ever was plotted in any civilized nation, wherein many members of both houses are concerned, the principal Ministers of State are named, and several ladies at court, who have had large stakes in this iniquity . . .[28]

It was imperative that Knight should never return, and George asked Melusine to intervene. She made it clear to the French diplomat Destouches that while parliament was baying to have Knight extradited, he should tell his master the Regent to ignore them; the king desired his government's official requests for Knight's return to be refused.[29]

But the caper continued as Knight unwittingly removed himself from the Regent's clandestine protection. The House of Commons placed a bounty of £2,000 on Knight's return and when he turned up in Brussels the British chargé d'affaires arranged for the issue of an Imperial arrest warrant. (Brussels was under the jurisdiction of the Emperor.) Knight, warned of his imminent arrest, fled to Liège, outside of Imperial authority. However, he was arrested before he arrived and imprisoned in Antwerp, firmly under the Emperor's control.

In March a debate in the House of Lords accused Melusine, Sophia Charlotte, Bernstorff and Bothmer of accepting bribes from the South Sea Company. Lord Guildford leapt to the defence of Melusine and Sophia Charlotte, saying: 'The ladies had had the right to receive such favours', although he did not speak up for George's Germans, specifically Bernstorff and Bothmer.

Now Melusine summoned her influence with the Emperor and her friendship with the Empress to block Knight's extradition. Events descended into farce. The Commons' demands for his return reached a crescendo when 300 MPs descended on St James's Palace in March, in an attempt to persuade George to press harder with the Emperor. (As with the Regent in France, behind the scenes Melusine was persuading Imperial diplomats of George's desire that Knight should be kept imprisoned in Antwerp.) George however assured the MPs: 'I am very well pleased that the instances which I have made for obtaining the delivering up of Mr Knight have given you satisfaction . . . I shall continue to employ my utmost endeavours for obtaining what you desire, and hope they will prove effectual.'[30]

But the Emperor, heeding Melusine and George, refused to comply, and in an elaborate subterfuge Knight was eventually allowed to escape from the Antwerp Citadel where he was being held, to France, on George's express orders. In September 1721 the British envoy, William Leathes, wrote to the Imperial envoy: 'he [George] is pleased to express the wish that Your Excellency should order the Governor of the Antwerp Citadel to enlarge Knight from confinement, allowing him not only to have liberty to walk on the Citadel, but to escape.'[31]

Knight did not suffer in exile. He bought a comfortable house in Paris, a country estate, and thrived financially as a banker. But he was homesick. In 1730 Lady Irwine, who met him in Paris, wrote:

Mr Knight lives always here, and is quite metaporphised [sic] into a fine gentleman; from being a man of business he is now become a gallant home, which character just as ill becomes him as a suit of embroidery would a country bumpkin. He keeps a great table, has always a vast deal of company, and being both generous and rich, is much visited and esteemed; but amidst all these caresses and plenty, he . . . is perfectly unhappy he can't breathe the air of dear England.[32]

Knight was only allowed to return in 1742, after Walpole's fall from power.

While Melusine had managed to keep scandal away from George's intimate circle, sacrifices had to be made to satisfy MPs and the public. The faithful Aislabie was one such casualty, victimized for his role in pushing the scheme through. He was accused of the 'most notorious, dangerous, and infamous corruption',[33] imprisoned in the Tower and forced to relinquish all funds and property he had acquired since 1718.

Aislabie in fact received better treatment than others who were found guilty, who were obliged to surrender everything they had made since 1716, and not, as in Aislabie's case, since 1718. Some historians believe that he received favourable treatment because the investments he made in the South Sea Company in his own name were actually made on behalf of various members of the royal family – George effectively gave him as lenient a sentence as possible to keep him quiet. For his part, Aislabie wrote in gratitude to Walpole in February 1722: 'I am extremely sensible of your generosity and am more ashamed of my own follies and mistakes, than any severe treatment I might deserve at your hands could make me. Since you have been so good to promise to forget what is past, I shall not put you in mind of it any further, than to return my most hearty thanks.'[34]

Charles Stanhope, the cousin of George's favourite English minister James Stanhope, was also accused. Stanhope was dismayed at the smearing of his cousin's name. He saw the ruin of all he had achieved for George with his careful diplomacy in Europe. He was so humiliated at the baying of the Lords, he fainted in the House. He died three days later. George was deeply affected by his death. He visited Stanhope's widow and 'assured her that next to her, he was the person who had suffered the greatest loss in being deprived of a good servant and good friend, that there was nothing she could ask he would not do for her and her children'. George arranged for a pension of £3,000 a year for her.[35] He also used his influence to have cousin Charles acquitted, although the young man was compelled to resign his junior position at the treasury.

Yet another ministerial death, that of James Craggs of smallpox only days after James Stanhope's, further depleted a shocked government. It was now essential that Sunderland, although accused, must survive or else the government would fall. He was saved, in a move of political expediency, by his old enemy Robert Walpole. The rash of casualties continued; James Craggs the elder chose to take his own life soon after his son's death to avoid the scandal – his guilt was known to all.[36]

Thomas Harley, hostile to the ministry, reported everything to the Earl of Oxford:

London: the deaths of Stanhope and Craggs have much perplexed Lord Sunderland. Walpole is to have the Treasury and choose his own creatures. And Lord Townshend will have Methuen in Craggs' place . . . The report of the secret committee made yesterday lays open Lord Sunderland for taking 40,000 l. Munster's nieces 5,000 l. each. Aislabie a vast deal in several shapes, Charles Stanhope 50,000 l . . . Walpole undertakes to screen Sunderland, and the German ladies, and to let Aislabie and the rest take their chance.[37]

He continued next day: 'The women are named, Aislabie very deep; never was such a group of felons ever got together.'[38]

As Harley so aptly put it, Walpole managed to 'screen' Melusine. Her predicament passed. Walpole was portrayed as the redeemer of the nation by many contemporaries and by his first biographer, Coxe. But his scheme to rescue the economy by merging part of it with the Bank of England never passed the House of Commons, and in fact an economy with strong underpinnings reasserted itself by the middle of the year, independent of his efforts. By the end of March the crisis was over; people and Commons had had their fill of blood. Walpole's course of remaining calm and shielding George, Melusine and Sophia Charlotte, as well as his sheer luck, both in not being associated with the passing of the original scheme and failing to purchase South Sea shares on the third subscription – his more financially cautious banker had not allowed him to – meant he was in the clear and free from scandal.

But he was not in fact unscathed. It is likely that he suffered huge losses, not least through his loans of £27,000 to Sir Caesar Child and Lord Hillsborough. They were financially ravaged by the Bubble and could not repay.

The next two decades would belong to Walpole politically. After Sunderland's death in 1722 he was very much in the ascendancy. By the end of 1722 he was beginning to be thought of as the first minister, and known by the nickname 'The Great Man'. George and Melusine would work closely with him until the end of George's reign in 1727.

14.

Venality

Money was with her [Melusine] the principal and prevailing consideration, and he [Robert Walpole] was often heard to say, she was so venal a creature, that she would have sold the king's honour for a shilling to the best bidder.
– William Coxe in his editorial reports on Reverend Etough's minutes of a conversation with Sir Robert Walpole[1]

The Bubble debacle did not leave Melusine as rich as she had hoped. As she grew older, she grew more and more anxious about money. Her pension from George was £7,500 per annum. She had £10,000 in Bank of England stock, and an estate in Holstein, which she had purchased in 1720.[2] But still she believed herself poor. She had too many dependents not to be driven in large part by money, and events between 1722 and 1725, perhaps unfairly, put the seal on her reputation for venality.

To make up for her losses with the Bubble, in 1722 George granted her the patent to produce copper coinage in Ireland. Her disposal of the rights to an ironmaster, William Wood, for a profit of £10,000, led to one of the biggest scandals of George's reign.

Melusine's actions were not illegal (although they were perhaps immoral). Sunderland had arranged for her to receive the patent and she was perfectly within her rights to sell it, following a centuries-old tradition in using her position at court to bolster her income. And equally she was not legally obliged to screen whom she sold it to. William Wood purchased the rights in July 1722, and began to mint the coins in London in January 1723. The coins were well made, but the brass content was low. Furthermore the Irish were up in arms because they were forced to accept English coins, and they resented the tax of between £6,000 and £7,000 that the measure entailed.

The Irish parliament was enraged, as was Jonathan Swift, who believed the coins to be inferior. In his role as dean of St Patrick's Cathedral, Dublin, he fanned the flames with his tuppenny pamphlets, which he wrote under the pseudonym M. B. Drapier. They were produced in their thousands and amongst the charges of bribery, corruption and the destabilization of the Irish economy levelled at William Wood, they implicitly attacked Walpole's government and blamed Melusine.

In October 1723 Walpole lamented Lord Carteret's attacks on himself and Melusine in parliament.[3] He complained to Townshend, who was with the king and Melusine in Hanover, that 'Lord Carteret . . . flings dirt upon me, who passed the patent, and makes somebody [Melusine] uneasy, for whose sake it was done . . .'[4]

And in another letter written to Townshend later in the month, Walpole justified and explained the careful process behind the production of the coins:

> Sir Isaac [Newton – Master of the Mint] was consulted in every step in passing the patent, that was to assay, try, and prove the finesse and goodness of the copper, and the weight of the coin, Sir Isaac Newton was himself made the first controller; but at his request Mr Barton, his nephew, was made the controller in his room. Upon the first apprehension of this trouble, the controller was directed to try and prove the coin; and he has reported, that it answered in all respects; this report of the controller's was, by order of the treasury, transmitted to Ireland; and I understand, was laid before the parliament of Ireland, but not at all regarded . . .[5]

But Swift's incendiary pamphlets and uproar in Ireland led to such an outcry that Walpole's ministry teetered. Melusine was desperately embarrassed and Wood's patent was finally withdrawn in August 1725. She was mortified not only because it placed George's government in jeopardy and led to uprisings in Ireland, but because of her vicious parodying in the penny press. Swift did not go so far as to fulminate against her in his *Drapier's Letters*, but he did lampoon her for her role in the sorry Wood affair on at least

two other occasions. In a poem of 1724, 'Prometheus: On Wood
the Patentee's Irish Halfpence', she is shown as Venus, one of the
pantheon of Roman gods and goddesses betraying a nation:

> There is a chain let down from Jove,
> But fasten'd to his throne above,
> So strong that from the lower end,
> They say all human things depend.
> This chain, as ancient poets hold,
> When Jove was young, was made of gold,
> Prometheus once this chain purloin'd,
> Dissolved, and into money coin'd;
> Then whips me on a chain of brass;
> Venus was bribed to let it pass.

And in another of 1725, 'A Simile on our Want of Silver, and the
Only Way to Remedy it', he writes:

> When late a feminine magician [Melusine],
> Join'd with a brazen politician,
> Exposed, to blind the nation's eyes,
> A parchment of prodigious size . . .

It is unfair to blame Melusine for the ensuing unrest in Ireland, but
elements of the pious chattering classes blamed her greed at least
in part for the uprisings. Worse was to come. Melusine's role in the
partial rehabilitation of Henry St John, Viscount Bolingbroke,
sealed her reputation for avarice with her contemporaries and with
historians up until the latter part of the twentieth century.

The hugely able and charismatic Bolingbroke had been Queen
Anne's Secretary for the North. After George's accession and the
ensuing Jacobite rebellions he fled to France, where he was

welcomed by the Pretender. But from as early as 1716 Bolingbroke attempted to obtain a pardon and re-entry into British political society through Lord Stair, the British ambassador to France. In a series of letters to Tory friends, he renounced the Pretender and attempted to justify his actions during the rebellions. This had little effect however, and neither did sporadic negotiations for his return with various Whig ministers.

In 1719, shortly after the death of his first wife Frances Winch-combe, whom he treated appallingly – a contemporary portrait by Michael Dahl shows a haunted young woman – Bolingbroke married Marie-Claire de Marcilly, marquise de Villette. She was the niece of Louis XIV's mistress and morganatic wife, Madame de Maintenon. It was through Marie-Claire's courtship of Melusine that Bolingbroke managed to come back to England. Marie-Claire travelled to the country specifically to plead for her husband. She spent a great deal of time in Melusine's company, charming her and winning her over to Bolingbroke's cause.

Bolingbroke was pardoned in May 1723, prompting a flurry of letters between him and Townshend. He promised: 'if my restitution can be completed, your lordship may have more useful friends and servants; a more faithful one you cannot have, than I shall endeavour to approve myself . . .' Within this letter to Townshend he included one to the king and one to Melusine, obviously perceiving them to be of equal importance in aiding him.[6] Melusine replied, through Townshend: 'to return your lordship very many thanks for your letter to her, with assurances of her grace's particular regard for your lordship, and the success of your affairs . . .'[7] Bolingbroke must have been hopeful of success with Melusine's assurances.

But he was desperately disappointed that nothing further happened. He was not readmitted to the House of Lords, his estates were not returned and he did not regain his title.

Melusine became very ill in the summer of 1724, beginning a series of ailments that would last for the rest of her life. In June Joanne Sophie wrote to her friend, Sophie Catharine of Münchhausen:

> our Duchess de Kendal became very unwell directly after the King's birthday and was brought sick to Kensington. She had a high fever with a heavy ache in the chest which seemed very dangerous at the beginning. The fever, however, thank the Lord, has left her and she has recovered so much that she left her bed the day before yesterday – and I was reassured today that she is recovering well. I thank God with all my heart for that, as we really are in need of this lovely princess [Fürstin] whose only goal it is to do good for everyone and to take special care of her loved ones.[8]

She recovered, and by May 1725 was able to intercede for Bolingbroke again. His situation changed and the king was persuaded that he could own and inherit property in England once more, although he remained without his seat in the House of Lords and his title. Contemporaries were convinced that George had arrived at this decision because Bolingbroke had bribed Melusine with the incredible sum of £11,000 – roughly one and a half million pounds in today's money.

Bolingbroke rightly blamed Walpole for his only partial restitution; Walpole was concerned that Bolingbroke would stir up trouble and advised George against giving him all he asked. What, then, of the bribe? Did Melusine really receive it, or was the speculation and gossip-mongering unfounded?

Fabrice, although he mentions other money presents to Melusine, does not mention Bolingbroke's gift. This does not mean that it was not made, only that no sources have been found. Coxe was convinced of it and quotes Reverend Henry Etough, Robert

Walpole's chaplain and the author of an early biography of the minister. Etough's minutes of a conversation with Walpole record:

> [Bolingbroke] gained the duchess of Kendal by a present of £11,000 and obtained a promise to use her influence over the king for the purpose of forwarding his complete restoration. Harcourt, with her co-operation, seems principally to have managed this delicate business; and as at this period Townshend was reconciled to Melusine, it was probably owing to her interest that he was induced to move the king to grant a pardon to Bolingbroke . . .[9]

Others thought that young Melusine was involved, and handled the gift on her mother's behalf. A nineteenth-century historian, Thomas Macknight, argued: 'The money was paid through William Chetwynd to Lady Walsingham, the niece of the duchess, who had assuredly an itching palm.' He cited Coxe's examination of the Walpole correspondence.[10]

Another strange rumour persisted after George's death, told by Horace Walpole. He reported that Bolingbroke was convinced George meant to replace Walpole, whom he trusted implicitly, with Bolingbroke, who had served the Pretender so closely. It was Melusine, he argued, who brought about the private meeting between rehabilitated traitor and monarch.

According to Coxe: 'Not long before his [Walpole's] death he said to his son, "Horace, when I am gone, you will find many curious papers in the drawer of this table," and mentioned, among others, the memorial which had been drawn up by Bolingbroke, and presented by the duchess of Kendal to the king . . .'[11]

Bolingbroke was erroneously convinced that George was ready to sack Walpole and make him prime minister. He believed he had such influence with Melusine that she would move heaven and earth to make it happen. Coxe reproduced Etough's intriguing report of a conversation with Walpole where he totally dismissed Bolingbroke's claims. It makes for fascinating reading:

I had an opportunity for full conversation with Sir Robert Walpole. I mentioned then to him, Bolingbroke's reports, of his often attending the late king at supper, and of his interest being so prevailing, that it was with the utmost importunity and address, he persuaded the king to defer the making him prime minister, till he returned from Hanover. He condescended to give me this explanation. He said lying was so natural to St. John [Bolingbroke], that it was impossible for him to keep within the bounds of truth. He might truly boast of his prospects, for they were very great; though things were not so fixed and near as he pretended. He had the entire interest of the duchess of Kendal, and having this, what consequences time would probably have produced, required no explanation. St. John, he averred, had only been once with the king, which was owing to his importunity.

The king had given Sir Robert a memorial [memo] of St. John's [Bolingbroke], consisting of three sheets of paper. He observed the cover was not sealed, and therefore the deliverer of it must certainly know from whence it came, and perhaps the contents. On the two Turks disclaiming all knowledge of the affair, he went to the duchess of Kendal, who owned the part she had acted . . . St. John, in this address, had desired an audience, and undertook, if admitted, to demonstrate the kingdom must shortly be ruined, if Sir Robert Walpole continued prime minister. Sir Robert Walpole himself, humbly and earnestly desired he might be admitted; he told the king, if this was not done, the clamour would be, that he kept him to himself, and would allow none to come near him, to tell the truth. This was repeated to the duchess, who promised her interest with the king.

When Sir Robert next attended her grace, she said the king was averse to seeing St. John, taking for granted, it must make you uneasy. He replied, he could not be easy till St. John was admitted. This was so much pressed, that he was soon after gratified with an audience. Lord Lechmere happened to come upon business at the same time, he enquired who was in the closet; he heard Walpole was also at court: he then imagined him to be sole director. Fully possessed with this conceit, he went in to the king. He began with reviling Walpole, as not being contented with doing mischief himself, but introducing one who was, if possible, much worse; and thus he departed, without offering the papers to be signed, which he brought as chancellor of the duchy. This diverted the king extremely, who made it the subject of conversation, when sir Robert waited on him; he slightly mentioned St. John's demonstrations, and called them bagatelles.

I have been thus minute and exact, because St. John and his friends have made the thing surer and more immediate, than can be justified from reality. On the other side, some of the great man's nearest relations and friends have deemed it as groundless, and have thought fit to represent him as under no sort of apprehension from his rival. I will therefore repeat what he said several times, and particularly at the end of the conversation, which was nearly in these words. 'As he had the duchess entirely on his side, I need not add, what must or might in time have been the consequence. He informed me the same day, that the bill in favour of St. John, is wholly to be ascribed to the influence of the duchess. Either the present Viscount Chetwind, or his brother William, conveyed eleven thousand pounds from St. John's lady to lady Walsingham, the duchess's niece.'[12]

It is highly unlikely that George would ever have admitted Bolingbroke into his ministry, and certainly not as his chief minister. George never forgot a misdemeanour and he could not forgive Bolingbroke, however talented and useful he might have been to him, for having made contact with the Pretender in 1714, despite his subsequent rehabilitation. George would have been unable to trust him. Furthermore he and Walpole worked well together; despite their differences, George had admired him as a politician since he came to the throne in 1714. He was well aware of Walpole's command of the House of Commons and the expediency of working with him.

Moreover Bolingbroke was a fantasist, although in his defence he may have been misled by Melusine. It is quite conceivable that when the bribe was offered, she accepted it with the intention of doing only a minimal amount for him. She may have felt that she had done her duty by Bolingbroke by arranging a meeting for him with George, and knowing George's favourable feelings towards Walpole, which she shared, did not push it further.

Bolingbroke was bitter for the rest of his life, and directed his animosity towards Walpole in the opposition newspaper, *The Craftsman*. But he continued to believe that had it not been for Walpole's intercession, he would have been George's chief adviser because of Melusine's good offices. In a rather unhinged letter of vitriol directed towards Walpole, he wrote to Sir William Wyndham in 1736:

> ... Though the late king durst not support me openly against his ministers, he would have plotted with me against them, and we should have served him, our country, and ourselves, by demolishing that power that is become tyranny in the paws of the greatest bear, and the greatest jackanapes upon earth ... I know not whether you may judge as despondingly as I do, concerning the present state of our constitution. But be pleased to dwell in your thoughts one moment on these short and obvious reflexions. The corruption now employed is at least as dangerous as the prerogative formerly employed ...[13]

15.

Diplomacy

The good duchess . . . [our] fast friend
– Townshend to Walpole on their friendship with Melusine

With the crisis of the South Sea Bubble behind her and the familial breach healed, Melusine was at the height of her influence. She had become the main conduit to George, and she would remain so from 1722 until his death in 1727. As Beattie explains:

> After the establishment of the Walpole ministry she looms large in the correspondence of Townshend, Newcastle [Secretary for the South from 1724] and Walpole. She became an invaluable intermediary for them with the king, and though her assistance does not of course explain Walpole's success, her management of George I and her help in securing the closet undoubtedly helped to establish and maintain Walpole's strong and stable administration . . .[1]

The French ambassador, Count Broglio, acknowledged her huge importance in his missives to Louis XV:

> As the duchess of Kendal seemed to express a desire to see me often, I have been very attentive to her; being convinced that it is highly essential to the advantage of your majesty's service to be on good terms with her, for she is closely united with the three ministers who now govern [Walpole, Townshend and Newcastle]; and these ministers are in strict union together, and are as far as I can judge, well inclined . . .[2]

Broglio also gives us fascinating information regarding Georg August's position after the family split:

The Prince of Wales endeavours to obtain information of what passes, from persons who are attached to him; but he learns nothing either from the king, the duchess [Melusine], or the ministers. The king goes every afternoon at five o'clock to the duchess, the ministers occasionally attend; and it is there that affairs which require secrecy are treated . . .[3]

Later in the month, Broglio continued, intriguingly: 'I am convinced that she [Melusine] may be advantageously employed in promoting your majesty's service, and that it will be necessary to employ her; though I will not trust her further than is absolutely necessary . . .'[4] Melusine's first loyalty, he noted, would always be to George.

Melusine enjoyed George's complete confidence, and for the last five years of his reign we see him entrusting her with diplomacy and his most private affairs to an extent that he never had before. She figured regularly in the correspondence of foreign diplomats in London, not only that of Count Broglio, but also in the letters of Pozobueno, the Spanish ambassador, and Karl Josef von Palm, the Imperial resident to his master the Emperor. It is Palm's letters that show us Melusine's high standing with the Empress, Elisabeth Christine of Brunswick-Wolfenbüttel: Melusine frequently corresponded with her as a way of enabling the Emperor and George to exchange views through discreet diplomatic back channels. In an interesting twist, Elisabeth Christine was the granddaughter of Anton Ulrich, who had fought so hard to undermine George's family's claim to the electoral cap. Had he succeeded, Melusine would have simply been the mistress of a minor German prince, and in no position to correspond with the Empress.

Here Melusine can be seen acting in a traditional queenly role as she pursued gentle, 'feminine', diplomacy. It was Melusine, for instance, who handled much of the correspondence with Charles Whitworth, the British envoy to Prussia – logical perhaps, as she was young Sophia Dorothea's regular correspondent. In May 1721 she wrote to Whitworth regarding the dismissal of George's Prussian granddaughter Wilhelmine's governess, Miss Letti, a very intimate family matter:

> I have not omitted to mention to the king the subject of your letter
> . . . He agrees with the reasons to dismiss Mme Letti and his Majesty
> is totally in agreement with the queen [Sophia Dorothea, queen of
> Prussia]. To tell you sir that I have never regarded Miss Letti as a
> person well qualified especially to raise a princess and I am ecstatic
> that in her place you have chosen Mme Sonsfeld . . . I have the
> honour to know her and I have always regarded her with good
> feeling and I am persuaded that the court will never regret the
> choice.[5]

According to Wilhelmine's memoirs, Miss Letti was something of a sadist and would regularly beat her, either on her own initiative or acting on Sophia Dorothea's orders. Miss Letti was also a protégée of Sophia Charlotte's, which may have had something to do with Melusine's approving her dismissal. After leaving the Prussian court, however, Miss Letti turned up in England, where Sophia Charlotte gave her a pension.

Melusine wrote to Whitworth later in the month, assuring him of George's high regard for him: 'that one could not be more in his majesty's favour than you are now and the full confidence that the king has in you . . .'[6]

And such was George's confidence in Melusine that in 1722 he persuaded the Emperor to honour her with the position of Princess of the Holy Roman Empire. The *Daily Journal* reported: 'The Duchess of Kendal, Countess of Schulenburg, is, of the Emperor's free inclination, advanced to the Dignity of a Princess of the Empire, without any charge.'[7]

But the relationship was not always entirely harmonious. We have at least one example of George losing his temper with Melusine. Worried for his health, she objected to his excessive drinking with Robert Walpole in Richmond Park:

> where the king after shooting . . . passed the afternoon drinking punch, of which he was excessively fond, in an easy and convivial manner. The duchess [Melusine], alarmed at this familiar inter-course, and anxious to render these visits less frequent, attempted, by means of some of her German friends, who were generally of the party, to break up the meeting sooner than the usual time of retiring; but their attempts having no effect . . .[8]

George was furious.

It was during the visit to Hanover in 1723 that Melusine's mutually rewarding relationship with the ministerial triumvirate – Walpole, Townshend and Newcastle – really came to fruition and worked in her favour to save her relationship with George.

Sophia Charlotte's sister-in-law, Sophie Karoline von Platen (she had married Sophia Charlotte's brother, Ernst August von Platen in 1697), had remained in Hanover, despite her husband's departure with George for England in 1714. They had separated some time before, and the countess preferred to stay in Hanover. As we have seen, contemporaries and later gossips such as Horace Walpole believed that when George came to England he had Sophie Karoline von Platen as one of his three mistresses, along with Melusine and Sophia Charlotte. They speculated that Sophie Karoline had only stayed behind in Hanover because she was Catholic, and was con-cerned that the 'militant' Protestant English might treat her badly.

George's payment of Sophie Karoline's daughter Amalie's dowry added fuel to the rumours that she was one of the king's mistresses, although as Hatton points out, George may have paid it because her husband was a trusted servant. It is more likely, however, that George paid the sum because he believed von Platen to be his half-brother, and Amalie his niece. The fact that von Platen was christened Ernst August makes it probable that he was another of the old Elector's children with his mistress, Klara.

George was very fond of Sophie Karoline. She was the niece of his old governess, Katharine von Harling, and as such George had known her for much of his life. Katharine was one of the Electress Sophia's dearest friends, and young Sophie Karoline must have been a part of the family's intimate circle. Clavering's letter to his sister Mary Cowper illustrates how Sophie Karoline disliked Melusine and was extremely jealous of her status at court. She was two years younger than Melusine and probably felt usurped by her lightning establishment as George's *mâitresse en titre* so soon after her arrival at the Hanoverian court in 1690.

1723 saw one of the longest sojourns of the reign in Germany, partly because George took the opportunity to make his only visit to Prussia to see his daughter and son-in-law. The party began at Bad Pyrmont to rest and revitalize, then moved to Herrenhausen, followed by Göhrde, then Hanover. Melusine entertained lavishly at all of their homes, particularly at Göhrde, where the hunting made it a favourite because George was at his most relaxed.

George and Melusine were accompanied by George's secretaries of state, Townshend and Carteret. After the deaths of Stanhope and Sunderland, Carteret had become the nominal leader of their Whig followers, and this faction was often at odds with Walpole and Townshend's group within the party. In Hanover events came to a head as Melusine championed Walpole and Townshend against Carteret. Sophie Karoline was the catalyst.

Carteret, mistakenly perceiving Sophie Karoline's influence with George to be such that if cultivated, it could rival Melusine's, sought to bring her to England. The plan prompted a flurry of letters between Walpole and Townshend, determined to keep her out.

At the end of August 1723, Walpole wrote to Townshend from London:

> Another report that has obtained very much is, that lord Carteret had endeavoured or procured the bringing over the countesse of Platen into England. 'Tis great pity, my lord, that some check cannot be given to these proceedings, which although they may seem trivial have their ill effects . . . And I find these reports are not confined to England; but my son [Horace Walpole], who returned hither last night from Paris, tells me . . . the lady's journey is received there as a settled point . . .[9]

Townshend however was able to reassure him at the beginning of September that: 'Count Lippe's story of the countess of Platen is certainly a lie. I am informed from very good hands, that she has not the least thought of going for England . . .'[10]

To gain Sophie Karoline's favour, Carteret attempted to raise the rank of Amalie's prospective in-laws. Amalie's fiancé was Henri Philippeaux, comte St Florentin, son of the marquis de la Vrillière. Now Carteret lobbied hard to have the de la Vrillières raised to the rank of *duc et pair*, or 'Peer of France'. This was the highest honour below that of the king and it was bestowed on only a very few of the nobility. Carteret's attempts however failed. (He was aided by Sir Luke Schaub, one of George's diplomats.) Louis XV evidently felt too much pressure, and George found himself embarrassed;[11] whereupon Carteret's standing with George fell somewhat, to the delight of a gleeful Walpole and Townshend.

But as late as November, Melusine remained fearful that Sophie

Karoline would contrive to get herself to England. She was used to coping with Sophia Charlotte and her sulks and tantrums, and found Caroline's dislike of George's half-sister a useful check. But Melusine feared the upset to her immediate family's equilibrium that the arrival of a hostile Sophie Karoline would mean. Townshend reflected these fears – he was plainly in Melusine's daily confidence – to Walpole:

> . . . the match . . . going on, his majesty has been pleased upon this occasion, to think of making a present to the countess of Platen, towards the charges of fitting the young lady [Amalie] out, and of removing with her to Paris. As the countess is none of the best economists, and her family affairs are by that means in no very good function, the king has thoughts of making her a present of three thousand pounds . . . I have acquainted the duchess [Melusine] with my writing to you on this subject, who is perfectly easy in our helping this matter forward, but is very much disturbed at the prospect . . . of the countess's making use of the interest this match will give her at the court of France, towards removing into England, which may so much easier be compassed from thence, than from this country . . .[12]

Sophie Karoline, encouraged by Sophia Charlotte, was particularly unbearable that year – she may have been rubbing Melusine's nose in her daughter's glorious match. Melusine had the still unmarried young Melusine with her, and according to Townshend, she too was enraged at Sophie Karoline's conduct. But it was not the enormous sum of money George gave to Sophie Karoline, or the rumours that George was infatuated with her and that Amalie was his daughter, or even the fear of her coming to England to live in close proximity to her that bothered her the most, it was a close friend's betrayal of her with Sophie Karoline that made her so miserable.

Christian Ulrich von Hardenberg formed part of George's most intimate circle. He had been in his service since 1707 and had accompanied him to England; he was one of the few Hanoverians to remain after 1716 and he was a close friend to both George and Melusine. But by 1723 he was desperate for promotion to first minister of Hanover, replacing the now elderly Bernstorff, who was to retire. Townshend, Walpole and Newcastle all favoured it, as did Melusine. George probably did from an early stage but typically was in no hurry to make a formal appointment. Melusine, under pressure from Hardenberg, pushed it as far as she could with George, but he was irritated and she had no success, at least not at first. She was devastated when Hardenberg, rather than waiting for her gentle influence to take effect, ran to Sophie Karoline to see what she could do for him with the king. Townshend reported all to Walpole:

> I am now able to send you an account of the whole progress and happy termination of an affair, which has given me the only solid uneasiness I have felt since my being here, and which looked so unpromising in some of its aspects, that I did not care to alarm you with any part of it, till all was over, and it had taken its turn one way or other. While we were extremely intent on guarding against the attacks of our enemies, and had all the success that way which could be desired; it happened, that the indiscretion of some of our friends, had like to have ended in worse consequences than the utmost efforts of the former could have brought about. The marshal [Hardenberg] even since his being here, has been labouring in the most eager and impatient manner to get himself declared minister [first minister]: and not being able to carry his point with that ease and expedition he wished for, he threatened, and certainly had thoughts of quitting the king's service altogether, and carried his indiscretion so far as to grow very negligent

in his attendance, and even to withdraw himself from court for some weeks, under frivolous pretences. But this was not all; for though the duchess [Melusine] acted a very sincere part towards him in this affair, and strained her interest, perhaps farther than was advisable, to gratify his eagerness and ambition; yet the marshal, partly through impatience and partly through a falsehood and indirectness, too habitual to him . . . could not forbear making his court privately to persons of the opposite faction [Sophie Karoline], and looking out for assistance in that quarter, from whence accounts of all his practices were constantly brought round to the duchess.[13]

Townshend went on to talk of Melusine's misery over the whole affair, and his own delight in its consequences which placed Melusine firmly in their camp:

This infidelity, in one whom the duchess honoured with her chief confidence has, you may be sure, given her great uneasiness. However, it has had the immediate good effect, of making her more open and unreserved towards me and I believe . . . she reposes a more entire confidence in me at present, than in any other person about the king. I was very true to the marshal in his grand affair, and notwithstanding the discoveries that have been made, advised the duchess to press his being declared minister, in which situation it is very possible, he may signify less than he did before. At least he will serve to exclude some more dangerous person [Sophie Karoline] from being brought over to England, and will save us from the difficulties and uncertainties that always attend a change of hands. I neither did, nor could (after some things that are come to my knowledge) endeavour to re-establish the marshal's character of integrity with the duchess, and as I believe it morally impossible, that he should ever regain her confidence entirely, the bringing him back to England must, I think, of course have the effect of throwing her into our hands . . .'[14]

Melusine was immensely loyal. Hardenberg would have known of the animosity that existed between her and Sophie Karoline, and although he achieved the position he coveted, she never felt the same affection towards him. Townshend though was delighted, and wrote in excitement to Walpole of the benefits of having Melusine completely on their side: 'I hope every thing will stand on the same good foot as formerly, with this only difference and advantage, that the marshal by his great dexterity will have transferred the ascendant with the duchess from himself to us . . .'[15]

Young Melusine, loyal like her mother, was livid on Melusine's behalf. She expected nothing less from Sophie Karoline, but was so disappointed in their old friend Hardenberg, and made her displeasure so well known, that 'he [Hardenberg] looks on Lady Walsingham [young Melusine was created Lady Walsingham in 1722] as his determined enemy . . .'[16] Here we catch a glimpse of the devoted relationship that existed between Melusine and her second daughter.

Sophie Karoline did not come to London; disaster was averted. Did George know of the tensions that existed amongst the women of his generation that he cared for most? It is hard to imagine the famously discreet Melusine speaking critically of Sophia Charlotte or Sophie Karoline to George – anything to maintain calm and equilibrium. Wherever possible she kept animosity amongst their circle away from her lover. Instead she confided her fears to her new allies, George's English ministers – Townshend, Walpole and Newcastle.

But there was to be no respite yet from an unusually stressful and unhappy holiday in Hanover. Before returning home the royal party was obliged to visit George's daughter Sophia Dorothea and her family in Prussia.

The visit did not begin well. George arrived exhausted, having driven himself from Hanover in his own chaise. On arrival at the feast thrown in his honour, he fainted. Melusine, who had been worried about his health for years, was so anxious that she persuaded Townshend to help her to prevent a trip to Hanover the following year, and they did not return until 1725.

One of the main reasons for the trip was to discuss the 'double marriage' project that Wilhelmine recorded in her extensive memoirs as being so dear to her mother Sophia Dorothea. The plan was to arrange for the marriage of Sophia Dorothea's and Georg August's children to one another. Wilhelmine, it was proposed, would marry Georg August's son Frederick Louis, and her brother Friedrich (who would be known to history as Frederick the Great) would marry one of Georg August's daughters, possibly Anne, as she was closest to him in age. Wilhelmine told of the importance of Melusine in advancing this proposal.

She wrote intriguingly that George was initially against the idea, having such a poor impression of Wilhelmine's character from her abusive governess Miss Letti, who was living in England on Sophia Charlotte's charity. She continued:

> The queen [Sophia Dorothea], in despair . . . had recourse to the Duchess of Kendal. . . . The latter told the queen that the aversion of the king of England to my marriage arose from certain malicious suggestions instilled into his mind concerning me: that Miss Letti had exhibited such a picture of me as was calculated to deter any man from marrying . . . 'Your majesty may judge,' concluded the duchess, 'whether, after hearing such reports . . . the king your father could consent to this marriage.' The queen, who could not conceal her indignation, told her how Miss Letti had behaved to me . . . At length the untruth of these rumours was so clearly demonstrated to the duchess that she was completely persuaded of the contrary . . .

she advised the Queen of Prussia to persuade the King of England to take a journey to Berlin, that he might with his own eyes undeceive himself respecting the calumnies that had been vented against me. Assisted by the duchess, the queen managed it so well that her father complied with her wishes . . .[17]

Wilhelmine's memoirs, written much later in life, were probably exaggerated. Her dates are incorrect: the incident described above appears in her memoirs as occurring in the autumn of 1724, when George and Melusine had been back in England for nearly a year. But the sentiments she expresses, of Melusine being able to gently steer George towards her will, are correct. Melusine, having fought off potential rivals and suffered disappointments in the immediate circle, would remain in the ascendant for the rest of George's reign.

The last obstacle to her singular place in George's affections was removed when Sophia Charlotte died at her apartments in St James's Palace on 20 April 1725; as she lay ill in her rooms the musicians were instructed by a distraught George not to play. She was buried four days later with all pomp at Westminster Abbey. Melusine finally had her lover to herself. She entered what was possibly the happiest and most secure period in her relationship with George. But it would last for only two short years.

16.

A Marriage?

How matters really stood between his Majesty and the Duchess of Kendal will remain, for the most part, a secret, until the great ones are pleased to make discoveries.

— Edward Calamy, *Own Life*[1]

On a freezing November day in 1726 George's estranged wife Sophia Dorothea died in her Ahlden prison. She was sixty years old and had been incarcerated for more than half her life. All hopes of freedom had long since evaporated. Depressed, she finally succumbed to a stroke or heart attack on 13 November. In death Sophia Dorothea continued in her state of limbo. George wanted her body buried in the grounds at Ahlden Castle, but the sodden earth, at the mercy of a cold wet winter, prevented it. Instead she remained unburied, and her body was placed in a coffin. It was not until the following May that George finally allowed her to be interred in the Old Church at Celle.

George's wife was dead. What then of the rumours that George and Melusine married, and how much credence can be given to them?

Many of their contemporaries were convinced that they were married before they came to England. Morganatic or left-handed marriages were reasonably common in Europe. The most high-profile example was Louis XIV, who had married his mistress Madame de Maintenon privately in the 1680s, and George's own Palatinate uncle had married his mistress Louise von Degenfeld morganatically*. Wilhelmine in her memoirs stated that Melusine was her grandfather's 'wife by the left hand'. Coxe believed that

*A left-handed, or morganatic marriage was the union between two people of different rank, usually a ruling prince with a commoner. Although the marriage was binding, neither the spouse nor any children of the marriage had rights of inheritance. It was called a left-handed marriage as during the ceremony the groom held the bride's left, rather than her right hand.

George 'espoused her [Melusine] with his left hand, a species of marriage not uncommon in Germany', and later he went on to say that the marriage took place, 'though his real wife, the unfortunate Sophia Dorothy, was still alive'. Lady Mary Wortley Montagu also repeated court gossip that George had entered into a morganatic marriage with Melusine before he came to England.

During the hysteria that surrounded George's breach with his son there were reports of Melusine being declared queen, which points to a marriage already having taken place. Edward Harley wrote to his mother at the end of January 1717: 'There is talk again of the Duchess of M—— [Munster] being declared Q[ueen].'[2]

But Liselotte, who enjoyed the Electress Sophia's complete confidence and as such was arguably a more reputable source than the tittle-tattle Lady Mary Wortley Montagu, or the eighteenth-century historian Coxe, who was writing after the events and often reported court gossip, was convinced that no such ceremony had taken place. On 17 March 1718, at the height of the crisis between the king and the prince, she wrote to her half-sister Louise:

> Everything goes from bad to worse in England. It is not safe to write anything about it. All Paris says that King George wants to declare publicly that the Prince of Wales is not his son, and that, in order to spite him still further, he wants to marry the Schulenberg woman who is now Duchess of Munster. I told Lord Stair all this, and he replied that nothing of the sort would happen, and that I had no need to alarm myself.[3]

Liselotte would not have written this letter had George and Melusine already been married. If she was privy to information that they had married, she was not in the habit of dissimulation.

George certainly treated Melusine as his wife. It is telling that even before the death of Sophia Dorothea he had often referred to her as his 'private wife'. The king was particularly conscious of social propriety, hence the Queen's Apartments at Kensington were shut up for the duration of George's reign – even if he had already married her in Germany, she was not allowed to use them because she was not queen consort. But he did everything possible to honour her. She was his hostess in Hanover and in England, she had the use of the best apartments at the royal palaces, he gave her a substantial pension, and most importantly he trusted her to act as an intermediary between himself and his ministers. He treated her as queen consort in all but name.

The painting recently discovered in the basement at Celle Castle shows the high esteem in which George held Melusine. Here she is indistinguishable from a queen, draped in sumptuous velvet, needing no ornament but the royal ermine she clasps so tightly in her left hand. Could it be that her firm hold of the fur in her left hand symbolizes George's intention to marry her 'by the left hand' at the earliest opportunity?

It is difficult to believe that George would have contemplated marrying Melusine while Sophia Dorothea lived. Although he was free to remarry under Continental law (Sophia Dorothea, as their divorce made clear, was not), George and his father had struggled hard to win electoral status for Hanover, and his remarriage might feasibly have endangered it. If George had taken another wife, popular opinion might have swept Sophia Dorothea to remarriage too. Remarried, there was every possibility that her new husband would have taken Celle from George – a significant portion of his territory – and endangered his position as Elector.

Furthermore remarriage was illegal in England while the divorced spouse lived, and George would have been sensitive to the laws of the country of which he expected to become king before 1714; after 1714 he would not have disobeyed the law of the land of which he was now monarch.

Equally it is very hard to imagine Melusine pressing George to marry her. She was too concerned for his wellbeing to request something of him that he was unable to give. Her family were obviously upset on her behalf at her status, as we can see from Johann Matthias's letter to Fabrice after George's death: 'If my sister is not one of the happiest human beings of her time, and if she is currently not in an agreeable situation and not completely independent, then she really only has herself to blame. She was wary of opening her heart to anyone, even those closest to her'.[4] This may be an oblique reference to the lack of any formal ceremony between them.

But Sophia Dorothea's death changed everything. And while her body awaited burial it is entirely credible that George should have finally felt free to marry the woman who had been his mistress for thirty-six years.

There is an intriguing letter in the British Library, written by Robert Walpole's chaplain, the Reverend Henry Etough, to his school friend Dr Birch. He claims that George and Melusine were married by the archbishop of York. Etough is an invaluable resource for the historian, as he wrote down many of his conversations with Walpole, who would have been privy to private information. Coxe uses him as one of his primary sources in his extensive biography of Walpole, although some historians suggest that he must be taken with a large pinch of salt.

The letter reads: 'The late king was expensive and vain in his amours. He had Kilmansegg and Platen besides Kendal to whom it is supposed the late Archbishop of York married him.'[5]

We have seen how the first part of the sentence was a repetition of erroneous contemporary rumours, and how they are perceived by most historians today to be mere gossip. But the death of Sophia Dorothea, coupled with the character of the archbishop of York, Lancelot Blackburne, who is supposed to have married them, makes it feasible that Etough was, in this instance, telling the truth.

The letter was written sometime after Blackburne's death in 1743. He was a maverick, not a typical conservative servant of the Church. In 1681 he was performing 'Secret Services' for Charles II, and it was widely rumoured that he was a pirate, capturing Spanish gold. Once he joined the Church in 1684, however, he quickly rose to become dean of Exeter, and then archdeacon of Cornwall in 1715. He accompanied George as his personal chaplain to Hanover in 1716 and the visit was obviously a huge success: Blackburne was appointed bishop of Exeter in 1717. He was a staunch supporter of the king and the ministry, and was rewarded by the archbishopric of York, which he assumed in October 1724 after the death of the previous incumbent, the more conventional Sir William Dawes. Dawes was a Tory who had supported the Prince of Wales during the row between father and son. It is unlikely that George would have asked him to perform so private a ceremony between himself and Melusine.

Blackburne was criticized by his contemporaries for not being spiritual enough and for indulging in worldly pleasures, and it is true that while archbishop of York he failed to perform any confirmations. He was reputed to have fathered at least one illegitimate son, Thomas Hayter, bishop of Norwich. Horace Walpole wrote of Hayter as: 'natural son of Blackburn, the jolly old Archbishop of York, who had all the manners of a man of quality, though he had been a buccaneer, and was a clergyman; but he retained nothing of his first profession, except his seraglio.'[6]

Blackburne's womanizing was lampooned in a verse written just after his death – 'Priest-Craft and Lust, or, Lancelot to his Ladies, an Epistle from the Shades' (1743) – in which he cries:

> No longer thro' the Town I range with raging Flame
> To seek the Virgin Nymph or married Dame.[7]

If anyone was going to marry George and Melusine, and assuage their fears of a disapproving Church (although a ceremony would no longer have been illegal), it was Lancelot Blackburne.

Unfortunately it is impossible to corroborate absolutely whether or not there was a marriage. There are no records of a ceremony in English or European archives, and it was only with Hardwicke's Marriage Act of 1754, specifically passed to thwart secret marriages, that English law required a written record of a marriage. Before this Act was passed, verbal consent alone was enough to make a marriage valid.

But knowing how devoted Melusine and George were to one another, and the love they gave to their daughters, it is probable that once George was free to marry her at the end of 1726, a secret ceremony would have taken place, simply because the opportunity had finally arisen.

17.

Endings

In a tender mood George the First promised the Duchess of Kendal, that if she survived him, and it were possible for the departed to return to this world, he would make her a visit . . .

– Horace Walpole[1]

At the beginning of June 1727 the family departed for a holiday in Hanover. Two days before they left, the young Horace Walpole met the king. He described the encounter many years later:

> How strange are the accidents of life! At ten years old I had set my heart on seeing George I – and being a favourite child, my mother asked leave for me to be presented to him, which to the first minister's wife was granted, and I was carried by the late Lady Chesterfield [young Melusine] to his hand as he went to supper in the Duchess of Kendal's apartment [1 June 1727]. This was the night but one before he left England for the last time . . .

For George and Melusine, possibly so recently married, it was something of a holiday. It was also an opportunity to grieve for the death of their youngest daughter Trudchen, who had died of tuberculosis in 1726 at the age of twenty-five, leaving her two sons William and George, aged two and four years old, motherless.

The entire family was devastated when Trudchen fell ill in 1723, with one newspaper reporting that she was 'past all hopes of recovery' in March of that year.[2] She recovered from this bout of illness however, and the family embarked on a round of spa cures and increasingly desperate visits to physicians, to no avail. There had been another death in 1726, that of Mehemet, whose association with George pre-dated Melusine's by five years.

Today many of Mehemet's family portraits hang in the convent at Barsinghausen, a small town near the city of Hanover, together with portraits of Melusine and Trudchen. That these portraits stand together in a remote part of the province of Hanover is testament to the closeness of the family to Mehemet, who served George for nearly forty years.

Despite these terrible losses, they looked forward to seeing George's only surviving sibling, Ernst August, and his daughter Sophia Dorothea in Hanover. As always, the girls, young Melusine and Louise, accompanied them.

George, in his eagerness to make good time, pressed on ahead with only Fabrice, Hardenberg and Mustafa for company. But on 20 June he suffered a stroke while still travelling through Holland. On the advice of his surgeon, George's courtiers decided to travel on to Osnabrück, the king's childhood home, where Ernst August was waiting for them at his palace. George managed to rouse himself on arrival to raise his hat in greeting, but he died in the early hours of 22 June, attended by Fabrice.

Melusine was not with him when he died. She arrived later in the morning, with young Melusine. The entire party left Osnabrück for Hanover the next day – and Melusine was amongst them.

George's death deeply affected his immediate family circle. Joanne Sophie, speaking for them all, wrote that they had 'lost a father and never would things be as in his lifetime'.[3]

Caroline, now queen, wrote immediately to Melusine: 'My first thought, my dear Duchess, has been of you . . . I know well your devotion and love for the late King . . . I hope you realise that I am your friend.'

Melusine was at a loss as to what to do with herself in the immediate wake of George's death. There was talk of her coming home at once, and *Mist's Weekly Journal* reported her imminent arrival on 24 June. The account ended with a note of her unpopularity in England: 'We hear at the rejoicing on the king's proclamation, a certain Duchess was burnt in effigy.' But it was not until the middle of August that Melusine even contemplated leaving Germany, when *The Daily Journal* reported that: 'The Duchess of Kendal's heavy baggage is put on board a ship at Hamburgh for England . . .'

But Melusine did not set foot in England until after Georg August's coronation as George II in October. She preferred to remain in Hanover to grieve with her surviving daughters and her closest friends. In England there was no official outlet for her grief because she held no official position within the royal family.[4] George had loved her from the very beginning, and may well have begun to think of her as his wife soon after he divorced Sophia Dorothea in the last days of 1694, but she was not a dowager queen and she chose to stay away.

Other members of Melusine's family attended the coronation, including her nephew the Baron von Spörken, her youngest sister's son. We can see here how intertwined the Schulenburg and the British royal families were. But young Melusine and Louise remained with their mother; they did not attend their half-brother's coronation.

Eventually Melusine made England her permanent home. She had bought an estate in Holstein, the Emkendorf Castle, from the Rantzau family in 1720. Now she decided to sell it. She finally disposed of the property in 1729 for 120,000 thaler, with a 4,000 thaler profit.[5]

She sent the head of her household, Mrs Schrieder, on ahead with her belongings in the middle of September. Joanne Sophie, still with Melusine in Hanover, urged her to stay with her at her home in Kew Green on her return to England, but Melusine was adamant, as so many widows are, that she must be independent. Now she had to decide where to live. The royal palaces were no longer available to her, not even the beautiful house George had built for her at Kensington, which had been so long in its construction that Melusine still had pictures to hang and furniture to buy: she would never enjoy it amidst the full glory of her furniture, fabrics and paintings.

At the end of 1727 Melusine set in motion the purchase of a beautiful house in Grosvenor Square. No. 43 was not the grandest of the new development, but it was elegant and comfortable, and she and young Melusine made it their main London home. It apparently cost her about £5,000.[7] She also possibly owned a house in Portugal Row; if so she did not live in it, but relied on its rental income of £90 a year.[8]

Whilst the work on her new house was being completed, she and young Melusine rented a house in Old Bond Street. Louise stayed behind in Hanover to sell her little palace; she would make her home with her mother and sister in England, where she eventually bought a house in Paddington. Ten years later we hear of her having such an argument with her tempestuous half-brother, now George II, when they holidayed in Hanover, that she was forced to leave Herrenhausen.

Melusine was desperately ill at the beginning of 1728; her health had been poor since her illness in 1724, and grief exacerbated it. Until the end of her life the newspapers were full of reports of her ill health. She rented the Swiss impresario John Heidegger's house in Barnes for the summer while she recovered.

Melusine's loss was compounded by Joanne Sophie's decision to return to Germany. After the death of her ex-husband in June 1728, her son Albrecht Wolfgang took up his position as ruler of Schaumburg-Lippe and Joanne Sophie went too. Henrietta Howard, Countess of Suffolk, wrote to John Gay: 'Count La Lippe's father is dead; by which he is become a count of the empire, and has a very great estate.'[6]

He took with him his and Trudchen's two young sons. It was a difficult decision for Joanne Sophie to leave her closest friend while she still mourned, but she and Melusine probably decided that the motherless boys, aged four and six, needed one of their grandmothers to help with their upbringing. It was far more practical for Joanne Sophie, and not Melusine, to go.

In addition to the townhouse, Melusine craved a country retreat. She had often visited Joanne Sophie at her house in Kew and had grown to love it there. Now she decided to build a house nearby, in Isleworth. And in the tradition of royal mistresses who no longer had a place at court, she created a perfect Palladian villa on the banks of the Thames, called Kendal House. (Henrietta Howard, George II's mistress, retired to Marble Hill House, the beautiful villa she built for herself on the Thames at Twickenham, when the king discarded her in 1734.)

After George's death Melusine virtually disappears from the sources. Her political importance as a conduit to the king was gone. Now Walpole thrust his energies into courting Caroline.

Through diplomacy, empathy and kindness, Melusine managed to maintain a good relationship with George's family after his death. Joanne Sophie notes in her extensive correspondence how kind Caroline and George were to Melusine, with Caroline, now queen, inviting her to tea on several occasions.

We see various donations to charity and increasing piety, we see her nursing Louise at Isleworth when she caught measles in 1736. In 1730 she showed her former feisty nature by pointedly asking Walpole for the money he held for her in trust from George.[9] She probably wanted it to build her country house. She wrote:

Sir
As his late majesty was pleased to make you my trustee, you will not wonder at this application. The little trouble I have given you on that head, is enough to convince you how great a regard I have had for your assurances. But having lately engaged in an affair that will require a large sum to complete, I hope you will now resolve to

accommodate me with the money entrusted with you, my occasions demanding the whole sum. This being a private trust that must one time or other be accounted for, it may be transferred without interfering with publick business. I can easily imagine one so continually employed, may not often think of me or my affairs, but you'll give me leave not to forget myself, especially in a thing of so great importance to me. I am, sir, your most humble servant.[10]

Young Melusine was her mother's constant companion. She acted as Melusine's nurse during her frequent illnesses, and remained with her even after her marriage to Philip Dormer Stanhope, fourth Earl of Chesterfield, in 1733.

We do not know why young Melusine married Chesterfield, since no contemporary wrote of the marriage from her point of view and she was as discreet as her mother in not committing her emotion to paper. She was certainly an attractive prospect for him. She had the geographical convenience of living next door to him in Grosvenor Square, she was rich – her dowry was reputedly £50,000, with an additional £3,000 per annum – attractive and clever. But she was also forty years old and probably beyond an age to bear children. She was kind to her husband's illegitimate son, but the relationship between husband and wife quickly ossified into one of courtesy. She turned a blind eye to his many mistresses, and he allowed her to spend most of her time with her mother. It was not the idyllic relationship she had witnessed between Melusine and George. Perhaps she was disappointed – she seems to have preferred her mother's company to that of her new husband.

Chesterfield meanwhile used his wife's enormous marriage portion to build a magnificent city mansion in South Audley Street and young Melusine moved back in with her mother soon after her marriage.

Melusine could barely tolerate her son-in-law. In turn he detested her and called her 'a half-wit', probably because he knew she disliked him. In her will she ensured that he was unable to touch any of the money she left to her daughter. She almost certainly knew of his mistresses, suspected that he gambled, and disapproved; on one occasion he kept a big win at Bath from her, he was so nervous of her silent wrath.[11] Hervey parodied the tense state of their domestic affairs. In October 1733, just after the marriage, he wrote: 'Lord Chesterfield has not stirred from Twickenham [Kendal House] since the declaration of his marriage. He talks, Lady Chesterfield kisses, and the Duchess of Kendal spins all day long . . . he has no resources to dissipate his boredom'.[12] Young Melusine seems to have barely permeated his consciousness, and we must conclude that he probably married her for her money. Chesterfield wrote extensive letters and he hardly mentions his wife in any of them. He did however write poems to his mistresses and misogynistic musings on the childlike nature of women.

Melusine was furious on her daughter's account. But for the most part she seemed only to wait for death when she would join George once more.

A remarkable anecdote is related by Horace Walpole:

In a tender mood George the First promised the Duchess of Kendal, that if she survived him, and it were possible for the departed to return to this world, he would make her a visit. The Duchess, on his death, so much expected the accomplishment of that engagement, that a large raven, or some black fowl, flying into one of the windows of her villa at Isleworth, she was persuaded it was the soul of her departed monarch so accoutred, and received and treated it with all the respect and tenderness of duty, till the royal bird or she took their last flight.[13]

Hatton believes that, as so often with Horace Walpole's scribblings, he took a remark and embroidered it. But his father or one of his other sources may have been party to an intimate moment between George and Melusine, where they whispered as lovers do of how they would manage when death took one of them away. George, playing the gallant lover who would never leave her, even in death, promised to return.

Melusine died on 10 May 1743. Horace Walpole wrote to his friend Horace Mann two days later:

> The Duchess of Kendal is dead, 85 years old [*sic*] she was a year older than the late king. Her riches were immense, but I believe my Lord Chesterfield will get nothing by her death but his wife: she lived in the house with the Duchess, where he had played away all his credit.[14]

She was buried, as she requested, in a vault at the South Audley Street Chapel in Mayfair. Her wealth at her death was roughly £60,000.

Melusine's beautiful home, Kendal House, became a 'place of public entertainment' after her death, and seven years later in 1750 *The Daily Advertiser* excitedly told its readers:

> Kendal House, Isleworth, near Brentford, Middlesex, eight miles from London, will open for breakfast on Monday. The room for dancing is 60 feet long, and all the other rooms elegantly fitted up. The orchestra is allowed to be in the genteelest taste, being housed in an octagon in the Corinthian order. Ladies and gentlemen may divert themselves with fishing, the canal being well stocked with tench, carp and all sorts of fish; near are two wildernesses, with delightful rural walks, and through the garden runs a rapid river, shaded with a pleasant grove of trees, so designed by nature that in

the hottest day of summer you are secured from the heat of the sun. Great care will be taken to keep out all disorderly people. There is a man cook and a good larder; all things are as cheap or cheaper than at any place of the kind.

Louise died in 1773. She was eighty-one years old and had lived in London for over half a century. Hervey tells us of her continued grace and wit as she grew older. She joined her mother in the chapel in South Audley Street.

Melusine and George's last surviving daughter died five years later, on 16 September 1778. Young Melusine's death was reported in the popular press, in *The London Chronicle*, *Lloyd's Evening Post* and others. She left a legacy of £80,000.

Young Melusine was the last to enter the vault in the church in South Audley Street. After that it was sealed, at her request.

Melusine's line did not endure. Trudchen's eldest son George Augustus died when he was only twenty years old, reputedly in a duel while studying at the University of Leiden.[15] William became the Graf zu Schaumburg-Lippe on his father's death and had a stunning military career. He was immortalized by Joshua Reynolds in a portrait now in the Royal Collection, painted sometime between 1764 and 1767. It shows a tall, dark, confident man sitting astride a cannon, in the midst of a battlefield. William married in 1765 and had two children, a son and a daughter. But his son died while still an infant and his daughter, Emilie, died when she was only three years old. Both Louise and young Melusine died childless, and with Emilie's death in 1774, Melusine's line died out.

It was Sophia Dorothea who trumped her rival with her status as ancestress to the British royal family. Melusine von der Schulenburg was the true love of Britain's first Georgian king, but she did not propagate the dynasty.

Bibliography

Archives
The British Library
The National Archives
Hannover Haupstaatarchiv

Books and Articles

Ackroyd, Peter, *London, the Biography* (2007)

Aiton, E. J., *Leibniz: a biography* (1985)

Arciszewska, Barbara, *The Hanoverian Court and the Triumph of Palladio* (2002)

Backschneider, Paula R., *Daniel Defoe: Ambition and Innovation* (1986)

Balen, Malcolm, *A Very English Deceit: The Secret History of the South Sea Bubble and the First Great Financial Scandal* (2002)

Baring-Gould, S., *Curious Myths of the Middle Ages* (1866)

Beattie, J. M., *The English Court in the Reign of George I* (1976)

Bentley, Richard (ed.), *Letters of Horace Walpole, Earl of Orford* (6 vols, 1840)

Bertram, Mijndert, *Georg II: König und Kurfürst* (2004)

Binney, Marcus, *Great Houses of Europe* (2003)

Black, Jeremy, *British Foreign Policy in the Age of Walpole* (1985)

——, *George II* (2007)

——, *Robert Walpole and the Nature of Politics in Early Eighteenth Century England* (1990)

——, *The Hanoverians: The History of a Dynasty* (2004)

Bristol, *The Diary of John Hervey, first Earl of Bristol*, ed. Sydenham H. A. Hervey (1894)

Buck, Anne, *Dress in Eighteenth-Century England* (1979)

Burton, Elizabeth, *The Georgians at Home* (1967)

Byrd, William, *The London Diary 1717–1721*, ed. Louis B. Wright and Marion Tinling (1958)

Calamy, Edmund, 1671–1732: *An Historical Account of My Own Life, With Some Reflections on the Times I Have Lived In (1671-1731)* (second edition, 2 vols, 1830), ed. John Towill Rutt

Callendar, Ann, *Godly Mayfair* (1980)

Campbell Orr, Clarissa, ed., *Queenship in Britain 1660–1837: Royal Patronage, Court Culture and Dynastic Politics* (2002)

Carswell, J., *The South Sea Bubble* (rev. edn 1993)

Chancellor, Edward, *Devil Take the Hindmost* (1999)

Chesterfield, Lord, *The Letters of Philip Dormer Stanhope, 4th Earl of Chesterfield*, ed. in 6 vols by B. Dobrée (1932)

Clavering, James, *The Correspondence of Sir James Clavering*, ed. and arranged by H. T. Dickinson (1967)

Colvin, H. M., ed., *The History of the King's Works*, vol. V, *1660–1782* (1976)

Cowper, Mary, *The Diary of Mary, Countess Cowper 1714–1720*, ed. The Hon. C. S. Spencer Cowper (1864)

Coxe, William, *Memoirs of the Life and Administration of Sir Robert Walpole, Earl of Orford: With Original Correspondence And Authentic Papers, Never Before Published* (3 vols, 1798)

Cruickshanks, Eveline, 'Charles Spencer, Third Earl of Sunderland, and Jacobitism', in *The English Historical Review*, vol. 113, no. 450 (Feb 1998)

Cumming, Valerie, *Royal Dress: The Image and the Reality 1580 to the Present Day* (1989)

Danneil, Johann Friedrich, *Das Geschlecht von der Schulenburg* (1847)

——, *Stammtafeln der von der Schulenburg* (1847)

Davies, Norman, *A History of Europe* (1996)

Deutsch, Otto Erich, *Handel: a Documentary Biography* (1955)

Dickson, P. G. M., *The Financial Revolution in England: A Study in the Development of Public Credit 1688–1756* (1967)

Doran, J., *History of Court Fools* (1858)

Downie, J. A., and Thomas N. Corns, ed., *Telling People What to Think* (1993)

Egmont, *Diary of Viscount Percival, afterwards First Earl of Egmont*, ed. R. A. Roberts (1920–3)

Ernst August, *Letters: Briefe des Herzogs Ernst August zu Braunschweig-Lüneburg an Johann Franz Diedrich von Wendt aus den Jahren 1703 bis 1726*, ed. Erich Graf Kielmansegg (1902)

Fabrice, Friedrich Ernst, *Memoiren: Die Memoiren des Kammerherrn Friedrich Ernst von Fabrice, 1683–1750*, ed. R. Grieser (1956)

Fara, Patricia, *Newton: the making of a genius* (2002)

Field, Ophelia, *The Kit-Cat Club: Friends Who Imagined a Nation* (2008)

Finke, Hans-Joachim, *The Hanoverian Junta* (DPhil dissertation, Univ. of Michigan, Ann Arbor 1970)

Franklin, Colin, *Lord Chesterfield, His Character and Characters* (1993)

Fraser, David, *Frederick the Great* (2000)

Fraser, Flora, *Princesses: the six daughters of George III* (2004)

George, 'George I's letters to his daughter', ed. R. L. Arkell, in *English Historical Review* (*EHR*) (1937)

Glendinning, Victoria, *Jonathan Swift* (1998)

Green, David, *Sarah Duchess of Marlborough* (1967)

Gwynn, J. *London & Westminster Improved* (1766)

Halsband, Robert, ed., Lady Mary Wortley Montagu, *Essays and Poems and Simplicity, a Comedy* (1977)

——, *The Complete Letters of Lady Mary Wortley Montagu* (1965)

Hamilton, *The Diary of Sir David Hamilton 1709–1714*, ed. Philip Roberts (1976)

Harding, Nick, *Hanover and the British Empire, 1700–1837* (2007)

Hatton, Ragnhild, 'In Search of an Elusive Ruler'. Source material for a biography of George I as elector and king in *Fürst, Bürger, Mensch*, ed. Friedrich Engel-Janosi, Grete Klingenstein, Heinrich Lutz (1975)

——, *George I, Elector and King* (1978)

Hervey, John, Lord, *Letter Books of John Hervey, First Earl of Bristol* (3 vols, 1894)

——, *Some Materials towards Memoirs of the Reign of George II*, ed. R. R. Sedgwick (3 vols, 1931)

——, *Memoirs of the Reign of George II by John, Lord Hervey*, ed. John Wilson Croker (3 vols, 1884)

Hibbert, Christopher, *London* (1980)

——, *London: the biography of a city* (1969)

Hill, Brian, *Sir Robert Walpole* (1989)

Historical Manuscripts Commission (HMC), *Manuscripts of the Earl of Egmont*, diary of the first Earl of Egmont (3 vols, 1920–3)

——, *Report on the Manuscripts of his Grace the Duke of Portland* (1899)

Holborn, Hajo, *History of Modern Germany 1648–1840* (1965)

Hopkinson, M. R., *Married to Mercury* (1936)

Howard, Henrietta, *Letters to and from Henrietta Howard, Countess of Suffolk, and her second husband, the Hon George Berkeley, from 1712 to 1767*, ed. J. W. Croker (2 vols, 1824)

Hughes, Michael, *Early Modern Germany, 1477–1806* (1992)

Hussey, Christopher, 'Kensington Palace, the Apartments of the Countess Granville', in *Country Life*, 1 September 1928

Israel, Menasseh ben, 'To His Highnesse the Lord Protector of the Commonwealth of England, Scotland and Ireland, The Humble Addresses of Menasseh ben Israel' (1665), in *Menasseh ben*

Israel's Mission to Oliver Cromwell: Being a Reprint of the Pamphlets published by Menasseh ben Israel to promote the Re-admission of the Jews to England 1649–1655, ed. Lucien Wolf (1901)

Jardine, Lisa, *On a Grander Scale: The Outstanding Career of Sir Christopher Wren* (2002)

Jesse, John Heneage, *Memoirs of the Court of England from the Revolution in 1688 to the Death of George II* (3 vols, 1843)

Jones, Clyve, 'Evidence, Interpretation and Definitions in Jacobite Historiography: A reply to Eveline Cruickshanks', in *EHR*, vol. 113, no. 450, Feb 1998

Jordan, Ruth, *Sophie Dorothea* (1971)

Keathes, Jonathan, *Handel: the Man and his Music* (2008)

Kemble, John, ed., *State papers and correspondence, illustrative of the social and political state of Europe, from the Revolution to the accession of the House of Hanover* (1857)

Kilburn, Matthew, 'Wallmoden, Amalie Sophie Marianne von, suo jure countess of Yarmouth (1704–1765)', *Oxford Dictionary of National Biography* (2004)

——, 'Kielmansegg, Sophia Charlotte von, suo jure countess of Darlington and suo jure countess of Leinster (1675–1725)', *Oxford Dictionary of National Biography* (2004)

——, 'Schulenburg, (Ehrengard) Melusine von der, suo jure duchess of Kendal and suo jure duchess of Munster (1667–1743)', *Oxford Dictionary of National Biography* (2004)

Komachi, Hanae and Queren, Henning, *Herrenhausen Gardens*, ed. Ronald Clark and Wilken von Bothmer, trans. Margaret Will (2008)

Kroll, Maria, *Sophie, Electress of Hanover: a personal portrait* (1973)

Lampe, Joachim, *Aristokratie, Hofadel und Staatspatriziat in Kurhannover* (1963)

Lewis, W. S., ed., *Selected Letters of Horace Walpole* (1973)

Liselotte, *A Woman's Life in the Court of the Sun King: Letters of Liselotte von der Pfalz, 1652–1722*, trans. Elborg Forster

——, *Letters from Liselotte*, trans. and ed. Maria Kroll (1998)

Mackay, Charles, *Extraordinary Popular Delusions and the Madness of Crowds* (1996)

Macknight, Thomas, *The Life of Henry St. John, Viscount Bolingbroke* (1863)

Mahaffey, Kathleen, 'Pope's "Artemisia" and "Phryne" as Personal Satire', in *The Review of English Studies*, New Series, vol. 21, no. 84 (Nov 1970), pp. 466–71 (OUP)

Malortie, Carl Ernst, *Der Hannoversche Hof unter dem Kurfürsten Ernst August und der Kurfürsten Sophie* (1847)

Marlborough, Sarah Duchess of, *Memoirs of the Duchess of Marlborough, together with her characters of her contemporaries and her opinions*, ed. William King (1930)

Matthews, William, ed., *The Diary of Dudley Ryder 1715–1716* (1939)

Melville, Lewis, *The First George in Hanover and England* (2 vols, 1908)

Michael, Wolfgang, *England under George I*, vol. 1, *The Beginnings of the Hanoverian Dynasty* (1936)

——, *England under George I*, vol. 2, *The Quadruple Alliance* (1939)

Montagu, Lady Mary Wortley, *The Complete Letters of Lady Mary Wortley Montagu*, ed. Robert Halsband (2 vols, 1965–6)

Morley, Henry, *Memoirs of Bartholomew Fair* (1880)

Newman, Aubrey, *The World Turned Inside Out: New Views on George II* (inaugural lecture, Leicester University, 1988)

Nicolson, William, *The London Diaries of William Nicolson, Bishop of Carlisle, 1702–1718*, ed. Clyve Jones and Geoffrey Holmes (1985)

Owen, John B., *The Eighteenth Century, 1714–1815* (1974)

Passingham, W. J., *A History of the Coronation* (1937)

Pearce, Edward, *The Great Man: Sir Robert Walpole: Scoundrel, Genius and Britain's First Prime Minister* (2007)

Perkings, Jocelyn, *The Coronation Book* (1911)

Plumb, J. H., *Robert Walpole* (1956)

——, *The First Four Georges* (1957)

——, *The Growth of Political Stability in England 1675–1725* (1967)

——, and Huw Weldon, *The Royal Heritage: the Story of Britain's Royal Builders and Collectors* (1977)

Pope, Alexander, *The Works and Correspondence of Alexander Pope*, ed. J. W. Croker (1871)

Prüser, Jürgen, *Die Göhrde. Ein Beitrag zur Geschichte des Jagd- und Forstwesens in Niedersachsen* (1969)

Redman, Alvin, *The House of Hanover* (1961)

Ribeiro, Aileen, *Dress in Eighteenth-Century Europe 1715–1789* (2002)

Richie, Alexandra, *Faust's Metropolis: A History of Berlin* (1998)

Robertson, R. G., *England under the Hanoverians* (1911)

Rudé, George, *Hanoverian London 1714–1808* (1971)

Ryder, Dudley, *The Diary of Dudley Ryder 1715–16*, ed. William Matthews (1939)

Saussure, César de, *A Foreign View of England in the Reigns of George I and George II: the Letters of Monsieur César de Saussure to his Family*, trans. and ed. Madame Van Muyden (1902)

Schaumburg-Lippe, *Letters: Briefe der Gräfin Johanne Sophie zu Schaumburg-Lippe an die Familie von Münchhausen zu Remeringhausen 1699–1734*, ed. Friedrich-Wilhelm Schaer (1968)

Schmidt, Georg, *Das Geschlecht von der Schulenburg* (1908)

Schnath, Georg, *Geschichte Hannovers im Zeitalter der neunten Kur und der englischen Sukzession 1674–1714* (4 vols, 1976)

Schulenburg, Johann Matthias, *Leben und Denkwurdigkeiten, Johann Matthias Reichsgrafen von der Schulenburg* (2 vols, 1834)

Scott Stevenson, Gertrude (ed.) *The Letters of Madame: the correspondence of Elizabeth-Charlotte of Bavaria, Princess Palatine, Duchess of Orleans, called 'Madame' at the court of King Louis XIV*, vol. 1, 1709–1722 (1925)

Sichel, W. S., *Bolingbroke and His Times* (1902)

Simms, Brendan, and Torsten Riotte, *The Hanoverian Dimension in British History, 1714–1837* (2007)

Sinclair-Stevenson, Christopher, *Blood Royal: The Illustrious House of Hanover* (1979)

Smith, Hannah, *Georgian Monarchy: Politics and Culture, 1714–1760* (2006)

Smith, W. H., *Horace Walpole: Writer, Politician and Connoisseur* (1967)

Sophia, *Correspondence with her brother: Briefwechsel der Herzogin Sophie von Hannover mit ihrem Bruder, dem Kurfürsten Kark Ludwig von der Pfalz*, ed. E. Bodemann (1885)

——, *Letters to the Hohenzollerns: Briefwechsel der Kurfürstin Sophie von Hannover mit dem Preussischen Königshause*, ed. G. Schnath (1927)

——, *Letters to the Raugravines: Briefe der Kurfürstin Sophie von Hannover an die Raugräfinnen und Raugrafen zu Pfalz*, ed. E. Bodemann (1888)

——, *Memoiren der Herzogin Sophie, nachmals Kurfürstin von Hannover*, ed. A. Köcher (1879)

Sophia Dorothea, *Der Königsmarck-Briefwechsel: Korrespondenz der Prinzessin Sophie Dorothea von Hannover mit dem Grafen Philipp Christoph Königsmarck, 1690 bis 1694. Kritische Gesamtausg. in Regestenform* (1952)

Speck, W. A., *Literature and Society in Eighteenth-Century England: Ideology, Politics and Culture, 1680–1820* (1998)

——, *Stability and Strife: England, 1714–1760* (1977)

Stair, *Annals and Correspondence of the Viscount and the First and*

Second Earls of Stair, ed. John Murray Graham (2 vols, 1875)

Stanhope, Philip Henry, *History of England 1713–1783* (7 vols, 1713–83)

Starkie, Andrew, 'Blackburne, Lancelot (1658–1743)', *Oxford Dictionary of National Biography*, Oxford University Press, 2004

Suffolk, Henrietta, *Letters to and from Henrietta, Countess of Suffolk*, ed. J. W. Croker (2 vols, 1824)

Summerson, John, *Georgian London* (1970)

Sundon, *Memoirs of Viscountess Sundon, Mistress of the Robes to Queen Caroline, Consort of George II*, ed. Mrs Thomson (1847)

Swift, Jonathan, *Poems*, 'A Description of Morning' (1709)

——, *The Correspondence of Jonathan Swift*, ed. Harold Williams (1963)

——, *The Journal to Stella AD 1710–1713*, ed F. Ryland (1924)

Thackeray, W. M., *The Four Georges: Sketches of Manners, Morals, Court and Town Life* (1909)

Thomas, Hugh, *The Slave Trade* (1997)

Thompson, Andrew, *George II: King and Elector* (2011)

Thurley, Simon, *Hampton Court: a social and architectural history* (2003)

Timms, Colin, 'Music and Musicians in the Letters of Giuseppe Riva to Agostino Steffani (1720–27)', in *Music and Letters*, vol. 79 (Feb 1998)

Toland, John, *An Account of the Courts of Prussia and Hanover, sent to a Minister of State in Holland* (1705)

Treadwell, J. M., 'Swift, William Wood, and the Factual Basis of Satire', in *The Journal of British Studies*, vol. 15, no. 2 (Spring 1976), pp. 76–91

Trevelyan, G. M., *England Under Queen Anne* (Longman 1936)

Tudor Tudor-Craig, Sir Algernon (ed.) *The Romance of Melusine and de Lusignan* (1932)

Turner, E. S., *The Court of St James's* (1959)

Uglow, Jenny, *A Gambling Man: Charles II and the Restoration* (2009)

——, *Hogarth: a Life and World* (1997)

Veale, J. M., *The Königsmarck Affair in History and Literature* (2001)

Verney, Margaret Lady, ed., *The Verney Letters of the Eighteenth Century* (2 vols, 1930)

Walpole, Horace, *Memoirs of the Reign of George II by Horace Walpole*, ed. Lord Holland (1847)

——, *Reminiscences written by Mr. Horace Walpole in 1788*, with notes by Paget Toynbee (1924)

Ward, A. W., *The Electress Sophia and the Hanoverian Succession* (1903)

Wentworth, Thomas, *The Wentworth Papers 1705–1739 selected from the private and family correspondence of Thomas Wentworth, lord Raby, created in 1711 earl of Stafford*, ed. James J. Cartwright (1883)

Wilhelmine, *Memoirs of Frederica Sophia Wilhelmina, Princess Royal of Prussia, Margravine of Baireuth, sister of Frederick the Great* (2 vols, 1877)

——, *The Misfortunate Margravine: the Early Memoirs of Wilhelmina Margravine of Bayreuth*, ed. Norman Rosenthal (1970)

Wilkins, W. H., *Caroline the Illustrious* (2 vols, 1901)

——, *The Love of an Uncrowned Queen* (1903)

Worsley, Lucy, *Courtiers: the secret history of Kensington Palace* (2010)

Young, Sir George, *Poor Fred, the People's Prince* (1937)

Young, Percy M., *Handel* (1965)

Notes

1. A Portrait

1. Many reputable historians of the Georgian era, such as J. H. Plumb, have perpetuated the erroneous theory that Melusine's primary motivation was greed.
2. Louis XV of France to Count Broglio, 18 July 1724. Quoted in Coxe, *Walpole*, vol. II, p. 304.

2. The Mermaid and the Girl

1. The castle did not survive the bombings of the Second World War.
2. Schmidt, *Das Geschlecht von der Schulenburg*.
3. Schmidt, vol 2.3, p. 418.
4. Friedrich Wilhelm was found a position first as Kammerjunker, then Kammerherr to George.
5. Danneil, *Das Geschlecht von der Schulenburg*.

3. Venice of the North

1. Redman, *The House of Hanover*, p. 16.
2. Davies, *History of Europe*, p. 568.
3. ibid.
4. Quoted in Uglow, *Gambling Man*, p. 91.
5. When Duke George moved his capital to Hanover in 1636, the Duchy of Calenberg-Göttingen became unofficially known as the Duchy of Hanover.
6. Hatton, *George I*, p. 24.
7. Sophia, *Memoiren der Herzogin Sophie*, ed. Köcher, p. 90.
8. ibid., p. 90.
9. ibid.
10. ibid., p. 91.

11. Liselotte, *A Woman's Life*, trans. Forster, p. 249.

12. Komachi and Queren, *Herrenhausen Gardens*, ed. Clark and von Bothmer, trans. Will, p. 38.

13. The canal was not built with the sole purpose of enhancing the carnival-goers' enjoyment. Its primary function was as a buffer against flooding. See Komachi and Queren, *Herrenhausen Gardens*, p. 74.

14. Frederick the Great, quoted in Richie, *Faust's Metropolis*, p. 72.

15. Hatton, *George I*, p. 29.

16. ibid., p. 45.

17. Kroll, *Sophie*, p. 178.

18. Hatton, *George I*, p. 34.

19. ibid., p. 82.

20. ibid., p. 38.

21. ibid., p. 40.

22. Sophia, *Memoiren*, p. 121.

23. It was probably symptomatic of Klara Platen's insecurity and jealousy of Sophia that she named her daughter by Ernst August Sophia Charlotte; Figuelotte, Sophia and Ernst August's only daughter, was christened Sophia Charlotte.

24. Liselotte, *Letters*, trans. and ed. Kroll, p. 78.

25. ibid.

4. The Mistress

1. See Schnath, *Geschichte Hannovers im Zeitalter der neunten Kur und der englischen Sukzession 1674–1714*.

2. Schnath, vol. 4, p. 60.

3. Jesse, *Memoirs of the Court of England*. The editor claims that Melusine was standing behind Sophia at the time.

4. Aurora von Königsmarck, sister of Count Philipp Christoph von Königsmarck, talking about the princess in 1693. Cited in Hatton, *George I*, p. 49.

5. Sophia, *Letters to the Raugravines*, to Louise, 24 Sept 1702.

6. For George feeling things deeply, see Hatton's essay, *George I: In Search of an Elusive Ruler.*

7. Richie, *Faust's Metropolis*, p. 6.

8. Thackeray, W. M., *The Four Georges: Sketches of Manners, Morals, Court and Town Life*, p. 45.

9. Hatton, *George I*, p. 57.

10. ibid., p. 54.

11. See Sophia Dorothea, *Der Königsmarck-Briefwechsel: Korrespondenz der Prinzessin Sophie Dorothea von Hannover mit dem Grafen Philipp Christoph Königsmarck, 1690 bis 1694. Kritische Gesamtausg. in Regestenform*, (Hildesheim 1952) p. 48.

12. Hatton, p. 55.

13. See Sophia Dorothea, *Der Königsmarck-Briefwechsel.*

14. ibid., p. 56.

15. Hatton, *George I*, p. 57, quotes *Königsmarck-Briefwechsel*, 23 June 1693.

16. For a full account see Hatton, p. 59.

17. Schnath, p. 59.

18. Liselotte, *Letters*, trans. and ed. Kroll, p. 87.

19. On her marriage to Friedrich Wilhelm of Brandenburg-Prussia young Sophia Dorothea became queen of Prussia. She was the mother of Frederick the Great.

20. Wilhelmine, *The Misfortunate Margravine*, ed. Rosenthal (1970).

5. Beloved

1. Ernst August, *Letters*, ed. Kielmansegg, p. 256.

2. Hatton quotes Prüser, *George I*, p. 69.

3. Ernst August, *Letters*, ed. Kielmansegg.

4. Schnath, *Geschichte Hannovers*, vol. 2.3, p. 418.

5. Toland, *Account of the Courts of Prussia and Hanover*, p. 54.

6. ibid., p. 70.

7. Hatton, *George I*, p. 99.

8. See HMC, *Report on the Mss of His Grace the Duke of Portland preserved at Welbeck Abbey*, pp. 437–8.

9. Scott Stevenson, trans. and ed., *The Letters of Madame from 1661 to 1708.*

10. Schaumburg-Lippe, *Letters*, 12/23 June 1724.

11. Thompson, Andrew, *George II: King and Elector*, p. 30.

12. George, 'George I's letters to his daughter', in *EHR* 1937, ed. Arkell.

13. ibid.

14. Arkell quotes G. Schnath, *Briefwechsel der Kurfürstin Sophie von Hannover mit dem Preussischen Königshause* (Berlin 1927), p. 105.

15. Schnath, p. 198.

16. Ernst August, *Letters*, ed. Kielmansegg, p. 89.

17. Schnath, pp. 156–7.

18. Hatton, *George I*, p. 78.

19. Ribeiro p. 42 quotes Swift, Jonathan, *The Prose Works of Jonathan Swift* ed. T. Scott (1877) p. 285.

20. Ribeiro quotes Edmond-Jean-François Barbier, *Chronique de la Régence.*

21. Ribeiro quotes *The Present Sate of the Court of France, and City of Paris, in a Letter from Monsieur Mxxx to the Honourable Matthew Prior* (1712) p. 35.

22. Ribeiro p. 38 quotes Mrs Delany, Delany, M., *Autobiography and Correspondence of Mary Granville, Mrs Delany*, ed. Llanover (6 vols. 1861–2) p. 99.

23. Ribeiro p. 41 quotes the anonymous author of *The Art of Dress*, p. 25.

24. Hatton, *George I*, p. 161.

25. Fabrice, *Memoiren*, pp. 156–7.

26. See Hatton, *George I*, p. 135.

27. Hatton, *George I*, p. 99.

28. Cowper, *Diary*, p. 13.

29. Wilhelmina, *The Misfortunate Margravine*, ed. Rosenthal, p. 86.

30. Quoted in Komachi and Queren, *Herrenhausen Gardens*, p. 22.

31. *The letters and diplomatic instructions of Queen Anne*, ed. B. C. Brown (1935), p. 413.

32. Diary of Sir David Hamilton, quoted in Edward Gregg, 'Anne (1665–1714)', *Oxford Dictionary of National Biography*, Oxford University Press, 2004; online edn, Jan 2009.

33. Quoted in Hatton, *George I*, pp. 109–10.

6. The Crown at Last

1. King James I, 21 March 1609, see Brian MacArthur, ed., *The Penguin Book of Historic Speeches* (1996).

2. The population of 1714 was eight and a half million; six million resided in England and Wales, one and a half million in Ireland, and the union with Scotland in 1707 had added a million more souls.

3. Quoted in Speck, *Stability and Strife: England, 1714–1760*, p. 2.

4. Menasseh ben Israel, "To His Highnesse the Lord Protector', in *Menasseh ben Israel's Mission to Oliver Cromwell*, ed. Wolf.

5. Uglow, *Hogarth*, p. 12.

6. Ackroyd, *London*, p. 307.

7. 'Trivia', John Gay, *Poetry and Prose* ed. Winton A Dearing, (2 vols. Oxford 1974) vol. 1, p. 138.

8. Daniel Defoe, *Review*, 11, 9; 6 March 1705. Quoted in Uglow, *Hogarth*, p. 42.

9. The impetus for William's 'invasion' was as much about trade as religious ideology.

10. In her last years Anne herself felt guilty at denying her half-brother James Frances Edward Stuart the throne, but as he refused to abandon his Roman Catholic faith the kingdom remained out of his grasp – at least legally. Both Bolingbroke and Oxford had corresponded with James. Bolingbroke was genuinely sympathetic towards him, while Oxford, a staunch supporter of the Hanoverian

succession, played the politician's pragmatic game of keeping his options open should a successful Jacobite invasion materialize on Anne's death.

11. G. deForest Lord, ed., *Poems on Affairs of State* (7 vols, New Haven, 1962–75), vol 7.

12. Michael, vol. 1, p. 28.

13. Quoted in Michael, *England Under George I*, vol. 2, p. 281.

14. Liselotte, *Letters*, trans. and ed. Kroll, p. 170.

15. HMC, *Report on the Mss of His Grace the Duke of Portland preserved at Welbeck Abbey.*

16. Quoted in Speck, *Stability and Strife*, p. 178.

17. ibid., p. 181.

18. Add. MSS 47028. Entry 26 Jan 1715.

19. Kroll, *Sophie, Electress of Hanover.*

20. ibid., p. 182.

21. *Memoirs of the Secret Services of John Macky*, ed. A.R. (1733), quoted in *DNB* entry on Charles, Second Viscount Townshend.

7. Germans in England

1. Beattie, *English Court*, quotes James Ralph, *A Critical Review of the Public Buildings . . . in and about London and Westminster* (1734), p. 48.

2. Gwynn, *London & Westminster Improved*, pp. 10–11.

3. *Cal. of Treasury Books*, ed. W. A. Shaw, xxix, 1957, *passim*.

4. Saussure, *A Foreign View of England*, trans. and ed. Madame Van Muyden, p. 68.

5. Swift, *Journal to Stella*, ed. Ryland, p. 328.

6. HMC, *Report on the Mss of His Grace the Duke of Portland preserved at Welbeck Abbey.*

7. *Letter Books of John Hervey, First Earl of Bristol* (3 vols. 1894), vol. II, p. 9.

8. *Daily Post*, Saturday 16 December 1721.

9. Cowper, *Diary*.

10. Hervey, *Memoirs*, p. 66, quoted in Beattie, p. 262.

11. Hatton, *George I*, p. 264.

12. See Beattie, p. 80.

13. ibid., p. 261.

14. Liselotte, *Letters*, trans. Forster, p. 96.

8. A Strange Family

1. Worsley, *Courtiers*, p. 109.

2. Worsley quotes Suffolk Records Office (SRO) 941/53/1, p. 219, William Hervey's commonplace book, 'Ballad of Molly Le Pell' (1726).

3. Worsley quotes Romney Sedgwick, *The House of Commons, 1715–54* (1970), vol. 2, p. 115.

4. Bonet, reprinted in Michael, vol. 2.

5. Hamilton, *Diary*, ed. Roberts, p. 87, n. 145.

6. Saussure, *A Foreign View*, trans. and ed. Van Muyden, p. 43.

7. ibid.

8. Thackeray – Punch, under the title 'George the First – Star of Brunswick'. Here, George is depicted as an illiterate and maleable buffoon with no taste in the arts, or in women. In Melville, L., 'The First George', vol. I, p. 217.

9. Walpole, *Reminiscences*, pp. 29–30.

10. Beattie, p. 136, note 1.

11. Franklin, *Lord Chesterfield*, p. 92.

12. Cowper, *Diary*, 4 Feb 1716.

13. ibid.

14. Kroll quotes Liselotte to Luise, Paris 14 January 1716, p. 197.

15. *Manuscripts in the Possession of his Grace the Duke of Portland*.

16. Letter from John Clavering to Mary Cowper printed in Cowper, *Diary*, Appendix E.

17. Quoted and translated from the original German by Hatton, p. 291.

(German text: Verlasse nie einen Freund Strebe, jeden Gerechtigkeit zu erwiesen, Fürchte niemand.)

18. Hatton, *George I*, p. 137.
19. *Daily Post*, 18 Jan 1724.
20. Hatton, *George I*, p. 137, quotes PRO, SPD Regencies 43 vol. 5 Townshend to Walpole, Hanover 17 and 23 Sept. NS 1723, on the money order composed of two bills of £500 each drawn on the treasury.

9. A City out of Rubble

1. Henry Kett, quoted in Ackroyd, *London*, p. 517.
2. Horace Walpole, quoted in Ackroyd, *London*, p. 309.
3. Swift, *Poems*, 'A Description of Morning' (1709).
4. Uglow, *Hogarth*, p. 13, quotes Lord Mayor's ordinance; Henry Morley, *Memoirs of Bartholomew Fair* (1880)
5. Bonet's description of the English court to the Prussian king, reproduced in Michael, vol. 2.
6. Uglow, *Hogarth*, quotes Betterton in Pat Rogers, *Literature and Popular Culture in Eighteenth-Century England* (Brighton, 1985) p. 44.
7. *London Evening Post*, Thursday 16 May 1728.
8. Uglow, *Hogarth*, Dabydeen, *Commercial Britain* (1987)
9. Gay, John, *The Letters of John Gay*, ed. C. F. Burgess (Oxford, 1966)
10. *Music Library Association*, September 1999, 'Supporting Handel Through Subscription to Publication: The Lists of Rodelinda and Faramondo Compared'.
11. *Royal Musical Association Research Chronicle* no. 36, 2003, Lowell Lindgren and Colin Timms, 'The Correspondence of Agostino Steffani and Giuseppe Riva, 1720–1728', Riva to Steffani, Feb 1721.
12. ibid.
13. Ackroyd, *London*, p. 319.
14. Quoted ibid., p. 320.
15. ibid., p. 308.

16. ibid., p. 320.

17. Printed in *The Scottish Historical Review*, vol. 8, no. 31, April 1911. The original is in the Douce collection in the Bodleian Library.

18. Bristol Selected Pamphlets, 1874, Charles Bradlaugh, *The Impeachment of the House of Brunswick*.

19. Drury Lane was notorious for its brothels.

20. Bristol Selected Pamphlets, 1874, Charles Bradlaugh, *The Impeachment of the House of Brunswick*.

10. Palaces

1. Saussure, *A Foreign View*, trans. and ed. Van Muyden, p. 130.

2. Colvin, ed., *The History of the King's Works*, vol. 5, *1660–1782*, p. 239. Much of the information in this chapter comes from this book.

3. ibid.

4. Saussure, *A Foreign View*, trans. and ed. Van Muyden.

5. Wilkins, *Caroline the Illustrious*, p. 266.

6. ibid., p. 335.

7. Hatton, *George I*, p. 262.

8. Colvin, ed., *King's Works*, vol. 5, p. 198.

9. For a full discussion see Christopher Hussey, 'Kensington Palace, the Apartments of the Countess Granville', in *Country Life*, 1 Sept 1928. The article includes many photographs.

10. Worsley, *Courtiers*, quotes John Murray Graham, ed., *Annals and Correspondence of the Viscount and the First and Second Earls of Stair* (1875), vol. 2, p. 94.

11. Politics and Players

1. Philip Stanhope, Earl of Chesterfield, *Letters written by the late right honourable Philip Dormer Stanhope, Earl of Chesterfield, to his son Philip Stanhope, esq* (1774).

2. Hatton, *George I*, p. 139.

3. ibid.

4. HM, Stowe MSS 251, fo. 30, quoted in Beattie, *English Court*, p. 142.

5. ibid., fo. 48.

6. Beattie, *English Court*, p. 223.

7. ibid., p. 221.

8. HM, Stowe MSS 57, vol. 14, pp. 177–8. Quoted in Beattie, p. 222.

9. Cowper, *Diary*, p. 6.

10. Panshanger MSS, Lady Cowper MS. Diary.

11. Wentworth, *Papers 1705–1739*, ed. Cartwright, p. 247.

12. Byrd, *The London Diary 1717-1721*, p. 259–.

13. Beattie, p. 135, quotes a copy made by Lady Cowper's daughter of 'An account of some matters of fact which relate to the Duchess of Marlborough's conduct at Court wrote by her Grace when abroad to some friends in England' (Panshanger MSS, Letterbooks II, 91–2).

14. Sarah Duchess of Marlborough, *Memoirs*, ed. King, p. 217.

15. See Beattie, p. 163.

16. Bonet's report to the Prussian king, see Michael, vol. 2, p. 377.

17. Hatton, *George I*, p. 147.

18. ibid., p. 149.

19. ibid., p. 150.

20. ibid.

21. Hatton, p. 149, quotes Craggs to Stanhope, 30 June 1717: Stanhope, Philip Henry, *History of England 1713–1783* vol. 2.

22. Cowper, *Diary*.

23. Count Palm to the Emperor, 17 Dec 1726, in Coxe, *Walpole*, vol. II, p. 508.

24. Hatton, *George I*, p. 155.

25. ibid., p. 152.

26. Hatton has reservations about Sophia Charlotte's lottery win. She suspects the entry in her account books may actually be for the £9,545 paid to her by the Duke of Chandos for her intercession with George in 1719 for his title.

27. Liselotte, *Letters*, trans. and ed. Kroll, p. 180.

28. Hatton, *George I*, p. 131.

29. See Mahaffey, 'Pope's "Artemisia" and "Phryne" as Personal Satire'.

30. For a full analysis of both poems see Mahaffey, ibid.

31. *The Morning Chronicle*, Friday 13 Feb 1818.

32. *Bonet's report to the Prussian court*, printed in Michael, vol. 2, p. 373.

33. HMC, *Portland MSS*, V, 501. Quoted in Beattie, *English Court*, p. 224.

34. Cowper, *Diary*, p. 118.

35. Cowper, *Diary*, p. 108.

36. William Coxe, *Memoirs of the Life and Administration of Sir Robert Walpole, Earl of Orford* (4 vols. 1816), Robert Walpole to Secretary Stanhope, 30 July/10 Aug 1716.

37. Coxe, *Walpole*, II, p. 507.

38. Montagu, *Letters*, ed. Halsband, vol. I, pp. 240–1.

39. Blenheim MSS. D 133, Stanhope to Sunderland, 3 Aug 1719. Quoted in Beattie, p. 242.

40. ibid., Wallenrodt to Sunderland, 18/19 Feb 1720. Quoted in Beattie, p. 242.

41. Coxe, *Walpole*, II, p. 265.

42. ibid., p. 59.

43. Lady Mary Wortley Montagu, *Works*, p. 127.

12. A Battle

1. I am indebted to Professor Aubrey Newman for his insights into this subject.

2. Lady Mary Wortley Montagu, *Account of the Court of George I*, p. 93.

3. This 'devotion' was probably twofold. Georg August loathed his father and would do anything to vex him.

4. Walpole, *Reminiscences*, ed. Toynbee, pp. 23ff.

5. The author was actually Karl Ludwig von Pöllnitz.

6. Walpole, *Reminiscences*, ed. Toynbee, pp. 22–3.

7. Bonet's report to the King and Queen of Prussia, July 1716, reproduced in Michael.

8. ibid.

9. The king's letter to his 'Dearest Son', 5 July (OS) 1716, is translated from the French in Coxe, *Walpole*, vol. 1, pp. 282–4. Reproduced in Hatton, *George I.*

10. J. H. Plumb, *The First Four Georges*, p. 46.

11. Hatton, p. 199.

12. ibid., p. 196.

13. ibid., p. 202.

14. Stair, *Annals of Stair*, ed. Graham, vol. II, p. 26, Quoted in Beattie, p. 270.

15. Beattie. p. 267.

16. HMC Onslow MSS, p. 509. Quoted in Beattie, p. 268.

17. The child was actually born with a polyp in his heart; he died in February 1718.

18. Hatton, *George I* , p. 207.

19. Liselotte, *Letters* trans. and ed. Kroll, p. 191.

20. Cowper, *Diary*, p. 108.

21. Beattie, p. 272.

22. ibid., p. 274.

23. ibid., p. 275.

24. Hervey, *Some Materials*, ed. Sedgwick, p. 303.

25. James Hamilton to the Pretender, 27 Nov 1721, n.s.: Royal Archives, Windsor Castle, Stuart Papers [RA, SP], 55/152. Reproduced Clyve Jones, 'Evidence, Interpretation and Definitions in Jacobite Historiography'.

26. *Letters of Madame*, ed. Gertrud Scott Stevenson, vol. 2, p. 167.

27. Quoted in Worsley, *Courtiers*, p. 41.

28. Cowper, *Diary*, 18 Dec 1714.

29. Nicolson, *London Diaries*, ed. Jones and Holmes.

30. Madame Gemmingen was dismissed by George on 4 April 1718. We

do not know why, but it could have been over a difference of opinion as the row between father and son progressed.

31. Liselotte, *Letters*, traans. and ed. Kroll, p. 210.
32. Hatton, *George I*, p. 210.
33. Hatton, *George I*, p. 242, quotes Frederick William Schulenburg's correspondence to Görtz of April 1718.
34. Quoted in Worsley, p. 43.
35. Coxe, *Walpole*, vol. I, p. 123, quoted in the *DNB* entry of Sir Robert Walpole.
36. Cowper, *Diary*, p. 142.
37. Cowper, *Diary*, p. 132.

13. A Bubble

1. Mackay, *Extraordinary Popular Delusions*, p. xv.
2. Quoted in *The British Poets: One Hundred Volumes* (1822), vol. II, p. xli.
3. Thomas, *Slave Trade*, p. 238, quotes Lord Erleigh, *The South Sea Bubble* (1935), p. 36.
4. Quoted in Thomas, p. 236.
5. Mackay, p. 16.
6. Carswell, *South Sea Bubble*, p. 127.
7. HMC, *Report on the Manuscripts of His Grace the Duke of Portland preserved at Welbeck Abbey.*
8. ibid.
9. Coxe, Walpole, Secretary Craggs to Earl Stanhope, 17 July 1720, vol. II, p. 189.
10. Carswell, p. 154.
11. Quoted ibid., p. 127: 'Poem in Honour of the Birthday of His Majesty King George', 1720.
12. *Original Weekly Journal*, Saturday 23 April 1720.
13. Carswell, p. 157.
14. Hatton, *George I*, p. 254.

15. Windsor, R.A.: 52844, copy of the duchess of Kendal's letter of 27 Sept. NS 1720, marked rec. 29 Sept. OS. Quoted in Hatton, *George I*, p. 252.

16. Quoted in Hatton *George I*, p. 253.

17. Hatton quotes drafts of letters to Johann Matthias in the Görtz archive.

18. Mackay, p. 55.

19. ibid., pp. 55–6.

20. Ackroyd, *London*, p. 322.

21. Quoted in Carswell, p. 195.

22. Coxe, vol. II, p. 195.

23. Coxe, Broderick to Middleton, 13 Sept 1720, vol. II, p. 190.

24. J. Oldmixon, *The history of England, during the reigns of King William and Queen Mary, Queen Anne, King George I* (1735), quoted in Stuart Handley, 'Knight, Robert (1675–1744)', *Oxford Dictionary of National Biography*, Oxford University Press, May 2005; online edn, Jan 2008.

25. Carswell, p. 210.

26. Balen, *A Very English Deceit*, p. 195.

27. Carswell, p. 231.

28. *Manuscripts in the Collection of His Grace the Duke of Portland.*

29. Carswell quotes Destouches's report of his conversation with the Duchess of Kendal. Archives des Affaires Estrangères, corr. Pol. Angl. cccxxxv 99–100.

30. Quoted in Balen, p. 204.

31. Quoted ibid., p. 208.

32. Carlisle MSS, 77, quoted in Stuart Handley, 'Knight, Robert (1675–1744)', *Oxford Dictionary of National Biography*, Oxford University Press, May 2005; online edn, Jan 2008,

33. Hatton, *George I*, p. 256.

34. Hatton, *George I*, p. 219, Aislabie to Walpole, Orford Papers, 2 Feb 1722, vol. II, p. 219.

35. Hatton, *George I*, p. 255.

36. ibid.

37. *Manuscripts in the Collection of His Grace the Duke of Portland.*

38. ibid.

14. Venality

1. Coxe, *Memoirs of the Life and Administration of Sir Robert Walpole, Earl of Orford* (4 vols, 1816)

2. Hatton, *George I*, p. 154, quotes Rudé, *Hanoverian London*, p. 40, listing holdings of 1721, and Dickson, *Financial Revolution*, p. 279, for holdings of 1723–4.

3. Carteret, Secretary of State for the South on Craggs's death, became the leader of those who had previously rallied around Stanhope and Sunderland. He and Walpole, although not enemies, had a fractious relationship.

4. Coxe, quotes the Townshend Papers, Robert Walpole to Lord Townshend, Whitehall 1/12 Oct 1723, vol. II, p. 276.

5. Coxe quotes Robert Walpole to Lord Townshend, Whitehall, 18–19 Oct 1723, Townshend Papers, vol. II, p. 283.

6. Coxe, quotes Lord Bolingbroke to Lord Townshend, 28 June 1723, Hardwicke Papers, vol. II, p. 311.

7. ibid., Townshend to Bolingbroke, 9/20 July 1723, Pyrmont, Hardwicke Papers.

8. Schaumburg-Lippe, *Letters*, pp. 77–8.

9. *Daily Journal*, Feburary 1723.

10. Macknight cites the Clough Papers; quoted by Coxe in the Walpole Correspondence, vol. II p. 345.

11. Coxe, vol. II, p. 338.

12. Coxe quotes Etough's minutes of a conversation with Sir Robert Walpole on the attempt of Lord Bolingbroke and the Duchess of Kendal to obtain his dismissal in 1727, Etough Papers, 13 Sept 1737, *Memoirs of Sir Robert Walpole.*

13. Coxe, quotes Lord Bolingbroke to Sir William Wyndham, 20 Feb 1736, Egremont Papers. Vol. II, p. 338.

15. Diplomacy

1. Beattie, p. 242.
2. Coxe quotes Count Broglio to the King of France, 6 July 1724, *Memoirs of Sir Robert Walpole*, vol. II, p. 300.
3. ibid.
4. ibid., 10 July 1724.
5. Add. MSS. 37385 ff. 88.
6. Add. MSS. 37384 ff. 80.
7. *Daily Journal*, 11 Feb 1723.
8. Lewis (ed.), *Selected Letters of Horace Walpole*, vol. 2, p. 455.
9. Coxe, quotes Robert Walpole to Lord Townshend, Townshend Papers, Whitehall, 30 Aug 1723, vol. 2, p. 265.
10. Coxe quotes Lord Townshend to Robert Walpole, Hanover, 8 Sept 1723, vol. 2, p. 287.
11. Hatton, *George I*, p. 275.
12. Coxe quotes Lord Townshend to Robert Walpole, Göhrde, 15 Nov 1723, Hardwicke Papers, vol. 2, p. 287.
13. Coxe, vol. 2, p. 271.
14. ibid.
15. Coxe quotes Townshend to Walpole, Hanover, 2 Oct 1723. Hardwicke Papers, pp. 271–4 .
16. Coxe quotes Townshend to the Duke of Newcastle, Hanover, 27 Nov 1723, vol. 2, p. 288.
17. Wilhelmine, *The Misfortunate Margravine*, ed. Rosenthal, p. 88.

16. A Marriage?

1. Edmund Calamy, 1671–1732: *An Historical Account of My Own Life, With Some Reflections on the Times I Have Lived In (1671–1731)*

(second edition, 2 volumes; London: Colburn and Bentley, 1830), ed. by John Towill Rutt.

2.   Hatton, *George I*; for English contemporary rumours of a morganatic marriage see Montagu, *Works* 1, p. 75; and Coxe, *Memoirs of the Life and Administration of Sir Robert Walpole, Earl of Orford* (3 vols, 1816), vol. I, p. 150, and vol. II, p. 258.

3.   *Manuscripts in the collection of Duke of Portland*. Edward Harley, junior, to Abigail Harley, 26 Jan 1717.

4.   *Letters of Madame*, ed. Gertrud Scott Stevenson, vol. 2, p. 167.

5.   Fabrice, *Memoiren*, pp. 153–9. Letter from Schulenburg to Fabrice from Venice. The letter is dated 1728.

6.   Add. MSS. 4326. B. f. 3.

7.   Andrew Starkie, 'Blackburne, Lancelot (1658–1743)', *Oxford Dictionary of National Biography*, Oxford University Press, 2004; online edn, Jan 2008 quotes Horace Walpole (*Memories* I, pp. 74–5).

8.   ibid.

17. Endings

1.   Lewis (ed.) *Selected Letters of Walpole*, v. 25, p. 248.

2.   *Daily Journal*, Friday 22 March 1723.

3.   Schaumburg-Lippe, *Letters*, 14/25 July 1727.

4.   Ernst August, *Letters*, ed. Kielmansegg.

5.   See Binney, *Great Houses of Europe*; Schmidt, *Schulenburg*, no. 742.

6.   Howard, *Letters*, ed. Croker, Mrs Howard to Mr Gay, 15 June 1728.

7.   *Weekly Journal*, Saturday 30 Dec 1727.

8.   Rudé, *Hanoverian London*, p. 146.

9.   George left Melusine £12,986.2s.2d. in South Sea shares. Its value when Walpole released it was only £6,993.1s.1d.

10. Hatton, The Duchess of Kendal to Sir Robert Walpole, London 18 Feb 1730, Orford Papers, Coxe, vol. II, p. 668.

11. Hatton, *George I*, p. 137.

12. G. S. Holland Fox-Strangeways, *Henry Fox, first Lord Holland* (2 vols,

1920), quoted in John Cannon, 'Stanhope, Philip Dormer, fourth earl of Chesterfield (1694–1773)', *Oxford Dictionary of National Biography*, Oxford University Press, 2004; online edn, Oct 2009.

13. Bentley, *Letters of Horace Walpole*, vol. 1, p. 65

14. Melusine was seventy-five when she died. She was seven years younger than George, not one year older as Horace Walpole erroneously believed.

15. Hatton, *George I*, p. 136.

Index

Achaz, Friedrich 12
Ackroyd, Peter
  London, the Biography 96, 144
Addison 96, 195
Aislabie, John 214, 216, 217, 219, 220, 227
Allanson, Mrs 198
Anne, Princess (daughter of George II) 40, 203, 217, 255
Anne, Queen 74, 98, 99–100, 102, 138
  childbearing history 38
  court of 111
  death 90, 164
  diamonds 3
  life in later years 111–12
  relationship with George I's father 40–1
  and slave trade 214
Anthony, Monsieur de 117
Archer, Thomas 138
Argyll, Archibald Campbell, Duke of 191–2
Augusta of Saxe-Gotha-Altenburg 156
Austria 99

Bank of England 213, 214, 228
baroque gardens 30
Bartholomew Fair 140
Beattie, J.M. 167, 195, 199, 245
Bedoghi, Lorenzo 29
Ben Israel, Menasseh 96
Benson, William 155, 158
Berens-Cohen, Elieser Lefmann 19
Berkeley, Bishop 143
Bernard, Francesco (Senesino) 142
Bernstorff, Baron Andreas von 164–6, 168, 169, 178, 181, 206, 225, 252
Bertram, Mijndert 201–2
Berwick, Duke of 105
Bílá Hora, Battle of (1620) 20
Blackburne, Lancelot (Archbishop of York) 262–4
Blenheim Palace 95
Blunt, John 224
Board of Works 155, 158, 159, 202
Bolingbroke, Viscount 99, 100, 101, 201, 235–41

Bonet, Frederick 114, 125, 141–2, 164, 168, 177, 189–90
Bothmer, Hans Kaspar von 44–5, 164, 167, 169, 206, 225
Brett, Anne 126
bribery
  and English court 166–71
Bristol, Lady 113
Broderick, Thomas 222
Broglio, Count 245–6
Brontë, Charlotte 51
Brunswick-Wolfenbüttel, Anton Ulrich, Duke 36, 37, 41, 59, 61, 62, 64, 246
Brunswick-Wolfenbüttel, Elisabeth Christine 246
Brunt, Captain Samuel
  A Voyage to Cacklogallinia 176
Brydges, Jones *see* Chandos, Duke of
Burroughs, Charles 128
Bussche, Albrecht Philipp von dem 37
Bussche, Johann von dem 43
Bussche-Ippenburg, Ernst August Philipp von dem 79–80
Byrd, William 167

Cadogan, William 177–8
Calamy, Edward 257
Campbell, Colen 158
Carlyle, Thomas 4, 123
Carnarvon, Lord 165
Carnival (Hanover) 31–2, 36
Caroline of Ansbach (wife of Georg August) 3, 189, 193, 194–5, 268
  death of son 204
  entertaining at court 118
  marriage 78
  relationship with Melusine 88, 271
  relationship with Sophia Charlotte 88
  separation from children 196–7, 205, 208
Caroline of Hesse-Cassel 21–2
Carswell, John 218–19
Carteret, Lord 234, 249–50
Caselius, John 11
Catherine of Braganza 98

Catholicism 98, 99
Celle 41
  unification with Hanover 62, 81
Celle Castle 5, 62–3, 261
Chandos, Duke of (James Brydges) 167–8
Charbonnier, Martin 30–1
Charlemagne 34
Charles I, King 95, 96
Charles II, King 22–3, 40–1, 98, 145
Chesterfield, Earl of 125, 128, 161, 206, 272
Chevreau, Urban de 33
Child, Sir Caesar 229
Christian Heinrich (brother of George I) 27,
  37–8, 39, 72
Christian Ludwig (brother of Ernst August)
  24, 25
Christina of Sweden, Queen 33
Chronicles of Newgate, The 141
Clavering, John 131
coffee houses (London) 145–6
Colt, Sir William Dutton 18
Colvin, H.M. 156
Conzbrücke, battle of (1675) 40
courtesans, court 49–50
Cowper, Lord 165–6
Cowper, Mary, Countess 116, 117, 126, 129,
  165–6, 170, 178, 179, 192, 197, 203, 207,
  208, 212, 216
Coxe, William 116, 231, 237–8, 259, 262
Craggs, James (the elder) 216, 228
Craggs, James (the younger) 129, 169, 205,
  215, 228
Creation of the World, The 140
Cromwell, Oliver 95, 96

Daily Courant 147
Daily Journal 247–8
Damaideno, Abbot Theodoro 34
Dawes, Sir William 263
Daye, Carey 106
de la Fosse, Rémy 71
Defoe, Daniel 97, 110
Degenfeld, Louise von 22
Delany, Mrs 83
Descartes, René 33
Destouches (diplomat) 225
Dryden, John
  Annus Mirabilis 138
Dupplin, Lady 102

East India Company 214
Egmont, Lord 103
Electoral College 28
Elizabeth of Bohemia (wife of Frederick V)
  20, 21, 197
Eltz, Philipp Adam 39
Emden castle 10
Emkendorf Castle 269
Enrico Leone (opera) 35–6
Ernst August, Elector of Hanover (father of
  George I)
  affair with Klara von Platen 35, 42–3,
  66
    attempt to secure the Hanoverian claim
      to electoral cap 28–9, 33–4, 35, 36
    and brother's anti-contract of marriage
      24, 25–7
    and Carnival 31–2
    and courtesans 50
    death 37, 66, 69
    dukedom of Hanover passes to 28
    marriage to Sophia 23–4, 39, 50, 66
    mistresses 52
    opposition to daughter-in law's affair
      with Königsmarck and ordering of
      murder of 59–60, 66
    plot against by son (Maximilian) 37
    primogeniture announcement and split
      within family over 36–7
Ernst August (brother of George I) 27, 72,
  76–7, 88, 218, 268
Etough, Reverend Henry 237–40, 262–3
Eusden, Reverend Laurence 217
Evening Post 147
'Excellent New Ballad, An' 147
exclusion crisis (1679) 97–8

Fabrice, Friedrich Ernst von 166, 237
fairs (London) 140–1
fashion 81–4
Figuelotte see Sophia Charlotte (sister of
  George I)
Flitcroft, Henry 138
Forster, Thomas 104
France
  peace treaty with England (1713) 99
Frederick the Great 32–3, 255
Frederick Louis (son of George II) 78, 156,
  199, 255
Frederick V, Elector Palatine 20–1

Frederick William of Brandenburg-Prussia 78
Friedrich August (brother of George I) 27, 36, 37, 49

Gallery, the (Hanover) 35
gambling 141
Gay, John 97, 121, 143
 The Beggar's Opera 143
Gemmingen, Madame 203
Georg August (future George II) 44, 77, 78, 131, 245–6
 acrimony between and rupture with father 64–5, 77, 179, 183, 187–206
 anger at father's dismissal of Argyll 191–2
 coronation 269
 and death of son 205
 devotion to mother 188–9
 expulsion from palace and separation from children 153, 183, 187, 196–7, 205
 marriage to Caroline of Ansbach 78
 reconciliation with father 206–7
 relationship with Melusine 193, 271
 relationship with own children 156, 187
 setting up of rival court in Leicester Square 117–18, 183, 197
George August (uncle to George I) 80–1
George of Denmark, Prince 40–1
George I, King 19
 acrimony and rupture between son and 64–5, 77, 179, 183, 187–206
 alleged incestuous affair with half-sister 87–8, 127–8, 130
 anti-Hanoverian ballads and pamphlets against 103–4, 125, 147–8, 150
 birth and childhood 27–8
 birthday celebrations 216–17
 break-down of marriage to Sophia Dorothea 45–6, 49, 54, 55
 bribery allegations at court of 166–76
 challenging of by the Pretender (James Stuart) 102–3, 104–5
 character and attributes 40, 51, 74, 188
 condemnation of for treatment of Sophia Dorothea 63–4
 conflict with brothers over primogeniture 37–8, 64, 187
 contesting of accession to the British throne 101–2
 coronation 102
 court of 111, 112–15, 119–21
 daily routine 119
 death 268
 and death of sister (Figuelotte) 80, 115–16
 dismissal of Argyle 191–2
 divorce from Sophia Dorothea and ordering of her incarceration 4–5, 63–4, 188
 as Elector of Hanover 71–2, 74–6, 81, 163
 enforced sociability at court due to rupture with son 194, 195, 197–8
 expulsion of son from palace and orders separation of children 153, 183, 187, 196–7, 205
 faction and discontent within first English ministry 176–8
 as father to illegitimate daughters 72, 79, 132–3
 flirtations and fondness of women 125–8
 grooming to be future king 39–40
 ill-health 193–4, 197, 255
 influence of 'German cabal' on 163, 164–6
 love of opera and theatre 142 85
 marriage to Melusine rumours 259–64
 marriage to Sophia Dorothea 41–2, 43–4, 53
 military campaigns 45
 mother's love for 27, 28
 movement between seasonal residences 118
 and parliament 97
 preferring intimacy of family life over court life 112–15, 117
 proclamation as king of England 90–1
 reconciliation with son 202, 206–8
 refusal to accept paternity of illegitimate children 53–4, 72
 and rehabilitation of Bolingbroke 237, 238–41
 relationship with half-sister (Sophia Charlotte) 43, 131, 132
 relationship with Melusine 4, 50, 53, 65, 80, 81, 84, 86–7, 163, 248, 260–1
 relationship with Sophie Karoline 251
 relationship with Walpole 241

George I (*contd*)
  renovation of Göhrde 71
  representation of by historians 50–1
  return visits to Hanover whilst king of
    England 91, 178, 190, 249
  romantic attachments before marriage
    42–3
  rumours of sexual rapacity of 125–9
  and South Sea Bubble 215, 218–19, 220
  and Stanhope's death 227–8
  takes up residence at St James's Palace
    100
  and Turkish servants 115–17
  and upbringing of son 190–1
  use of British resources in Hanoverian
    matters 178–9
  and Whigs 100–1, 105–6
  and wife's affair with Königsmarck 5, 62,
    63–4
  will 171
George II, King *see* Georg August
George William of Brunswick-Lüneburg,
  Duke (brother of Ernst August) 23, 24,
  25–6, 41, 62, 64, 78
German Protestant Union 20
Germany
  and Thirty Years War 21
Gibbs, James 138
Giusti, Tommaso 35
Glorious Revolution (1688) 38, 95
Gloucester, William, Duke of 38
Göhrde, hunting lodge at 70–1
Görtz, Friedrich Wilhelm von 40, 106, 165,
  168
Grand Alliance 99
Great Fire of London (1666) 138
Great Northern War 76
Grote, Otto 40
Guildford, Lord 225
Gwynn, J. 110

Habeas Corpus, suspension of 104
Halifax, Lord (Charles Montagu) 176–7
Hamilton, Duke of 200
Hamilton, Elizabeth Gerard, Duchess of
  200, 201
Hammerstein, Alexander von 80, 206
Hampton Court 118, 154–6, 197–9
Handel, George Frideric 85, 142, 143–4, 203
  Water Music 144

Hanover 17–19, 73
  admission to Electoral College (1708) 61
  as ally of the Grand Alliance 99
  and Carnival 31–2, 36
  claim to electoral cap 29, 35, 36
  court at 18–19, 73–4
  courtesans at court 49–50
  electoral cap conferred on House of
    (1693) 39, 61
  enhancing glory of through architecture
    and portraiture 34
  establishing of primogeniture (1683) 36
  fashion 81–4
  Gallery 35
  genealogy of House of 33–4
  and Herrenhausen 18, 29–31, 70, 158
  illegitimacy in 43
  and Leineschloss 18, 28, 29, 34
  opera 35–6
  population 81
  unification with Celle 62, 81
Hardenberg, Christian Ulrich von 252–4
Harley, Abigail 102
Harley, Edward 216, 224, 260
Harley, Robert *see* Oxford, Earl of
Harley, Thomas 228
Harling, Frederick von 204
Harling, Katharine von 249
Hatton, Ragnhild 51, 77, 128, 190, 206, 214,
  215
Hattorf, Baron 154
Hawksmoor, Nicholas 138
Hayter, Thomas 263
Heidegger, John James 142, 270
Henry the Lion 24, 28, 34, 36
Henry VIII, King 154–5
Herrenhausen (Hanover) 18, 29–31, 70, 158
Hervey, Lord John 118, 130, 199, 275
Hillsborough, Lord 229
Historia Domus 33–4
Hogarth, William
  Southwark Fair 140–1
Holy Roman Empire 18
Howard, Henrietta *see* Suffolk, Countess of
Hugo, Ludolf 40
Hussey, Christopher 159
Hyde, Anne 98

Irby, Sir William 163–4
Irish copper coinage patent scandal 233–4

Irwine, Lady 226

Jacobite rebellions 61, 103–5, 142, 235–6
Jacobites 64, 90, 101, 104
James I, King 21, 95
James II, King 38, 95, 98, 102
James, John 138
James Stuart (Pretender) 99, 101, 102–3,
    104–5, 199–200, 236
Jardine, Lisa 155
Jews 96
Joanne Sophie *see* Schaumburg-Lippe,
    Countess of
Johann, Adolf 23
Johann Friedrich, Duke 24, 25, 28, 29
Jones, Inigo 139, 159

Karl Ludwig (uncle to George I) 21–2, 23,
    25, 70
Karl Philipp (brother of George I) 27, 37,
    44, 49
Kendal House 271, 274–5
Kensington Palace 116, 118, 156–60, 197,
    202
Kent, William 116, 153, 158, 159
Kielmansegg, Johann Adolf von 88, 166,
    170, 171, 197
King's Theatre (London) 142, 144
Kinnoull, Abigail, Countess of 216
Knesebeck, Eleonore von dem 45, 57, 60,
    61, 63, 65
Knight, Robert 222, 224, 225–7
Königsmarck, Hans Christoff von 55–6
Königsmarck, Count Philipp von 66, 77,
    201
    affair with Sophia Dorothea 4–5, 51,
        55–60, 77
    background 55–6
    murder of 60, 61–2, 65
Königstreu, Mehemet von 71, 115–16, 154,
    194, 267–8

Law, John 215, 218, 221, 223
Leathes, William 226
Leibniz, Gottfried Wilhelm 19, 30, 33–5, 74,
    76
Leicester House 153
Leineschloss (Hanover) 18, 28, 29, 34
Leinster, Duke of 119
Leopold I, Emperor 18, 36, 39, 81

Lepell, Molly 125
Letti, Miss 247, 255
Licensing Act 147
Liselotte (Elizabeth Charlotte) (daughter of
    Karl Ludwig) 21, 25, 27–8, 52, 62, 102,
        103–4, 133–4, 197, 200–1, 204, 260
London 96, 137–46
    architecture 138
    building activity 139
    coffee and chocolate houses 145–7
    fairs 140–1
    gambling 141
    Great Fire of (1666) 138
    as important commercial centre 96
    life on streets of 137
    opera 142–3, 144–5
    population 137
    theatres 141–2
London Bridge 139
London Stock Exchange 146
lottery, state 117, 141
Louis XIV, King of France 33, 34, 39, 69, 95,
    99, 102, 104, 193, 259
Louis XV, King of France 4
Louise, abbess of Maubuisson 20
Louise (daughter of Melusine) *see*
    Schulenburg, Anna Louise von der
Lubomirska, Princess Ursula Katherina 81

Macaulay 146–7
Macclesfield, Lord 73
Mackay, Charles 212, 215, 220–1
Macknight, Thomas 238
Macky, John 105–6
Madonetto, Pierre 32
Mahaffey, Kathleen 172
Maintenon, Madame de 69, 236, 259
mantua 82
Mar, Earl of 104–5
Marlborough, Duke of 95, 99, 177, 178, 191
Marlborough, Sarah, Duchess of 111, 126,
    153, 167, 183
Marriage Act (1754) 264
Mary II, Queen 38, 98–9, 158
Mary of Modena 98, 102
Masham, Abigail 111
masks
    wearing of at Hanover court 83–4
Matthias, Johann 217, 220
Mauro, Hortensio 36

Maximilian Wilhelm (Max) (brother of George I) 27, 36–8, 44, 59
Mecklenburg 179
Mehemet see Königstreu, Mehemet von
Melusina story 9
Melusine see Schulenburg, Ehrengard Melusine von der
Melusine (daughter of Melusine) see Schulenburg, Petronella Melusine von
Mencken, Otto 60, 62
Methuen, Paul 129
Meysenbug, Maria Katherine von 42–3, 50
Mississippi Scheme (1720) (France) 212, 215, 218, 221
Mistra, Mustapha de 71, 115–16, 154
Molesworth, Lord 223–4
Moltke, Joachim and Otto Friedrich von 37
Montagu, Charles see Halifax, Lord
Montagu, Lady Mary Wortley 18, 171, 172, 181–2, 188, 259
Montalbano, Nicolò 60
Morning Chronicle 175–6
Mustapha see Mistra, Mustapha de

Navius, Accius 34
Newcastle, Duke of 196
Newgate prison 141
Newton, Sir Isaac 234
Nicolson, William (Bishop of Carlisle) 203
Nottingham, Earl of 101, 105, 177

Oates, Titus 98
Oeynhausen, Margarethe Gertrud von (Trudchen) see Schaumberg-Lippe, Margarethe Gertrud
Oeynhausen, Rabe Christoph von 12, 73
Oeynhausen, Sophie Juliane von (sister of Melusine) 10–12, 73
Olbreuse, Eléanore d' 25–7, 63
Onslow, Arthur 195
opera
    and Handel 143–4
    Hanover 35–6
    London 142–3, 144–5
Orléans, Philippe duc d' 25, 82
Ormond, Duchess of 214
Oudernarde, Battle of (1708) 190
Oxford, Earl of (Robert Harley) 90, 99, 100, 101, 111, 177, 213

Paleotti, Marchesa 52
Palm, Karl Josef von 246
Peerage Bill 207
Perrault, Charles 51
Peter the Great 35
Peter the Wild Boy 116
Philippeaux, Henri (comte St Florentin) 250
Platen, Ernst August von 248
Platen, Franz Ernst von 42
Platen, Klara von (mistress of Ernst August) 35, 39, 42–3, 66, 74, 171
Platen, Sophia Charlotte von (illegitimate sister of George I) 3, 74, 251
    alleged incestuous affair with George 87–8, 127–8, 130
    antipathy between Melusine and 88, 119, 130–1, 251
    appearance 127–8
    bribery allegations 171
    character 89, 130, 172
    court rumours over lovers 129–30
    creation of discord 88
    death 256
    and death of husband 197
    finances 171
    lodgings at St James's 153–4
    lottery win 141, 171
    marriage 88
    popularity 171–2
    relationship with Caroline of Ansbach 88, 251
    relationship with George 43, 131, 132
    and South Sea Bubble 215, 225
    titles bestowed on to by George 131
    vilification of by Pope 174–5
Platen, Sophie Karoline von 88, 248–51
Plumb, J.H. 191
Pope, Alexander 172–4
    'Artemisia' 174–5
    Moral Essays 116
    'Phryne' 172–4
    on South Sea Bubble 213
Popish Plot 98
Portland, Jane, Countess of 202–3, 204
Pozobueno (Spanish ambassador) 246
Pretender see James Stuart (Pretender)
Prussia 78
Pulteney, William 125, 221–2

Ralph, James 110
Redman, Alvin 19
Reynolds, Joshua 275
Ribeiro, Aileen 82
Riva, Giuseppe 145
Robartes, Lady Essex 165
Robethon, Jean 166, 167, 168–9
Royal Academy of Music 142–3
Rupert, Prince 22

St James's Palace 109–10, 120, 153–4, 199
    fire (1723) 154
St James's Park 110–11
St Paul's Cathedral 138, 155
Sarah, Duchess of Marlborough see
    Marlborough, Sarah, Duchess of
Saussure, César de 119–21, 126, 127, 151,
    154, 156–7
Schaumberg-Lippe, Margarethe Gertrud
    (Trudchen) (daughter of Melusine) 73,
    85, 109, 132–3, 176, 201–2, 205–6, 218,
    267
Schaumburg-Lippe, Albrecht Wolfgang zu
    (son of Joanne Sophie) 132, 176, 202,
    270
Schaumburg-Lippe, George Augustus zu
    (son of Trudchen) 275
Schaumburg-Lippe, Joanne Sophie,
    Countess of 77–8, 89, 91, 132, 197, 201,
    202, 205, 268, 269, 270
Schaumburg-Lippe, William zu (son of
    Trudchen) 275
Schnath, George 62
Schulenburg, Anna Elisabeth von der(née
    von Stammer) (stepmother) 11
Schulenburg, Anna Elisabeth von
    der(sister) 10, 12
Schulenburg, Anna Louise (Louise)
    (daughter) 53, 70, 79–80, 109, 130, 133,
    176, 205, 270, 275, 176205
Schulenburg, Daniel Bodo von der
    (brother) 10, 12, 170
Schulenburg, Ehrengard Melusine von der
    (later Duchess of Kendal)
    in Hanover
        acknowledgement of status as
            George's mistress and rise of
            position in court 69–70
        becomes George's mistress 49
        birth of daughters and refusal of

George to accept paternity 53–4, 65,
    72
diplomatic role 78, 81
and divorce and imprisonment of
    Sophia Dorothea 63
leaves for England 91
lifestyle and routine 85–6
living at Göhrde 70–1
as maid of honour to Sophia,
    Duchess of Hanover 12, 49
pivotal to maintenance of friendly
    relations between George and rest of
    family 77
popularity at court 73
presiding at official functions 69
relationship with Sophia (George's
    mother) 20, 51–3, 63, 69–70, 71–2,
    89
rise of after Ernst August's death 69
in England
allowance 119
apartments at St James's 110–11, 153
attack on by Swift 82, 175
and betrayal by Hardenberg 252–4
bribery allegations against and
    reputation of corruption 170, 171,
    172–4, 201, 225, 237–8
diplomatic role 246–7
dislike of Townshend and role of in
    downfall 179–81
elevated to Irish peerage 179–80
and George's quarrel with his son
    193
honours and titles bestowed on 91,
    147, 247–8
household and servants 117
influence and power of 4, 180–3, 245
instrumental in rise and fall of
    George's English ministers 180–3
involvement in political affairs and
    intermediary between George and
    his ministers 4, 5, 163–4, 179–83,
    182, 205, 253–4, 261
Kensington Palace accommodation
    202
life at court 118–19, 119
looting of Queen Anne's diamonds
    allegation 3
mastering of English 91
and opera 144–5

Schulenburg, Ehrengard Melusine von der
(*contd*)
 overtures to the Pretender claims
  199–200, 201
 Pope's attack on 172–5
 preferring of intimacy of family life
  and close friends over court 112–13,
  117
 and rehabilitation of Bolingbroke
  235–6, 237–9, 241
 return visits to Hanover 91, 178, 190,
  249
 selling of copper coinage in Ireland
  patent 233–5
 and Sophie Karoline 250–1, 253–4
 and South Sea Bubble 4, 201, 211,
  213, 215, 219–20, 223, 225, 228,
  233
 theatre visits 141–2
 unpopularity of 268
 and upbringing of Georg August and
  Caroline's children 201–3
 vilification and lampooning of in
  publications 91, 147–50, 172–6,
  234–5
 and Wren's dismissal 155
Personal Life
 antipathy between Sophia Charlotte
  and 88, 119, 130–1, 251
 appearance and figure 3, 51–2, 84
 attitude towards money 170
 birth and childhood 9, 12
 charity giving 170
 closeness of relationship with siblings
  11, 53, 54, 75–6
 and death of brother (Frederick
  William) 211
 death and burial 274
 and death of daughter (Trudchen)
  267
 and death of father 53
 and death of George 268–9
 and death of mother 10–11
 and death of youngest brother
  (Frederick William) 211
 dislike of daughter Melusine's
  husband 272–3
 education 11
 fashion worn by 84–5
 finances 4, 170–1, 233

 generosity and kindness of 77–8, 170
 ill-health 132, 217, 237, 270
 insecurities felt over relationship with
  George and finances 86–7, 170–1,
  199–200, 233
 kindness of 77–8
 life after George's death 269–72
 marriage to George rumours 259–64
 parental background 9–10
 pension 170, 233
 portraits 5, 84–5, 128
 relationship with daughter (Louise)
  80
 relationship with daughter
  (Melusine) 254, 272
 relationship with and devotion to
  George 4, 50, 53, 65, 80, 81, 84,
  86–7, 163, 248, 260–1
 relationship with George's children by
  Sophia 77–8
 and religion 85–6
 reputation 3
 sense of fun 134
 will 273
Schulenburg, Frederick William von der
 (half-brother) 11, 12, 75, 166, 194, 197–8,
 211
Schulenburg, Gustav Adolph von der,
 Count (father) 9–11, 53
Schulenburg, Johann Matthias von der
 (brother) 10, 12, 49, 75–6, 86–7, 118, 170,
 262
Schulenburg, Johanna Auguste von der
 (stepsister) 11, 12
Schulenburg, Margarete Gertrud von der
 (sister) 10, 12, 54, 72–3
Schulenburg, Petronella Melusine von der
 (Melusine) (daughter of Melusine) 65, 70,
 109, 176, 205, 206, 238, 254, 270, 272–3,
 275
Schulenburg, Petronilla Ottilia von der
 (mother) 9, 10
Schulenburg, Sophie Juliane (sister) *see*
 Oeynhausen, Sophie Juliane von
Schutz, Baron 101, 169
Scotland
 and Pretender's cause 104–5
 union with England (1707) 104
Settlement, Act of (1701) 38, 74, 163
Shrewsbury, Duchess of 125–6

Shrieder, Mrs 117
slave trade 137, 214
   and South Sea Company 214–15
Sophia Charlotte (illegitimate sister of
   George I) *see* Platen, Sophia
   Charlotte von
Sophia Charlotte (Figuelotte) (sister of
   George I) (later Queen of Prussia) 37, 44,
   72, 77, 80, 115–16
Sophia Dorothea of Celle (wife of George I)
   affair with Königsmarck 4–5, 51, 55–60,
      77
   appearance and figure 52
   birth 27
   birth of son (George II) 44–5
   break down of marriage to George I and
      divorce 4–5, 45–6, 49, 54, 55, 60–1
   death 259, 262
   as focus of opposition to Hanover 61
   and husband's affair with Melusine 55
   incarceration in Ahlden prison and
      separation from prison 5, 61–3, 64, 65,
      188, 259
   marriage to George I 41–2, 43–4, 53
   motherhood 64–5
   popularity at Hanover court 44
   relationship with mother-in-law 44
Sophia Dorothea (daughter of George I and
   Sophia Dorothea) 27, 77, 78–9, 255
Sophia, Duchess of Hanover (mother of
   George I) 12, 17–24
   admiration of Versailles 33
   birth of children 27
   birth of George 27–8
   childhood 21
   court of 33
   death 89
   and Eléonore's marriage to George
      William 25–7
   Grand Tour of Italy and France (1664)
      33, 34
   and husband's mistresses 42, 52
   and illegitimate granddaughters 70
   and Leibniz 33, 34
   lineage and parental background 19–21
   love for son (George) 27, 28
   and marriage of George to Sophia
      Dorothea 41
   marriage to and relationship with Ernst
      August 23–4, 39, 50, 66

quest for husband 21, 22–3
rebuilding of Herrenhausen and
   re-creation of gardens 29, 30–1
relationship with Melusine 20, 51–3, 63,
   69–70, 71–2, 89
relationship with Sophia Dorothea 44
succession and Act of Settlement 38–9
suspected of treason against husband 37,
   39
Sophie Karoline *see* Platen, Sophie Karoline
   von
Sorosina, Benedetta 145
South Sea Bubble 4, 143, 182, 201, 211–23
   Aislabie made scapegoat 227
   bribe list 222–3, 224
   bursting of 217–18
   ending of crisis 229
   failure of Sunderland to inform George
      of disaster 218–19
   flight of Knight and failed attempt to get
      extradited 222–3, 225–6
   losing of fortunes and bankruptcies
      221–2
   and Melusine 4, 201, 211, 213, 215,
      219–20, 223, 225, 228, 233
   ministerial casualties 227–8
   origins 213–16
   Pope on 213
   and Walpole 228–9
South Sea Company 213, 214–15
Speck, W.A. 96
Spencer, Charles *see* Sunderland, Earl of
Spörken, Baron von 269
Stafford, Earl of 101
Stair, Lord 236
Stanhope, Charles 227, 228
Stanhope, James 101, 176, 179, 180, 181,
   182, 196, 205, 207, 215, 227, 227–8
Steel's Company 199
Steffani, Agostino 19, 85, 145
Suffolk, Countess of (Henrietta Howard)
   51–2, 153, 270, 271
Sunderland, Earl of (Charles Spencer) 177,
   178, 179, 180, 182, 192–3, 196, 205, 207,
   216, 218, 228
Sunderland, Lady 83
Swift, Jonathan 96, 111, 143, 200, 221,
   233–4
   attack on Melusine 82, 175
   Gulliver's Travels 175

Swift, Jonathan (*contd*)
   lampooning of Melusine in Irish coinage
      patent scandal 234–5
   on London 139–40
   'Prometheus' 235
   'A Simile on our Want of Silver' 235
   The South Sea Project 209

theatre, London 141–2
Thirty Years War 18, 21, 28, 32, 56
Thomas, Hugh 214–15
Toland, John 73–4
Tories 97–8, 99, 100–1
Townshend, Charles, Viscount 105–6,
   163–4, 168–9, 176, 177, 178–9, 182–3,
   192, 197, 205, 211–12, 250, 251
Townshend, Dorothy (née Walpole) 105
Tract of the National Interest, A (1757) 96
trade, British 137
Trudchen *see* Schaumburg-Lippe,
   Margarethe Gertrud zu
Tulip Mania (Netherlands) 212

Ulrich (tailor and fool) 154
United Provinces 99
Utrecht, Treaty of (1713) 99, 100, 139,
   213

Vanbrugh, Sir John 153, 155, 157, 168
Venice 29
Versailles 33, 81–2
Villette, marquise de 236

Walpole, Horace 126, 127–8, 137, 188–9,
   238, 265, 267, 273

Walpole, Robert 100, 105, 106, 163, 177,
   178, 211–12
   background and character 106, 180
   and Bolingbroke 237, 241
   and Georg August 192, 194
   and Irish copper coinage patent scandal
      234
   and Melusine 106, 180–1, 183
   and reconciliation of George I with son
      206–8
   relationship with George I 205, 241
   and Sophie Karoline 250
   and South Sea Bubble 212, 228–9
War of the Spanish Succession 75, 99
Weekly Journal 149
Wentworth, Peter 166
Wesley, Samuel 149
Westminster Bridge 139
Westphalia, Treaty of (1648) 18, 28
Wharton, Duke of 172
Whigs 97–8, 176
   and George I 100–1, 105–6
   rift amongst and reconciliation 192, 194,
      205–8
Whitworth, Charles 247
Wilhelmine (granddaughter of George I)
   88–9, 187, 247, 255–6, 259
William III, King 38, 39, 80, 95, 98, 99, 157
Windham, William 221
Windsor Castle 156
Wood, William 171, 233, 234
Worsley, Lucy 125
Wren, Sir Christopher 138, 153, 154, 155,
   157
Wyndham, Sir William 104